**DENIS BALY and
ROYAL W. RHODES**

The Faith of Christians

An introduction to basic beliefs

THE FAITH OF
CHRISTIANS

With the constant help and advice of the following contributors:

Christopher L. Anderson

Mary E. Bolton

Louis M. Boxer

Joseph C. Caperna

Binney H. Connell

Lori K. Dibble

John P. Gerace

Jonathan K. Han

Sheryl D. Hankins

Elizabeth B. Honea

Jeffrey L. Kovach

Ross A. Miller

Laura S. Peale

Suzanne C. Poznanski

Michael A. Renne

Marc M. Rose

James E. Rossman

Susan A. Smith

David R. Watson

Jerome H. Witschger

THE FAITH OF CHRISTIANS

Denis Baly
and
Royal W. Rhodes

FORTRESS PRESS   PHILADELPHIA

Biblical quotations have normally been made from the Revised Standard Version (RSV). However, we have also used the King James Version (KJV), the Jerusalem Bible (JB), the New English Bible (NEB), and for the Psalms and Canticles occasionally the Coverdale translation. From time to time we have ventured to make our own translation, indicated by the initials D.B.

Library of Congress Cataloging in Publication Data

Baly, Denis.
  The faith of Christians.

  Bibliography: p.
  Includes indexes.
  1. Theology, Doctrinal.   2. Christianity—20th century.
I. Rhodes, Royal W.   II. Title.
BT75.2.B32 1984   230   84–47914
ISBN 0–8006–1790–8

CONTENTS

INTRODUCTION

This book is the work of a considerable number of people. It began in the first place from the realization by some of us at Kenyon College that ordinary people in this country are often startlingly ignorant of even the elements of the Christian faith, but are at the same time full of questions about it. This by itself is not a very profound observation, but it stimulated us to introduce a semester course on the subject, based partly on the reading of some fifteen books, but even more upon questions submitted at the beginning of each week by all the student participants. The Rev. Norman Hjelm of Fortress Press, hearing about the course, suggested that it would make a good foundation for a book. Encouraged by him, we embarked upon the process of writing one.

The method adopted was very similar to that used with success in the production of *God and History in the Old Testament* (Harper & Row, 1976), with the difference that this time there were two authors rather than one. Twenty students were involved, ranging from sophomores to seniors, who represented a wide variety of disciplines. Although Kenyon College makes no inquiry into the religious faith or otherwise of its students, it soon became evident that the group included people from very different church backgrounds, as well as those who were critical of religion, and some members also of the Jewish faith. This diversity has been of the greatest value. We must also record our gratitude to those students who had taken the course in its previous form, and whose questions and ideas provided the basis for the first draft of the book.

The method adopted was as follows. The course was planned to last over the whole academic year, and the group met once every two weeks in the evening, so that there would be plenty of time for discussion. At this meeting one of the two authors presented the draft of a chapter in the book, copies of his text being provided for all the student contributors. During the intervening two weeks the contributors studied the draft chapter, both individually and in small groups, usually on their own, although one group in rotation met with the two authors. The contributors had complete freedom to make any criticisms or suggestions they wished, ranging from a matter of punctuation to advice for complete rewriting. Only two provisos were made: (1) if a contributor thought that a passage was unclear, he or she must suggest how it should be rewritten, and (2) serious criticism involves assessing both what is good as well as what is bad. Also, during the two weeks all contributors were asked to read books relevant to the subject of the chapter, and comment on their value. At the same time the two authors were working on chapters still to come.

The authors cannot be sufficiently grateful to the contributors for the thoroughness of their work, the seriousness with which they took their responsibilities, and their readiness to take time out of a busy college life to come in for private, and sometimes lengthy, discussions with one or another of the two authors. It is very salutary for a college professor to find written in the margin of his work, "You have *totally* misunderstood this biblical passage," or "The last four pages of this chapter are *trash*," as well, fortunately, as more encouraging comments, such as "This is a brilliant paragraph," or "Excellent! I never thought of looking at it this way before." Not all comments, of course, went to such extremes, but it soon became apparent that if one contributor said that a passage was inferior and should be omitted, another would be bound to say that it was admirable and should be kept!

An impressive feature of the year's work was the wide variety of reading done by the contributors, and the suggestions made on the basis of that reading. Although suggested reading lists were occasionally provided, complete freedom of choice was allowed, and even encouraged, and the reading evidently ranged far and wide, and included at the final count some three hundred books and journal and magazine articles. From these have been selected the books included in the annotated bibliography.

A very important feature of this book is the annotated notes at the end of each chapter. Because of the rich diversity of opinions, it was impossible to find room for all suggestions. The principle adopted was to include the majority opinion in the text, but where there was serious disagreement, or useful material for which we could not find space, this is included at the end of the chapter and forms an essential part of the book. Our aim was never to tell the readers what they ought to believe, or to attempt a compendium of what all Christians do believe, which would be an impossible task. Our hope has been rather to provide a helpful basis for consideration, discussion, and further reading.

A careful record was kept of every suggestion and comment made, however apparently minor. Then during the summer months the entire book was rewritten, not a single page remaining unaltered, a very large proportion of the book being completely revised, and much new material included. The rewriting was done by one of the two authors, with a view to preserving unity of style. He confesses that he did his best, but found the task extremely complicated because of the need to preserve in the different chapters material approved by the contributors. Nevertheless, it is to be hoped that the final result reads smoothly and contains no awkward seams.

The contributors then read and commented on the revised edition, though at this point comments had to be confined to questions of accuracy and style. The book was then given its final form. The contributors assisted with all the tedious duty of seeing the book through the press: assuring the accuracy of the manuscript before it was sent to the publishers, proofreading, checking biblical references, and preparing the indexes.

Finally, our thanks are due to Norman Hjelm and Harold Rast of Fortress Press for their support, advice, and encouragement, to Patricia Bosch for typing the final manuscript, and to Louise Baly for help with proofreading and preparing the index.

Denis Baly
Royal W. Rhodes

1

FAITH AND BELIEF IN THE WORLD OF TODAY

The Purpose of This Book

The purpose of this book is to examine the basic tenets of the Christian religion, as they have been handed down through the centuries, and to ask what relevance, if any, they still have in the modern world. This seems indeed an arrogant goal, and it would be if we should claim to give any final answers. But our aim is a great deal more modest. We propose to set out on a journey of exploration in a territory where there is no lack of maps, but where they often seem to contradict each other and where there are unexpected swamps and seemingly impenetrable thickets. We shall therefore do no more than feel our way toward answers, and even when we arrive at some, and state them as such, they will be in no sense final, but positions set forward for argument and debate.

Equally, if there are no final answers, there are also no a priori positions. We cannot begin by stating that something is true because the Bible says so, or because any other book or person says so. This is not to decry the Bible, or any other long-trusted source of knowledge and understanding, but only to say that we can take nothing for granted, as if it were absolved from all questions. Certainly, the Bible has to be the primary source for any examination of the Christian faith, and in the next chapter we shall look at its authority and the question of its inspiration. But the Bible itself needs careful study and interpretation. It is an ancient book, and the meaning of much of it is not immediately obvious. Furthermore, it is not the only source. There are also the writings of the great Christian figures throughout the centuries, and we need to make use of their experience. We may, indeed, have to go further, and ask whether there might be other sources for understanding the faith of Christians, sources much older than the Bible, or sources which are foreign.

There is no need to be afraid of such questions, for truth is exactly that

1

which cannot be destroyed by any inquiry, which can endure all things, and survive every test. It is, in the last resort, its own authority. It demonstrates its validity by being indestructible. To refuse to ask the searching questions is not, as some people imagine, to have faith. It is to be doubting and faithless.

"Believing in" and "Believing that"

This brings us, then, to the question of what we mean when we use the words "faith" and "belief," words that occur constantly in religious discussion, so much so, in fact, that many people think of religion as primarily concerned with faith and belief. However, they are also thoroughly secular terms. But here we are faced with a difficulty. These two nouns both describe something that people do. Neither of them indicates a static, passive attitude. Admittedly, we can say that people do, or do not, have faith, or that they do, or do not, hold a certain belief, but in each case we are speaking of an activity of the mind, which may, perhaps, lead to direct action. But one verb has to do duty for both activities, the verb "to believe," and the problem is rendered more complex by the fact that we can "believe that" something is true or "believe in" somebody or something, and these two activities, though related, are nevertheless distinct. We are therefore dealing with what may be called "slippery words," that is, words which can mean more than one thing, and that are only too often used loosely, so that speakers slide from one meaning into another.

Both faith and belief begin where knowledge ends. What we know as fact, what we have been able to discover by patient inquiry, by experiment and proof, or from accumulated experience, constitutes the foundation stone and the building blocks for the structure of our society and of our personal lives. But there are limits to knowledge, to personal knowledge and communal knowledge, and to the total knowledge of humanity. For instance, a person may not know from direct personal experience that strychnine is poisonous, and yet accept the statement as true because of faith in the observation of others. The direct personal knowledge of individuals is always strictly limited, but they share in the communal knowledge of the group to which they belong, built from the personal knowledge of all the members. There are, therefore, "knowledge groups," often overlapping with each other, and held together within the very much larger community of knowledge which we call "society." But the accumulated knowledge of each group, and also of the whole society, is always itself limited. Even if we extend the boundaries to include everything that belongs to Western civilization it is still limited. Indians, Chinese, and

Africans know as facts of experience what is altogether beyond the limits of Western knowledge.[1]

What all this demonstrates is that belief and faith are perfectly normal features of everyday life, and are, indeed, essential to human existence. We could not continue to function if we did not every day of our lives believe to be fact what we ourselves have no means of verifying. We have to go forward trustingly, steadfast in faith. Otherwise, we could not act at all, because we cannot know everything.

Moreover, humanity as a whole cannot know everything. The limits of human knowledge are rigidly imposed by the very fact of humanness. To know what it is to be human is not to know, and to be forever excluded from knowing, what it is to be a dog, a cat, a mosquito, or a whale. It is to live always at a particular time, never to know the future as fact, and to know the past only as memory, which is always selective and distorting. But to be human is also to be continually conscious that beyond these limits is not necessarily nothingness, not merely a void. There is a past behind us, about which we can discover a great deal, though still only a fraction of the whole truth. The future is not a vast emptiness, but is instead overflowing with facts, some of which in due course we shall learn. Cats, dogs, whales, and even mosquitoes do have a life of their own, hidden though it may be. Therefore, we rely upon belief. We construct models and develop concepts, using such facts as are available to us. These are not fantasies. Some may contain a great many facts and all are the result of rational, intelligent thought. But they are not themselves facts. They are always beliefs.

Until now we have spoken mainly about "believing that" certain things are true, and acting upon these beliefs. We believe that future events will take a certain form and have a certain pattern, and we act accordingly. We believe that the foreign policy of this or that nation has certain definite goals and objectives, some of which may seem inimical to this country, and so we shape our own foreign policy to take these perceptions into account. We believe that the past had a certain character—we may look back upon it with nostalgia as the good old days or we may view it with loathing as something from which we have been delivered—and we struggle to shape the society of our own day on the basis of these beliefs, either to recapture something of our earlier heritage or to build a better world in the future.

---

1. A perfectly true anecdote may serve to illustrate this. A few years ago an Englishman visiting Jerusalem said to an Arab, a close friend of his, that he thought the Palestinians would be wise to be more cooperative with the Israeli authorities. The Arab replied, "You do not know what you are talking about. You are English. For nine hundred years you have never been conquered. You have no idea at all what it is like to be an occupied people."

But already we are on the borderline between "believing that" certain things are true and "believing in" certain things or people. The two activities certainly overlap, but they are also distinct. "Believing that" may well be complete in itself, for although it may lead to subsequent actions, it does not necessarily do so. It is, for instance, perfectly possible to believe seriously that alcohol, or cigarettes, or marijuana are bad for one's health, and nevertheless to disregard this belief and do nothing about it. It is also presumably possible for, let us say, a well-read Hottentot in the recesses of Africa to believe that the founding fathers of the United States established certain principles for American government and the American people, but to see this as having no relevance to his own society.[2]

However, when we "believe in" someone or something we commit ourselves in a manner beyond that demanded by "believing that." To believe *that* democracy is a good form of government commits one to very little; it is an academic, intellectual matter. But to believe *in* democracy requires the believer to participate in it, and if necessary, to take action to protect it, to ensure that government by the people, and for the people, shall not perish from the earth. To believe that Jesus is the savior of the world can perhaps remain as no more than a theological opinion, an intellectual concept, but to believe in Jesus as the Savior of the world commits the man or woman who thus believes to living a life of obedience to him.

Here we step over the boundary between "belief" and "faith." Belief can remain within the intellectual sphere, the sphere of "believing that," as, for instance, when a scholar says, "I believe that this hypothesis is correct, but I do not yet have the evidence necessary to prove it. Further research is needed before I know whether I am right or wrong." But faith demands trust, committal, and involvement. In the realm of belief it is possible to stand on one side and observe dispassionately, but in the realm of faith one is indissolubly related to, bound up with, the person or thing in which one has faith.

Although we are forced by poverty of language to use only one verb, we can to some extent keep the nouns separate, and in the rest of this chapter it will be helpful to speak of "faith" when we mean personal trust and involvement, and of "belief" when we mean that kind of believing that is dispassionate and observing. The boundary, however, is not a rigid one. A person can both "believe in" and "believe that," i.e. have both faith and belief, at the same time, doing both, but being conscious of their difference. In a college or university, for instance, it is essential to do so. It is necessary to act again and again in faith—faith in the educational principles, in the value of the discipline, and in those with whom one works.

2. There is at least one important exception to this general principle, which will be dealt with a little later on.

The instructor must have faith in the students and in his or her colleagues, and the students must have faith in the faculty and in each other. Both must have faith in the institution. Yet both must also be continually objective, believing that certain things are true, but taking nothing for granted, being ready always to examine and question them. They must be ready to suspend faith and criticize honestly and objectively even that to which they are altogether committed. Only thus can truth be separated from error.

It is, of course, perfectly possible to lose faith, to discover or imagine that one has discovered that the object of faith is unworthy, that the god had feet of clay. It is even possible to lose faith altogether, to consider nothing as worthwhile, to have no faith left, even in oneself, a situation which may lead to suicide. But it is not possible to dispense altogether with belief. To lose faith, even to lose it totally, involves believing that the object of faith is unworthy. No one acts or makes decisions without reasons, and reasons depend upon believing that certain things are true.

Belief Systems

Without belief it is impossible for human beings to live. Indeed, it is impossible without beliefs in the plural, for no one has only one belief; everyone entertains a whole complex of beliefs. Some are based upon serious thought and inquiry, but an even larger number upon general reading, upon hearsay, and upon things taught and remembered from childhood. Some indeed may be based upon prejudice and misunderstanding. These beliefs, however ill thought out, provide the basis and framework for action. They may seem jumbled and incoherent to an outside observer, but in the mind of the one who believes they are always related, though often unconsciously and instinctively. He or she draws upon these beliefs when it is necessary to make a decision.

Furthermore, all these beliefs are in some way related to the society in which the person lives, and upon which he or she is wholly dependent. It is in society, and only in society, that men and women "live and move and have their being."[3] In society we live, because it is only in collaboration with other human beings that we can obtain the physical necessities of life: food, clothing, and shelter. We move, because apart from society we are disoriented and have no sense of direction. This is immediately recognized by anyone who goes to live in a foreign society and culture. The familiar guideposts and pathways are nowhere to be found, and the

---

3. One contributor wrote, "You have *totally misused* this passage. The Bible uses it differently." Admittedly, it is something of a misquotation, taken from Paul's address to the Athenians on the Areopagus (Acts 17:28), but Paul himself seems to have been quoting rather at random, possibly from Epimenides.

newcomer is compelled to start afresh and learn new patterns before he or she can function effectively in the new society. The Islamic world uses the word *sunnah*, the "beaten path" in the otherwise trackless desert, to describe the proper behavior of human beings, and in many other cultures the metaphor of the road or way is similarly used.[4] It is the path of experience, cleared, paved, and signposted by society in the course of its long history.

Finally, we have our being, because it is our society that endows us with identity, with a certain recognizable character, so that other people know who we are. Our speech and our involuntary gestures proclaim our identity, sometimes even betray it. In occupied Europe during World War II British spies were apt to look to the right instead of the left before crossing a road. This was, as their instructors told them, a "dead giveaway," and they had continually to be on their guard against such ingrained but treacherous motions. Moreover, every time a person joins a new society, such as going to school, to college, into business, or the armed forces, he or she is refashioned and given a new identity. This is done with love and affection in a true family relationship, rather more impersonally in school or college, and altogether more forcefully in military basic training. In totalitarian regimes it may be done ruthlessly by deliberate and contrived brainwashing. What cannot happen is that the remaking of the identity be omitted. The newcomer remains an uncomfortable misfit until refashioned to conform to society's understanding of itself.

Although society gives its members security, it is itself constantly insecure, threatened from both inside and outside. From inside it is threatened because the old and experienced die off, and at the same time new and ignorant children are born. It is threatened from outside because beyond its border dwells a multitude of people with quite different beliefs and patterns of behavior. The internal threat is heightened when the behavior of some of the members goes beyond what society is prepared to tolerate. It finds their actions incomprehensible, and can explain such behavior only by saying that there is something wrong with such people, that they are either bad or mad, criminal or crazy.

All these threatening insiders, whether they be children or adults, are placed under some kind of restraint, though, of course, it varies in severity. The children are by law sent to school, and do not achieve full membership in society until they are educated and mature. The others are placed in prisons or asylums until it seems safe to readmit them to free citizenship. It may certainly seem harsh to lump together under one heading children who, though ignorant, are normally thought of as innocent, and such obviously evil people as murderers. But children, if untaught and

---

4. Other examples are the *tao* in Chinese thought, or the Noble Eightfold Path in Buddhist teaching. Serious infringements of society's patterns are often said to be "unheard-of behavior."

unrestrained, can be exceedingly dangerous. They may take only too easily to crime and violence, largely because they do not perceive these to be wrong. This was abundantly illustrated in Russia in the period immediately following the Revolution.

The outsiders are "foreigners," people with different patterns of behavior and therefore different identities. All societies in the world perceive the outsiders as potentially dangerous, and treat them at best with caution, and at worst with suspicion or even outright rejection. Even so very tolerant a society as that of the United States requires visas and entry permits for non-Americans, and when such people appear to threaten the livelihood of the insiders, it places obstacles in the way of their admission. It is, for instance, a very complicated process for a foreigner, invited to teach for a semester at an American institution, to obtain the necessary visa.[5]

It is certainly true that societies may sometimes welcome the outsiders, as the United States welcomed immigrants in the nineteenth century,[6] or political parties welcome new adherents, or religious groups welcome converts. But these newcomers are always required to conform.

Society, therefore, is the structure within which we live. It is "our world." But, and this is very important, it is a human construct, something made by men and women to provide a shelter from the unknown, from the storms and tempests "out there" in the dread realm of all that lies beyond our own experience. It is always, in the eyes of its members, a rational structure, built upon unquestioned facts of experience, but, of course, interpreted facts, distilled in the human understanding of them. The primary facts are those of the natural environment in which men and women find themselves, and every migration into a new environment requires a new search for information, since without such a discovery there can be no certainty of producing food. But these newly discovered facts have themselves to be interpreted. From the very beginning it is not the environment as such that provides the earliest foundation for society, but the environment *as perceived by human eyes and interpreted by human brains.*[7]

Yet these interpretations are not themselves facts, save only in a

---

5. In times of apparently acute danger the most stringent demands are made before outsiders are granted admission. This was made abundantly clear in the U.S.A. during the McCarthy era of the 1950s. One contributor added this comment: "My Italian professor this summer is no longer allowed into the U.S.A., although he is married to an American, because the two of them marched in a peace rally in Boston several years ago. The CIA took pictures of him, and classified him as dangerous to the public peace. However, his wife is allowed to continue as before."

6. To its everlasting credit the United States still does welcome immigrants, but there is now a quota, and a stringent examination before citizenship is possible.

7. Some authorities would go so far as to say that we cannot ever speak of the actual facts of the environment, since we can speak only of what we perceive, but this is probably going too far. Such things as mountains and rivers certainly exist, and earthquakes take place, whether they are perceived correctly or incorrectly by human beings.

restricted sense; they are *beliefs*, and a society is, therefore, a *belief system*, a highly complex and complicated structure of interlocking beliefs, sometimes in apparent conflict with each other, but nevertheless interrelated, all under the umbrella of the unitary concept. This unitary concept, the America or France or China or Russia, in which the citizens of each country believe, which is to them their true home, fatherland and motherland, completely transcends the actual America, France, etc. The actual country may be marred by poverty, crime, and much unhappiness, but the country for which men and women are prepared to die is altogether more glorious. It lies beyond the limits of factual knowledge. It is an exalted vision, a passionate belief.

This brings us to the exception mentioned earlier to the statement that "belief that" does not require action. Unfortunately, an apparently all-embracing belief system, such as democracy, the native country, or human rights, seems inevitably to involve both believing *in* the system, and believing *that* those who reject it, or dwell outside it, are inherently wrong, rebellious, and wicked, and must therefore be steadfastly opposed. There is a very strong tendency in this country to follow in the steps of John Foster Dulles during the Eisenhower regime, and to divide the world into "democratic" and "nondemocratic" countries, applauding the first as children of light and condemning the second as children of darkness—completely failing to recognize that an autocracy can be benevolent and a democracy, alas, be racist and tyrannical.

This disastrous simplification results from the fact that it is, unfortunately, a great deal easier to think in this way. The belief system, whatever it may be, to which people belong is itself highly complex and confusing—inevitably so, since it claims to be all-embracing. It is much easier for people to accept their belief system as being "obviously right," and to dismiss the others as not worthy of consideration, or as "obviously wrong." We are also under great pressure from our society to hold firmly to these beliefs, to be above all things loyal to our own people and our own community, whether it be large or small. Moreover, we are limited human beings. We cannot see what the Chinese see, what the Arabs see, what the Pakistanis see. What is so obvious to them is often invisible to us, and we blame them for being blind to what we see so clearly. Our world is for most of us all the world there is, and what lies outside does not make sense until it is incorporated within our world.

One has only to consult almost any textbook on the history of civilization to see the truth of this. "Civilization," for the purposes of an introductory course on the subject, is always Western civilization, and the rest of the world enters civilization only when it becomes closely involved with the West, penetrated by Western traders and missionaries, or invaded by Western armies. Moreover, when the student advances further and takes courses in the History of China, or Women in the Muslim World, the emphasis is usually on learning *about* these people and their countries. It seems that only a few instructors and students ever consider the course as a means of discovering what we can learn *from* them.

Political Beliefs

What people believe is itself a political fact, even when what they believe is factually incorrect, or in the understanding of others downright wrong. They believe in a certain system of government, a certain pattern of society, a certain way of administering justice, and so on. These have developed out of their historical experience and have been tested and found profitable. The people possess a great deal of remembered history, which they teach to their children so that they may also believe, and in due course carry on the task of maintaining unharmed the society that nurtured them.

The history which children learn is often a mixture of fact and legend, and sophisticated scholars tend to despise the legends as inaccurate and therefore misleading. They point out, for instance, that we have in fact no evidence that the young George Washington ever cut down a cherry tree, and that our modern picture of the origin of Thanksgiving has little basis in fact. But these stories are valuable for inculcating at a very early age the importance of telling the truth so that the various members of the society may trust each other, and for keeping alive in the community the memory, however much simplified and even distorted, of the early hardships and also sense of community with the Native Americans so as to encourage and maintain a deep feeling of gratitude that we live together in *this* society. It is not by accident that those applying for citizenship in the United States are required to learn English as the common language, and also to learn American history and the American structure of government and justice. By this means they enter fully into the American society, and its history becomes *their* history and American beliefs *their* beliefs.

These beliefs all lie beyond the frontiers of objective knowledge. It is not an observable fact, proved by empirical study, that all men and women are created equal and are endowed with certain inalienable rights. People in many other societies would strongly dispute the statement. It is equally not a fact in any scientific sense of the word that democracy is the best form of government, since it is highly doubtful that the majority of the voters are the wisest and best informed of the community, and democracy as we know it today relies on balancing the selfish desires and wants of different groups in the country against each other. Nevertheless, we believe strongly in democracy, and would do all in our power to preserve it for ourselves and for our children.

A most important, and probably almost universal, feature of political belief is that of territorial possession. Almost every human community feels the need to stake out and insist upon a certain area of land (often also including part of the sea) as belonging inalienably to them, and are ready, if necessary, to fight to maintain possession of it. To fail to do so would seem to them to guarantee their own extinction. But the basis upon which these claims to ownership are made lies almost entirely beyond the limits of factual knowledge. That a particular people occupy a certain area of land is clearly an observable fact, but whether that occupancy confers right of exclusive ownership is often disputed. It is even more open to dispute when the basis of the claim lies in some now long-distant ownership, as when the Chinese assume that all the land that once formed part of the Han Empire two thousand years ago is therefore Chinese, or when Israelis base their claim to the whole of Palestine on their possession of it much more than two thousand years ago, or upon the promises of God to Abraham.

No attempt is being made here to say whether these claims are right or wrong but merely to point out that are vehemently contradicted by other people with different, but no less powerful, beliefs. Whether it is right to speak of the Arabian or the Persian Gulf can be answered only in terms of the beliefs of the speaker. No one can establish as fact universally admitted by outside observers, who has the right of possession in Jerusalem. Muslims believe in the depths of their being that Jerusalem is fundamentally Muslim, and that it cannot, therefore, belong to anyone else. But this is a claim hotly opposed by the Jewish people, and also by many Christians, who, no less than the Muslims, speak from the depths of their being.

Almost all political action is based upon belief. Certainly, facts enter into the decision to act, but no government can act upon the facts alone. The facts need to be interpreted, and the interpretation depends upon how the facts are perceived and understood. This perception and understanding must draw upon the transcendent realm, the realm that lies beyond the limits of factual proof, the realm of belief.

Religious Belief

Until now, although this book is about the faith of Christians, little mention has been made of religion. This has been quite deliberate, for we need to recognize from the beginning that belief and faith are fundamental and necessary human activities. There must always be both "belief that" and "belief in," and these beliefs must be held with conviction, and often passionately. To imagine that human beings could continue to be human and live together in community without belief is to imagine the impossible.

But this raises the question of whether what we call religious belief is in any way different from the ordinary down-to-earth belief of human beings, which we may describe as secular beliefs. Belief, as we have seen, is concerned with all that lies beyond the limits of factual knowledge, and the two most absolute limits are those of birth and death. The realm that lies beyond these is, as far as humankind has ever been able to discover, the realm of the absolutely transcendent, where there are no discernible "facts." It is the realm of sheer belief.

Moreover, as we peer into this realm, we encounter a sharp distinction between secular and religious belief. Within the limits of birth and death there can be much overlapping, and even agreement, between secular and religious thought. But beyond birth and death the secular mind sees only nothingness, believing that all that is meaningful must lie within these absolute limits. All religious thought, however, strongly disputes this. It seeks to proclaim the meaning of birth and death, and this it can do only by venturing boldly beyond the absolute limits, asserting that out there is not nothingness, but the source of all meaning. Drawing upon its own conviction concerning the absolutely transcendent, it claims to put birth and death in their proper place, to reveal their significance and therefore, inevitably, the significance of life itself. Of course, neither can prove their confident assertion, and it may be that a truly secular society is not possible, and that human beings long to believe that death is not the end of all meaning. The continual pilgrimage to Lenin's tomb in the secular Communist Russia suggests that some form of belief in meaning beyond death, i.e., religious belief, may well be inescapable.[8]

Two concluding words of warning are necessary. First, "religion" is being used here in an entirely neutral sense. Religion shares with all other forms of belief the possibility of being false, misleading, and dangerous, as well, of course, of being helpful and right. There is nothing inherently good about being religious. Religious people are of all sorts. They can certainly do a great deal of good, but they can no less certainly do an immense amount of harm.

Second, religion does not always involve belief in God, or in gods. Confucianism and Theraveda Buddhism do not include such a belief, and it would clearly be quite false to define religion in such a way as to leave well over a quarter of the human race outside. The Christian faith, with which this book is concerned, certainly insists upon belief in one God as a fundamental necessity, and so also do Judaism and Islam. In chapter 3 we shall examine what this belief involves, but first we must ask what authority Christians have for their beliefs, and this we shall do in the next chapter.

---

8. It would probably have been more correct in this section to speak of conception rather than birth, since we can discover a lot about the human embryo, but "birth" is a far more evocative word, and, in any case, we cannot discover what the embryo is thinking.

2

THE AUTHORITY OF SCRIPTURE

Whatever was written in former times was written for our instruction, that by steadfastness and by the encouragement of the scriptures we might have hope.

Romans 15:4

What Is the Bible?

So far we have been speaking about faith and belief in general terms, but now we must turn to the more specific question of what Christians believe, and what authority they claim for their faith. They are, as are also Jews and Muslims, "people of a book," but their book, which they speak of as the Holy Bible, is more complicated than the sacred book of either Muslims or Jews. The Qur'an is a unity, containing only the divine revelations made to Muhammad. *Tanak*, the Jewish Scripture, which Christians call the Old Testament, is a collection of books, containing very varied material; law, history, prophetic oracles, songs used in worship, ancient proverbial teaching, philosophical writing, and other matter as well. All this was committed to writing over a period of at least a thousand years. To this exceedingly rich body of literature Christians have added a further twenty-seven books. These include the four Gospels, which are accounts of the life and work of Jesus, all laying the major emphasis on his crucifixion and resurrection; the Acts of the Apostles, written by the author of the Gospel According to Luke, to show how the Christian message was carried out from Jerusalem, first to the Jewish communities and then to the pagan Gentile world, until it reached the city of Rome, the heart of what was then thought of as the civilized world; the epistles, or letters, by different authors and of varied length, giving teaching and counsel to the early Christian communities; the Book of Revelation, a profoundly symbolic work written to encourage and strengthen the Christian communities suffering persecution by the Roman imperial government.

13

This may all sound very complicated, and indeed it is. Yet the sixty-six books of the Bible,[1] diverse though they undoubtedly are, have a fundamental unity on at least two levels. First, at the secular level, is the cultural unity. Every one of the books belongs to, and has taken shape in, the ancient Jewish society and reflects the thinking and the centuries of experience which characterized that society. This is no less true of the New Testament than of the Old. Even though the language of the New Testament is Greek, its thought forms are thoroughly Semitic,[2] and even when the writers of the New Testament letters are addressing largely Gentile groups of Christians, it is to the Jewish scriptures that they always appeal in support of their arguments.

The second level is the religious one. Here Christians part company with those who do not share their beliefs, for it is the universal Christian conviction that the Scriptures, both New and Old Testament, are given unity by the person of Jesus of Nazareth. That the New Testament writings are concerned from beginning to end with this person is evident to anyone who reads them. However, the New Testament argument, constantly emphasized, is that the Old Testament writings are brought to fruition in the person of Jesus, and that apart from Jesus the full depth of meaning in the Old Testament can never be grasped.

This is clearly a faith statement, since it cannot be proved empirically, and it is not accepted by those for whom the New Testament is not authoritative Scripture. But, as we have seen in the last chapter, faith statements are not necessarily false; they are often perfectly true. As with all faith statements, care must be taken not to treat them lightly. Those people who do not share them tend to reject them almost automatically, without serious consideration, and those who from their youth have thought of them as true tend to think of them as so obvious that they need no further study. The great majority of Christians in this country fail to grasp how bold and controversial a claim the New Testament writers were making, and their interpretation of the claim is often superficial. It is, for instance, very revealing to study the liturgies of the churches in this country, especially the new prayer books which have appeared in recent years, and see with what readiness all the glorious promises of the Old Testament proph-

---

1. Although today we speak of the Bible in the singular, the word is really a translation of the Greek *Ta Biblia*, meaning "the Books." The sixty-six books are those universally recognized by Christians. The Septuagint, or Greek translation of the Old Testament, used by the early Christians, contained some other books, the Apocrypha, which Roman Catholic bibles include, but are printed separately by Protestants. The Eastern Orthodox Church accepts some of these books as authoritative.

2. The one possible exception to this is the author of the Gospel of Luke and the Book of Acts, who may very probably have been a Gentile—we cannot be absolutely certain. Nevertheless, he also uses the Jewish scriptures as his primary literary source.

ets are claimed by Christians as pertaining to them, and how little the severe judgments and drastic warnings are included in the Sunday readings. These are treated as less relevant and are left to those outside. Christians would do well to meditate on Peter's warning that judgment begins with the household of God, by which he means the Christian church (1 Pet. 4:17).

What Is Meant by Authority?

There is no one meaning of the word. It can refer to the legal or rightful power to act or give orders, and such authority does not belong in advance to the person who wields it. It has to be bestowed by some person, or group of persons, themselves possessing authority. This is clearly recognized in the Constitution of the United States, which begins with the phrase, "We the People . . . ," thereby rejecting more traditional sources of authority, and claiming that the people as a whole possess inherent authority to settle their own affairs. The Constitution then goes on to confer authority upon certain groups of people—the President, the two houses of Congress, the Supreme Court, and so on. It was in this sense that the chief priests and elders of the people challenged Jesus in the Temple, when they asked him, "By what authority are you doing these things, and who gave you this authority?" (Matt. 21:23).

Another quite distinct meaning is evident when what is challenged is not an action or executive order, but a statement, especially a statement of fact. In such a case the question, "What authority do you have?" means "What factual evidence is there for this statement?" But a different meaning comes into play when what is at issue is a statement of faith, and what is being challenged is a belief system. Here the question, "What authority do you have for believing as you do?" may certainly include the sense of "What facts can you adduce in support of your belief?" But it goes much further, for as we have seen faith and belief systems reach out beyond the limits of factual knowledge. The answer to the question, therefore, must go well beyond the empirical, ascertainable facts.

We in this country take it for granted that the people have inherent authority to choose their own leaders, but we would have difficulty in providing factual evidence, clearly recognizable by anyone, in support of this belief, and we would, moreover, have considerable doubts about the authority of a people to choose a brutal, dictatorial regime. If we were challenged to justify our own democratic system, we would probably appeal to experience, and especially to the experience of the American Revolution. Many other societies in the world similarly look back to a landmark, a transforming event which has reoriented their experience and given them a new sense of power and being. People are motivated to accept the authority of this experience, not primarily because they have been compelled to do so, but because they perceive it as right, as the appropriate response to the transforming event.

The Authority of the Bible

It should be clear from what has already been said that the question so often asked, Is the Bible true? is by itself too simple. We must begin by asking, What kind of authority is there for accepting or rejecting what we read in the Bible? As with the question of the unity of the biblical writings, this question also has a secular and a religious level.

On the secular level the biblical claim to authority rests upon the transforming event and the consequent reorientation of communal experience. There are above all two specific events: (1) the going out of the people from Egypt in about 1250 B.C. and their subsequent wanderings in the desert, and (2) the work of Jesus of Nazareth, and particularly his agonizing death at the hands of the Roman government. These took place in ordinary secular history, and they established the foundations of society for the peoples concerned. In terms of these events all subsequent history was interpreted.

But they were not the only formative events. On a number of later occasions the validity of the foundation experience was called in question by new and largely unforeseen events.[3] For the Jewish people these included replacement of a confederacy by a kingdom under David in 1000 B.C., with a centralized government at Jerusalem; the forced submission to foreign dominance under the Assyrians in the eighth and seventh centuries B.C.; and the profoundly traumatic experience of the exile in Babylon during the sixth century. In the New Testament period the critical and challenging events were the unexpectedly rapid development of Christian communities in pagan countries far from Palestine, the spasmodic, but often brutally cruel, persecution by the imperial government, and the devastating destruction of Jerusalem and the Temple in A.D. 70.

All these events are secular in the sense that they all actually happened and are all fully open to detailed study and analysis by scholars of any persuasion. That the events provided the authority for the societies which developed out of them is altogether evident, although the exact nature of the events and the character of the later interpretations are, and will continue to be, subjects for constant research. But an essential and inescapable feature of the interpretations is the argument that the authority for both

---

3. None of the events mentioned was altogether unforeseen, as the prophetic warnings make clear, but it is also evident that the great majority of the people of the time were taken by surprise.

the events and the interpretation is not to be found in the events themselves, but in the activity and power of God. For this reason, and for this reason only, the records were preserved and are still available to us today.

Here we are inescapably transposed from the strictly secular level to the wholly religious. Obviously, for those who accept the belief system outlined in the first chapter, that the universe is fully comprehensible in terms of itself, the introduction of what we may call the "God-concept" makes no sense at all. But for those who perceive the universe as deriving its meaning essentially from that which is not itself, the God-concept is an absolute necessity.

Yet, God cannot remain merely a concept. Who and what is meant when Christians speak of God will be explored in the next chapter, but for the moment we must be clear that God is not merely "a god," not just "somebody" sitting up in heaven, giving orders, answering prayers, and intervening in the world's affairs from time to time. All three great monotheistic religions insist that in using the word "God" we speak of what is beyond all human comprehension, but certainly of overwhelming and transcendent power, active and purposeful, maintaining the whole universe in existence and giving coherence and meaning to everything in it. "God" is a word we use for absolute and ultimate truth and reality, so far outreaching what finite human minds can envisage that we can speak of God only with awe and humility.

No man or woman by searching can find out God, for all our researches are confined within the limits of the universe, and God is other than the universe. Therefore, if God is to be known at all by human minds, He must reveal Himself, and Himself make known His purposes.[4] It is this self-disclosure of God that is meant when the biblical writers speak of God's Word, and when Christians today speak of the Word of God. The entire Bible took shape within the rich heritage of Semitic culture, and the Semitic mind was always intensely conscious of the power of words.[5] Words were for them alive and active, spoken for a purpose, and intended by the speaker to achieve that purpose. For every idle word that men speak, said Jesus, they will be judged (Matt. 12:36).[6] Indeed, the ancient Hebrews thought of the activity of words very much as we might think of an electric circuit, where the pressing of a switch here causes power to rush out and ignite a lamp over there, or perhaps to set off an explosion.

---

4. The question of what pronoun (he, she, or it) is appropriate in speaking of God will be discussed in the next chapter (see pp. 33–35). For the moment it is convenient to keep to the conventional "He."

5. This is still profoundly true today. Westerners constantly misinterpret Arabic rhetoric because they do not share this strong sense of the active power of words once spoken.

6. The KJV is better here than the RSV. The Greek word is *argos*, which means "idle" or "inactive," either because the person is unemployed (Matt. 20:3, 6), or because he is lazy (Titus 1:12).

So shall my word be that goes forth from my mouth;
   it shall not return to me empty,
but it shall accomplish that which I purpose,
   and prosper in the thing for which I send it.
                                                    Isaiah 55:11

Is not my word like fire, says the LORD, and like
a hammer which breaks the rock in pieces?
                                                    Jeremiah 23:29

The "Word," therefore, is not only the self-disclosure of God. It is the
sheer power of bringing into being, of creation where before there was
nothing, of producing order where before was chaos and confusion.

By the word of the LORD the heavens were made,
   and all their host by the breath of his mouth.

For he spoke, and it came to be;
   he commanded, and it stood forth.
                                                    Psalm 33:6–9

It is in this sense that the Gospel of John speaks of Jesus as being the
Word of God, the power of making all things new, of producing piercing
light where before there had been darkness, of establishing meaning and
order, where before men and women had been groping and confused,
indeed of creating an altogether new kind of person. The Word was there
in the beginning, but in due time, at a specific point in history, in Jesus
of Nazareth the Word became flesh (John 1:1–18).

The Bible itself is not God, but in the Bible we are confronted and
challenged by God. In the Bible the all-powerful Word has become incarnate in words, has taken human shape in the Hebrew and Greek languages,
has become subject to human manipulation, which is to say, translation
into a thousand other languages, and to human study and interpretation,
or perhaps misinterpretation.

Is the Bible True?

We cannot now avoid this question, but it is a question which can have
more than one meaning. Is the Bible factually accurate? Is it inerrant,
which means incapable of containing mistakes? Does it present a faithful
portrayal of God and of His actions and purposes? Is every part of it of
equal value, or are some parts more completely God's word than other
parts? Does it tell the truth about humankind and the function, duties, and
responsibilities of human beings? These and other questions as well can
be contained in the query, Is the Bible True?

What is often termed the "conservative view" is that "the Bible has as
its ultimate source God himself, and . . . because God cannot lie or con-

tradict himself, the Bible cannot contain any errors or inconsistencies."[7] In other words, the Bible is inerrant. The so-called "liberal view" is that the biblical material is inevitably culturally affected, because it took shape in specific cultural situations, and was expressed in limited cultural languages, and that therefore some parts are less inspired than others, which display an "extraordinary stimulation and elevation of the powers of men who devoutly yielded themselves to God's will, and sought, often with success unparalleled elsewhere, to convey truth useful to the salvation of men and nations."[8]

There is an obvious weakness in this liberal view, for who has the right to say which parts of the Bible are more inspired and to condemn others as less inspired? Nevertheless, the position adopted in this book is that of the liberal rather than the conservative school.[9] This is because there are enormous difficulties about ascribing unbroken factual accuracy to the biblical records. Gone are the days when it was possible for such great scholars as William Foxwell Albright, Miller Burrows, John Garstang, and Nelson Glueck to claim that archaeological research has confirmed rather than challenged the biblical accounts. The wealth of discoveries that have taken place since their day have made archaeologists and biblical scholars much more cautious, for though these discoveries have thrown a flood of light upon the rich history of the biblical period, they have also challenged a great many apparent statements of historical fact in the Bible.[10]

The conservatives, it is true, are fully justified when they accuse the liberals of having undermined the authority of the Bible. Certainly, the liberal scholars never intended to do anything of the kind. What they set out to do, with full sincerity, was to use all the tools of modern scholarship to understand the Bible more profoundly, and to perceive the relevance of the rich biblical literature to the problems of the modern world.[11] Nevertheless, as they probed more deeply, and tried to disentangle all the different literary materials and sources, as well as the later additions by

---

7. Paul J. Achtemeier, *The Inspiration of Scripture: Problems and Proposals* (Philadelphia: Westminster Press, 1980), 50.

8. L. Harold DeWolf, *A Theology of the Living Church*, rev. ed. (New York: Harper & Brothers, 1960), 76. Quoted by Achtemeier, *Inspiration of Scripture*, 41.

9. This was the majority opinion among the contributors, but two argued strongly for biblical inerrancy. See additional notes.

10. Outstanding examples are the accounts of the capture of Jericho and Ai in Joshua 6—8. In fact the only conquest story in Joshua which seems really compatible with archaeological evidence is the capture of Hazor in 11:10–11. Another serious problem is the kingdom of Edom, which recent evidence indicates did not exist before about 700 B.C.

11. "Modern" here means the last 230 years, which is a very short time when one considers that the Exodus took place over three thousand years ago. The first attempt at documentary studies was a book published by Jean Astruc in 1753 in France. The two people who did most to establish the idea were K. H. Graf and Julius Wellhausen, writing in Germany between 1866 and 1883.

scribes diligently copying the manuscripts, they seemed to very many to have reduced the treasured text to little more than "a thing of shreds and patches."

Their intentions were honest and serious, but they tended to set on one side the question of "authority," and it is only in recent years that this question has become again in this country a subject for deep thought and serious discussion. In the fifteen or so years after World War II biblical scholarship in the United States was often exceedingly arid, and so anxious were departments of religion to get the subject accepted as a serious academic discipline that the Bible was taught as if the study of it were a purely intellectual exercise, making no demands at all upon the life and conscience of the reader. The situation changed greatly in the 1960s and 1970s, but we are still to some extent heirs of it.

But if the liberals have misused Scripture, so also have the conservatives, for they have tended only too often to impose upon it a preconceived interpretation, and to squeeze all the doubtful passages into this straitjacket. They have tended also to reject in advance all results of scientific and historical research that do not agree with their preconceptions. In short, the adherents of both schools of thought have been guilty of the essentially human sin of saying, "We are they that ought to speak; who is lord over us?" They have acted as if they were the masters rather than the servants of the text.

Liberal scholarship may have raised all sorts of uncomfortable questions about factual accuracy in some of the biblical accounts, but it has in no way undermined the authority of the Bible to make God known to us, nor has it destroyed the Bible as a major and essential source for ancient Israelite and early Christian history. What it has done has been to undermine biblical authority in scientific questions. But it is very doubtful whether any part of it was written for that purpose. All the biblical writings, from the first chapter of Genesis onward, were written for the instruction of men and women concerning the power, majesty, glory, love, and honesty of God. In this sense, and in this sense only, can the Bible be said to be altogether true. It is, of course, very often accurate in the factual pictures it presents, but it seems impossible in the light of all our modern knowledge to say that it is inerrant, incapable of making any factual error at all. In this matter, as in all others, "we have this treasure in earthen vessels, to show that transcendent power belongs to God and not to us" (2 Cor. 4:7).

Inspiration and Revelation

If nobody by searching can find out God, then it follows that if God is to be known at all by human beings, He must reveal Himself to them. If they are to speak of Him, He must inspire them, for from the resources of their own spirit alone they cannot speak truth concerning Him. This is axiomatic and few would deny it, but who or what is inspired, and what exactly is revealed—the biblical text, or God by means of the text?

Those who claim that the Bible is revelation directly inspired by God frequently quote three passages in support of their view:

All scripture is inspired by God and profitable for teaching, for reproof, for correction, and for training in righteousness, that the man of God may be complete, equipped for every good work.

2 Timothy 3:16–17

First of all you must understand this, that no prophecy of scripture is a matter of one's own interpretation, because no prophecy ever came by the impulse of man, but men moved by the Holy Spirit spoke from God.

2 Peter 1:20–21

Scripture cannot be broken.

John 10:35

Unfortunately, none of these critical passages is easy to translate exactly. The Greek wording in the quotation from 2 Timothy could just as well be translated "Every scripture inspired by God is also . . . ," indicating that not all scriptural material is so inspired. In the passage from 2 Peter it is not clear whether the word translated "moved" (in the Greek, literally "carried") means that the Holy Spirit dictated what the men were to say, or whether it means "encouraged" or "supported" them in what they said. Finally, in John 10:35 the translation "broken" is inadequate. The Greek word *luo* really means "broken into little pieces," and therefore "rendered useless, done away with, got rid of." When the same word is used in John 5:18, Jesus was being accused not merely of breaking the Sabbath, but of doing away with it altogether.

In the Christian understanding the true revelation, the true self-disclosure, of God is in the person of Jesus Christ. Here we can see God as completely as it is possible for limited human beings to see Him. "No one has ever seen God; the only Son, who is in the bosom of the Father, he has made him known" (John 1:18). If this claim is true, then all revelation and all inspiration must be tested against this supreme revelation. In other words, if anywhere in the Scriptures God is presented in a manner which clearly conflicts with the revelation in Jesus Christ, that presentation must be reckoned at best inadequate, or even perhaps seriously misleading.

This conclusion resolves some of the problems people have about revelation in the Scriptures, but creates some others. Thus, when we read that God commanded King Saul, "Now go and smite Amalek, and utterly destroy all that they have; do not spare them, but kill both man and woman, infant and suckling, ox and sheep, camel and ass," and then punished Saul for not carrying out this genocide to the full (1 Sam. 15:1–

23), we do not need to interpret this as an actual command of God, even though both Samuel and Saul understood it as such. Equally, when we read in Ezekiel 25 that God would utterly destroy the Ammonites, the Moabites, and the Edomites east of the Jordan, we are not required to see in this an assurance that their descendants are therefore destined to be themselves destroyed, and their cities and villages laid waste. And even more, when we read in Matt. 27:25 that the people of Jerusalem took full authority for the death of Jesus, saying, "His blood be on us and on our children!" we are not justified in saying, as Christians have done constantly, that the Jews throughout the ages must be punished for the crime.[12]

But if we adopt this position, we are faced with two major problems: (1) why are these passages in the Bible at all? (2) has not the Bible ceased to be the Holy Bible if readers can pick and choose in this manner? In response to these problems we need to return to Paul's statement already quoted, "We have this treasure in earthen vessels." The entire Christian faith rests upon the conviction that God revealed Himself most fully in Jesus of Nazareth, a Jew, brought up in a little village in Palestine, obedient to his parents (Luke 2:51), speaking Aramaic, and expressing himself always in terms of the Palestinian culture of his day. We should surely be making a great mistake if we tried to make the Bible more "holy" than Jesus, and did not recognize it as no less culturally conditioned. That both Saul and Samuel saw the slaughter of the Amalekites as something commanded by God is certainly true, but they interpreted the purposes of God in terms of the culture of their day. There was for them, indeed, no alternative. The passages are in the Bible because men and women are within the framework of time, and therefore the self-disclosure of God comes to them gradually, here a little and there a little, and the Bible is the priceless record of that disclosure, and of how men and women continually grew in knowledge and understanding. Were the Bible to contain nothing but "timeless truths," we would all be the poorer, because we would be the less aware of our own frailty, of the inadequacy of our understanding, and of our constant need to learn. "God hath yet a blessing to add to the reading of His holy word."

Revelation and the Role of Reason

If it is granted that human beings are created by God, then it follows that human reason is the gift of God and an essential part of His purposes

---

12. Despite notable exceptions, the history of Christian treatment of the Jews, to whom they owe so great a part of God's teaching, has been abominable, and the result of taking such passages a great deal too literally. And sadly, it is true that books by Christians are still published arguing that the Arabs east of the Jordan must inevitably be displaced and crushed, because this is the fulfillment of biblical prophecy.

for humanity. Yet it must never be forgotten that human reason is in fact human, and not in itself divine. Since it is the gift of God, we are intended to make full use of it, and indeed will have to answer to God if we neglect it. Since it is by nature human, it is therefore fallible, capable of brilliant and glorious achievements, but also capable of error, and altogether incapable of encompassing and comprehending God as He reveals Himself to the human heart and mind.

This problem of how revelation and reason are related to each other has haunted Christian minds from the very beginning. Some have argued that the self-disclosure of God so completely transcends human reason that reason has in fact no part to play. The second-century Christian writer Athenagoras said that the Spirit so entranced men that they became "its instruments, as a flute-player might play a flute." Tertullian in the early third century went further and appeared to reject reason altogether. "What indeed has Athens to do with Jerusalem? What concord is there between the Academy and the Church? . . . Away with all attempts to produce a mottled Christianity of Stoic, Platonic and dialectic composition! We want no curious disputation after possessing Jesus Christ, no inquisition after enjoying the Gospel."[13] And again, in an oft-quoted passage, "I believe because it is absurd." But he did not in fact reject reason, and at times extolled it: "Before all things existed God was alone. He was himself his own universe, his own place, everything. He was alone in the sense that there was nothing external to him, nothing outside his own being. Yet even then he was not alone; for he had with him something which was part of his own being, namely, his Reason."[14] He goes on later in the same passage to say that human reason is derived from the divine reason.

Tertullian's argument is that human reason, however brilliant it may be, cannot by itself be the arbiter and judge of revelation, which is the self-disclosure of God, since the less cannot assess the greater. Nevertheless, the Christian community from very early days, and constantly thereafter, has been suspicious of what might be called "unbridled revelation," ecstatic utterances, and behavior going far beyond what is considered rational speech and action.

It has done so both because extravagant ecstasy, even though authentic, seemed to do little, if anything, toward building up a solid and well-informed community, and also because it could only too easily get out of control and produce false and destructive beliefs. Thus Paul, though fully recognizing that the divine revelation may take unintelligible form, warns

---

13. Tertullian, *On Prescription against Heretics*, chap 7. Quoted by Etienne Gilson in *Reason and Revelation in the Middle Ages* (New York: Charles Scribner's Sons, 1938), 9–10. See additional notes.

14. Henry Bettenson, *The Early Christian Fathers* (New York: Oxford University Press, 1956), 162–63.

against speaking in tongues: "For one who speaks in a tongue speaks not to men but to God; for no one understands him, but he utters mysteries in the Spirit. On the other hand, he who prophesies speaks to men for their upbuilding and encouragement and consolation" (1 Cor. 14:2–3). The First Epistle of John likewise urges caution: "Beloved, do not believe every spirit, but test the spirits to see whether they are of God; for many false prophets have gone out into the world" (1 John 4:1). In other words the revelation, or at least the interpretation of revelation, must submit to constant, and at times ruthless, questioning.

On the other hand, reason cannot be allowed to dictate to revelation, since it is only by revelation that God can make Himself known, and a thoroughly rational and reasonable Christian community would not, in fact, be Christian at all, for it would exclude God altogether, or at best admit Him only on human terms. To be truly Christian the community must on the one hand be sensible and rational, and on the other display a healthy skepticism about the human capacity to deal in rational terms with ideas and forces in our lives that are nonrational or plainly irrational. The seventeenth-century mystic and mathematician, Blaise Pascal, knew this well when he wrote, "The heart has its reasons, of which reason knows nothing."[15]

The concept of an inspired scripture, rooted in belief in the one unchanging, trustworthy God, provides us with a source of confidence that we have an account of the world that is both wise and compatible with reality, despite the limits and changes in human experience. Christianity is therefore reasonable, but it demands something beyond reason. The mathematical equation $2 \times 2 = 4$ is rationally true within the accepted system of mathematical functions, and can within that system be proved to be true. But the statement, "Jesus Christ died for us while we were yet sinners," is a statement of a quite different kind of truth. One statement cannot be treated like the other, nor can one contradict the other. Each can be true within its own sphere. The second, however, cannot be proved by the exercise of reason; it can be proved (or disproved) only by experience, by committing oneself to it, by betting one's life that it is true.

For Augustine (354–430), true reasoning begins with faith in God, but it is "faith seeking understanding." Human reason with its own integrity, its powers and limits, is necessary to understand, accept, and appropriate what has been revealed, if there is to be true faith, and not just thought control. God's self-disclosure demands that we use our reason to comprehend it. "Far be it from us to think that God would hate in us that which distinguishes us from the beasts."[16] Revelation is necessary for men and

---

15. *Le coeur a ses raisons que la raison ne connait point.* Pensées, sect. 4, 227.
16. *Epistle* 120.3.

women, since it comes to heal the damaged human mind, which can comprehend the piercing light only dimly. It is not brainwashing.

The role, therefore, of reason is to comprehend revelation, and the role of revelation is to enlighten reason.

ADDITIONAL NOTES

9. One of the contributors wrote concerning inerrancy: "The biblical writers, inspired by God, wrote the words of God, and because these are God's words they must be perfect and without error in all matters, faith and practice as well as history and science. This is a position considered by many to be normative of the church throughout history.

"Inerrancy does not necessarily mean that God dictated the message, but it does mean that the biblical writers wrote what God intended them to write, and thus what they wrote is without error. They may have written out of a lifetime of experience or knowledge, as a result of observation, or by a more direct revelation. Most importantly, inerrancy does not always entail a strict literalism in interpretation. Where the Bible is intended to be literal, it should be taken literally; where it is intended to be symbolic, it should be interpreted symbolically; where a simile is intended, it should be taken as such. Inerrancy, however, does not include spelling and grammar, which have fluctuated over the centuries, and therefore belong to the realm of human fallibility.

"In scientific and historical matters the same rule applies: The Bible is to be taken in its natural and intended sense. Thus, when we are told in Joshua 10 that 'the sun halted in the middle of the sky; not for a day did it resume its swift course,' the reader is to understand that a miracle actually happened and that it remained day for much longer than normal. The natural and intended sense of this scripture does not include a scientific statement.

"One of the problems is that the manuscripts we possess today are none of them the actual originals, and only these can properly be called 'inerrant.' Mistakes in copying and corruptions may have crept into the text. However, because of the great amount of manuscript evidence, especially for the New Testament, scholars are confident that the text we have today is extremely reliable. It cannot be denied that apparent discrepancies exist, but in the present state of our knowledge the doctrine of inerrancy gives God's Word the benefit of the doubt.

"Essentially the problem is one of the authority. The doctrine of inerrancy affirms that the whole of Scripture, being the Word of God and inseparable from the divine, is the authoritative guide for Christian belief and practice, rather than reason or tradition. All things are to be measured according to it, even the Bible having to be understood in the light of itself."

This contributor wished to disassociate himself entirely from the argument presented in this chapter, which he regarded as thoroughly misleading. He said that it seriously misrepresented the position of believers in inerrancy, and imposed upon the Bible a purely human interpretation.

13. Tertullian said, "The Son of God died; it is by all means to be believed, because it is absurd. And he was buried and rose again; the fact is certain because it is impossible." This paradoxical statement, coming from a man deeply schooled in classical philosophy and rhetoric, was meant to shock the reader. We should understand it as a vivid way of saying that what he found revealed in the Christian message did not fit into the easy assumptions about the divine expressed in the classical intellectual tradition. In Christian belief Tertullian found himself confronted by an entirely different standard

from human rationality, but he sensed it as an authentic clue about reality insofar as it had broken radically from that rational order. A falsehood would have sought continuity with the accepted range of traditional human knowledge, rather than undermining it.

3

ONE GOD AND FATHER

Can you find out the deep things of God?
Can you find out the limit of the Almighty?
Job 11:7

What Is Meant by the Word "God"?

In considering the meaning of the universe, of which we form such a very tiny part, we have really only two choices: to argue that the universe is ultimately the source of its own meaning, or to argue that it is not, that its meaning must be in some way dependent on that which is not itself. The first may be described, but only *very* roughly, as the "scientific," and the second as the "religious" approach. In this chapter we shall be concerned with the religious understanding, but first three things must be made clear:

First, there is no suggestion here that the scientific approach is somehow less important. That would be absurd, for without the scientific method the universe cannot be properly understood at all. For Christians to speak disparagingly of science, or to ascribe to it a secondary place, would be sheer folly.

Second, *both* arguments are assumptions; they are faith statements. We cannot prove either of them.

Third, the word "meaning" does not, and cannot, signify "inherent meaning," for that is something which we can never discover. Whenever we speak of the meaning of anything, we are saying no more than what it means for us, the meaning as perceived by human beings. The meaning of the sun, the endlessly revolving planets, the nebulae, or of atoms and subatomic particles, can be only that meaning that we, the observers, attribute to them. It is restricted to what we believe we are able to detect.

27

When we study the universe, or even just this planet earth and its inhabitants, we are compelled, for the time being, to set on one side the religious approach. To introduce the divine activity in any form at all would be to render the research useless. All serious intellectual and scientific inquiry, using the word "scientific" in its broadest sense, proceeds by the method of identifying the thing to be studied, isolating it from any external influence which might interfere with the study, and then examining it for what it is in itself, as far as it is possible to discover this. It is by this process of isolation and examination that our now enormous and still rapidly expanding mass of knowledge about the universe has been achieved.[1]

Nevertheless, the study has to proceed further, since the object to be studied cannot be allowed to remain in lonely isolation. It must be put in its place, so to speak, and be seen where it really belongs—in relation to other things. Nothing that the human mind ever studies can be properly understood except in terms of relationship, for nothing exists all by itself, but only as part of a complex pattern of other things, and it is only in relation to these things that it takes on meaning.[2] Therefore, everything of which we have any knowledge at all depends for its meaning, not upon itself, but always upon that which is not itself. Consequently, it is not unreasonable to conclude that the entire vast universe also derives its meaning from that which is not itself, from "something other." But what that "something other" may be is altogether beyond human research, for the universe, the space-time continuum, is the totality of what the human intellect can discover and examine. In speaking of something other than the universe we peer into that realm which lies altogether beyond the frontiers of human knowledge, as it were into the realm of "otherness" itself, transcending human comprehension.

Not all men and women, of course, would accept this conclusion. Very many, indeed, proceed upon the other assumption, that "out there" is merely nothingness and that ultimate meaning, if it is to be glimpsed at all, can be sought nowhere else but in the universe itself. All that is being said here is that belief in "something other" is by no means irrational. So far along the path belief and reason may still walk hand in hand, and about one thing they may fully agree: the essential oneness of ultimate truth.

That truth cannot in the last resort conflict with truth is, of course, also an assumption, but for all scientific and intellectual inquiry it is a necessary assumption. If in the course of prolonged research two apparently contradictory conclusions appear to be true, neither may be rejected. Both

1. See additional notes.

2. The classic statement of the two types of relationship, "I-It" and "I-You," is to be found in Martin Buber, *I and Thou* (New York: Charles Scribner's Sons, 1970).

must be accepted for the time being, in the assurance that some day further research will disclose their unifying relationship.[3] All the so-called great religions also base their teachings upon this same conviction that ultimate truth is fundamentally one. They speak, therefore, of the one God, the one *Tao*, the essential unity of *Brahman* and *Atman*, and so on.[4]

It follows, then, that the Christian believer, wholeheartedly committed to faith in the One God, the source of all truth, is not merely taking refuge in irrational fantasy, and also that such a believer would have no fear of scientific and intellectual inquiry. Rather, he or she should delight in it, being assured that every step toward the truth brings the believer closer to God Himself.

But one further question remains before we turn to Christian belief in particular. It is the problem of how men and women can have any solid basis for religious belief beyond the conviction that the universe depends for its meaning on a vague "something out there." Left to themselves, of course, they cannot have such a basis, for they can never by their own endeavors discover what lies beyond the further limits of human perception. There is only one hope for them. The Truth beyond the limits must somehow make itself known. There must be disclosure, revelation, or, to use the Buddhist word, enlightenment.

It is, of course, the firm conviction of religious believers throughout the world that such disclosure does take place. The secularist is apt to dismiss these claims as deceptions, either purely subjective or else culturally conditioned. Certainly, many religious beliefs, once sincerely held to be truths of revelation, have had to be abandoned, but that does not invalidate the concept any more than now discarded beliefs of science[5] discredit the scientific method. Moreover, we have to remember that *all* human thought is to a large extent subjective, and is always culturally conditioned. Our constant temptation is to believe this to be true of the past, and of thought forms foreign to us, such as Communism, but not true of our own "enlightened minds."

Indeed, all so-called fundamental truths, even though less than the one ultimate Truth, can be discovered only very partially by inquiry. They must demonstrate their own trustworthiness. For this reason we assert, "We hold these truths to be self-evident, that all men are created equal. . . . " It is by no means necessary that revelation is separate from, or the enemy of, reason, nor that reason is either superior or inferior to revelation. Both have a part to play in a full understanding of the universe and the human situation within it.

---

3. An excellent example of this kind of situation is the nineteenth-century conflict between the wave and the corpuscular theories of light.

4. See additional notes.

5. E.g., the phlogiston theory of the late eighteenth and early nineteenth centuries.

Believing in One God

We must not suppose that the early Christians arrived at their belief in One God by the kind of intellectual argument with which this chapter has begun, or that the One God revealed Himself in the first century A.D. to a people who had not known Him before. All the earliest Christians were in fact Jews, and it was only with much hesitancy that non-Jews were admitted to their community.[6] The Jews of that time were firmly monotheist, wholeheartedly committed to being a "light to the nations" (Isa. 49:6), to demonstrating to a world accustomed to a multiplicity of gods the inadequacy of such beliefs, and they had been conscious of this function for more than five hundred years.

In earlier centuries, however, the God whom they had encountered in the desert wastes of Sinai, whom they knew as Yahweh and with whom they entered into covenant, did not seem to them to be the only god, but one among very many. In the covenant, the terms of which are found in the Ten Commandments (Exod. 20:1–17; Deut. 5:6–21), they had certainly committed themselves to worship only this god. Yet they recognized that other nations had other gods and, right up to the end of the monarchy and the destruction of Jerusalem in 587 B.C., they often succumbed to worshiping some of them, despite the angry protestations of the prophets.[7] The prophet Amos in about 750 B.C. seems to have been the first to recognize that Yahweh, the God whom they worshiped, must be the God of the whole earth (Amos 9:2–4, 7), but the prophet known today as the Second Isaiah,[8] teaching in Babylon about 540–530 B.C., was the first person to proclaim in absolute terms that there could be no other gods (for example, Isa. 44:8).

Monotheism, the belief that if there be God at all there is and can be only one, seems to most westerners today to be so obvious that it can be taken for granted without further discussion. But it is, in fact, obvious only in theory. In practice it seems far from evident. Both Hindus and Mahayana Buddhists accept the concept of more than one god, and though Christians cannot accept this themselves, they would be wrong to dismiss such people as benighted heathens without careful and honest study of their religious beliefs. Even more disturbing is the fact of enormous evil in the world, which cannot easily be reconciled with belief in one God, understood to be inherently loving and righteous. Dualism, the belief that

---

6. See, for example, Acts 10, especially v. 28, and also Acts 13:44–52.

7. Jer. 44:15–28; Ezekiel 8. Evidence of the worship of the mother-goddess in the seventh century B.C., only a few hundred yards south of the Temple, was found by Kathleen Kenyon, *Jerusalem: Excavating 3000 Years of History* (London: Thames and Hudson, 1967), 101.

8. The teachings of the Second Isaiah are found in chapters 40—55 of the Book of Isaiah.

opposing the righteous God is another power, demonic and evil, and also transcending the universe, has been throughout the centuries a persistent and very tempting alternative to monotheism. The problem of evil is in fact so frightening and intractable that many who "profess and call themselves Christian" prefer to close their eyes to it. The Bible gives no explicit answer, and it seems that the answer is known only to God Himself.

Indeed, only relatively few people, even among committed Christians, adhere steadfastly to trusting in only one God. To believe sincerely in one God means to reject all alternative sources of authority for life and behavior. In theory, of course, all Christians do this, but for very many of them the God made known to them in the pages of the Bible, and whom they worship on Sunday, retreats into the background on Monday, when in the hurly-burly of day-to-day life other principles, that is, other gods, begin to make absolute demands, notably the gods of the marketplace—the "mammon" of the New Testament (Matt. 6:24)—and gods of the political forum. So vast a country as the United States, though claiming in principle to be "one nation under God," has to admit that many in the country do not share this belief, and have to be granted full rights of worship after their own manner, or even allowed to reject the concept of God entirely. Here we make a virtue out of necessity, and speak proudly of religious freedom and pluralism, but "pluralism" could easily become a code word for polytheism.[9]

The early Christians had to come to grips with this problem when they became more and more involved with the foreign, Gentile world during the second half of the first century and the second century A.D., and when consequently an increasing number of their members came from a Gentile, polytheistic background. Although they had to wrestle with the problem intellectually, they did not approach it as a purely intellectual question. They could not be disinterested. When they thought about God, it was always as historic communal beings and as believers. Talk about God was for them the story of their life. "When a Christian says 'God' he does not mean that a being exists who is the beginning of the solar system or of the cosmos, or the great mathematician who figured out a world in which mathematicians can take delight. What he means, what he points to with the word 'God,' is a being infinitely attractive, which by its very nature calls forth devotion, joy and trust. This God is always 'my God,' 'our good,' 'our beginning,' and 'our end.'"[10]

---

9. See additional notes.

10. H. Richard Niebuhr, *The Meaning of Revelation* (New York: Macmillan Co., 1960), 25.

Our Father in Heaven

These words come from Jesus himself, who constantly addressed God
as "Father," and taught his followers to do the same (Matt. 6:9; Luke
11:2). They form the opening words of the Lord's Prayer, which Christians
throughout the world have used since the very beginning of the Christian
community. Yet today they are being called in question by many, who see
in the use of the term "Father" a perpetuation of male dominance over
women. This protest is part of a very much wider revolt against paternalism, against the idea that any group of people should remain in tutelage
to another people, however well-intentioned they may be. "Humankind
has come of age,"[11] say the protesters, "and human beings are all by their
very nature mature enough to look after themselves."[12]

There is unfortunately plenty of evidence that throughout history Christians have used the Bible to justify various forms of human domination—
male supremacy, colonial rule, religious discrimination, privileges of
wealth, white superiority, and so on. Yet the New Testament gives little
support to such arguments. Certainly, it urges respect for authority.

> Let every person be subject to the governing authorities. For there is no authority
> except from God, and those that exist have been instituted by God. Therefore he
> who resists the authorities resists what God has appointed, and those who resist
> will incur judgment.
>
> Romans 13:1–2

It supports the role of the father as head of the family.

> Be subject to one another out of reverence for Christ. Wives, be subject to your
> husbands, as to the Lord. For the husband is head of the wife as Christ is head
> of the church.
>
> Ephesians 5:21–23

It even supports the continuation of slavery.

> Slaves, be obedient to those who are your earthly masters, with fear and trem-
> bling, in singleness of heart, as to Christ.
>
> Ephesians 6:5

Yet at the same time it urges love and generosity on the part of those in
authority (Eph. 5:25; 6:9).

But while insisting upon authority and subservience, the same writers
urge that, whatever may be true of the world outside, in the Christian community all men and women are equal.

---

11. The phrase originated with Dietrich Bonhoeffer in his *Letters and Papers from Prison* (New
York: Macmillan Co., 1953), though he wrote, "Mankind has come of age."

12. A very helpful short book on the subject is W. A. Visser 't Hooft, *The Fatherhood of God
in an Age of Emancipation* (Geneva: World Council of Churches, 1982).

> There is neither Jew nor Greek, there is neither slave nor free, there is neither male nor female; for you are all one in Christ Jesus.
>
> Galatians 3:28

> Christ is our peace, who has made us both one, and has broken down the dividing wall of hostility, by abolishing in his flesh the law of commandments and ordinances, that he might create in himself one new man in place of the two, so making peace.
>
> Ephesians 2:14–15

This apparent contradiction stems from the fact that the writers of such passages were convinced that Christ would soon return in glory and that the world would end. They saw the structure of society, therefore, as temporary, and they urged compliance with it for the sake of peace and order. The essential equality of all men and women, however, was part of the new creation and destined to endure. Nearly two thousand years later we have to recognize that they were mistaken in expecting the immediate end of the world, but this does not mean that they were mistaken in insisting upon equality. Authority and obedience are necessary features of any human society if there is not to be anarchy and disorder, but it is an essential Christian conviction that no human beings have *inherent* authority over other people and, moreover, that authority, when it is granted, bestows no superior nature, but imposes upon the recipient the role and function of a servant:

> And he said to them, "The kings of the Gentiles exercise lordship over them; and those in authority over them are called benefactors. But not so with you; rather let the greatest among you become as the youngest, and the leaders as one who serves."
>
> Luke 22:25–26

Therefore, Christians who quote the Bible in support of authoritarian systems and structures are almost certainly wrong. The fatherhood of God gives no support for any kind of absolutism.

The early Christian writers insisted that power and authority belonged to God alone, and were in no sense the prerogative of any human being, however exalted and majestic. Human beings were no more than His deputies. About this they were adamant. Other people might drop a pinch of incense upon the altar of the Emperor, in recognition of him as the ultimate arbiter of human affairs, but Christians would not. The Roman rulers saw this refusal as nothing less than dangerous sedition, and many martyrs suffered because of it.

The term "Father" applied to God suggests to many people today what they would call sexist language, but this was never the intention of the New Testament writers. They were certainly opposed to the adoration of Artemis and the whole cult of the mother goddess, which was strongly sexual, and very powerful in Anatolia, the modern Turkey. But then they never thought of attributing sex to God in any way. Sex was for them a human and animal phenomenon, an aspect of the creation, but not an aspect of the Creator. Instead, when they addressed God directly as "Father," following the example and teaching of Jesus, they thought of the intimate relationship of a father with his family, full of affection for his wife and children, working to ensure that they were both clothed and fed, occasionally severe, as a father must sometimes be, but longing for their welfare, comforting and strengthening them in times of trouble and distress. In the Gospels the true father is exemplified in the parable of the Prodigal Son (Luke 15:11–32), in which the father is ready and willing to grant his son complete freedom, and no less ready to restore him to full fellowship, even after he has completely disgraced himself.

The idea of God as Father, and also, though this is often overlooked, as Mother, was already there in the Jewish heritage:

Yea, like as a father pitieth his own children; even so
is the LORD merciful unto them that fear him.
                          Psalm 103:13 (Coverdale)

As one whom his mother comforts,
    so will I comfort you.
                          Isaiah 64:13

Can a woman forget her sucking child,
    that she should have no compassion on the
    son of her womb?
Even these may forget,
    yet I will not forget you.
                          Isaiah 49:15

In the thinking of the day, the father was understood to be the one who initiated the process of producing life, of making the necessary decision, but, of course, the child was born from the mother. So the will of the child was thought of as coming from the father, but the mother endowed him or her with physical identity. Consequently, in speaking of God as Father, they spoke of Him as the One who by sheer dynamism of will and purpose brought into existence the universe and every part of it. The mother image for God, though certainly less frequent, was confined to the relationship between God and human beings, and it is an image that needs to be rediscovered today.

Jesus showed his followers the full depth of this rich heritage. He addressed God as *Abba* (Father) and he taught his disciples to do the same (Mark 14:36; Rom. 8:15; Gal 4:6). No one before him had dared to address the almighty creator of the universe in such intimate terms. Unfortunately, Abba defies translation into English. Certainly it means "father," but it means very much more. It is one of the very first words that a baby learns, equivalent to "daddy," but it is also a word of dignity and respect, as well as affection and concern; an elemental word that is not to be discarded with childhood. Fully grown men and women, established in the world and with a family of their own, would still say *Abba* to their father, and in doing so they honored him.

Jesus' own human father disappears early from the gospel story, having only a marginal part to play even in the story of the child Jesus in the Temple (Luke 2:41–51), but his mother remained very close to him, to the point of staying with him as he died on the cross. We have, of course, no direct information, but it would seem that very much of what he learned as a child, and even as a young man, he must have learned from her. The Roman Catholic and Orthodox churches are much more aware of this important fact than are Protestants, but probably all need to meditate upon it, and to reflect on its significance in relation to the fatherhood of God. "There is neither male nor female, for all are one in Christ Jesus," and both are one, therefore, in the Godhead.

How, then, shall we speak and write of God? What pronoun shall we use? All pronouns, he, she, and it, are inadequate and misleading, for they are human words for phenomena of this world. We are probably committed to "he," since it is the language of the New Testament and above all the Lord's Prayer, but it would do us good, in saying this prayer, to think of both father and mother. We shall, therefore, continue to use "he" in this book, as we have done already, but spell it always with a capital, to indicate that in speaking of God we do not use it in its normal human sense.

Believing in God Today

The argument that God is, and must be, other, altogether beyond the limits of human discovery and comprehension, seems to set God at such an infinite distance from us that He is irrelevant. How can we speak of Him at all? Two biblical books, Job and Ecclesiastes, are fully aware of the problem posed by God's absolute transcendence:

Lo, he passes by me, and I see him not;
 he moves on, but I do not perceive him

How then can I answer him,
 choosing my words with him?

If I summoned him, and he answered me,
 I would not believe that he was listening to my voice.
Job 9:11–16

Be not rash with your mouth, nor let your heart be hasty to utter a word before God, for God is in heaven, and you upon earth; therefore let your words be few.
Ecclesiastes 5:2

Devout Muslims insist that we can say nothing about God except that He is, and He is eternal. To assert more is for them blasphemy. Nevertheless, as we have seen, the Jewish people, wholeheartedly monotheistic, have always maintained that God does indeed make Himself known, and Muslims delight in repeating and meditating upon the ninety-nine "beautiful names" of God.[13] There is an unbroken body of human experience which insists that although God is in principle unknowable, He nevertheless can in fact be known. How can this be so?

If it be true that the whole vast universe is not the source of its own meaning, but can be said to have meaning only in terms of what is not itself, in terms of the other, for which we use the word "God," then God can have meaning, that is, "meaning for us," only in terms of the unierse. God, therefore, is revealed to us in the universe, which is altogether other than Him, but to which He is and must be intimately related.

We must take this concept of otherness seriously. What the universe is, God is not; what God is, the universe is not. The universe is a space-time continuum, which means that it has a beginning and an end. God is unlimited, infinite, altogether other than both space and time. But when we speak of infinity, we do not speak only of the infinitely great, for a true understanding of infinity involves recognizing that it transcends all conceivable methods of measuring. The infinite God, therefore, must be also infinitely small, or, as Blaise Pascal put it in the seventeenth century, "an infinitely minute point moving at infinite speed." God so understood not only transcends the greatest that we can conceive, but is infinitely close to us, immeasurably concerned with things that to us seem too trivial to bother about. "The very hairs of your head are all numbered" (Matt. 10:30 KJV).[14] God does not experience past or future; for Him all is present, everything is "now." Moreover, the infinite must be the source of the finite and not the other way around, since time cannot produce eternity, nor space infinity. We quite rightly, therefore, speak of God as Creator. Indeed, we are compelled to do so, for as far as we can see, the universe did not bring itself into existence.

Whatever else, then, God may be said to be, He is certainly sheer, unadulterated power. However, to many in the world today power has become something of a dirty word, and power politics an opprobrious term. But this is a misunderstanding. There is no other kind of politics except power politics, for that is what politics is all about. There are, of course, many other kinds of power in the world: economic power, techno-

---

13. These are such names as the *Merciful*, the *Compassionate*, the *All-knowing*, the *Alive*, the *Self-subsisting*, the *Wise*, the *Protector*, the *Avenger*, etc., all of which describe the character of God.

14. See additional notes.

logical power, military power, nuclear power, electricity, tides, intellectual power, physical strength, social pressure, and so on. Without the constant presence of power actively at work we should be imprisoned, motionless, and without hope in an entirely static universe. Indeed, we should never have been born.

Power, energy, force—by these the entire universe was brought into existence, and is unceasingly controlled and maintained. But all have this curious characteristic: we can never say exactly what they are. We can study only how they act and what they do. We cannot say what gravity is, what electricity is, what the ability of one human being to dominate another actually is, although we know how and when they operate and can utilize this activity for our own purposes. We can recognize the thrusting power of life, which enables a blade of grass sometimes to break through a rock, but we cannot say exactly when a human body is no longer alive, and the more precise our measurements, the less precise are our statements about physical death.

All power, therefore, lies in one important sense "beyond the limits," apparently beyond the frontiers of human discovery and knowledge, and must be said to *belong*, not to human beings, nor to anything else that we can discern in the universe, but to the realm of the other, the realm, Christians would say, of God. From this we may proceed to the suggestion that God is most effectively disclosed to the human mind, not in static or philosophic terms, but in terms of *dynamism*, or *activity*, that is to say, in terms of power, force, energy at work, maintaining all that is in existence.

The New Testament is almost as cautious as the Muslim about daring to say what God actually is, but the Johannine writings contain three such statements: "God is spirit" (John 4:24); "God is light" (1 John 1:5); and "God is love" (1 John 4:8). To these we should almost certainly add the opening words of John's Gospel: "In the beginning was the Word, and the Word was with God and the Word was God." Since the writer of the Gospel was beyond doubt thinking of the opening words of Genesis,[15] what he is saying here is that the fundamental reality of our existence is the sheer power of bringing into *being*, constantly at work in our world. It is the essential newness of everything, and of every moment and every day, which he insists upon before ever he starts to tell the story of Jesus.

When, shortly afterward, he recounts how Jesus said to the Samaritan woman, "God is spirit, and those who worship him must worship him in spirit and truth" (John 4:24), the same sense of dynamic power making everything new is present. Both in Hebrew and in Greek one word is used

---

15. "In the beginning God created the heaven and the earth." But see the whole chapter, with its emphasis on God speaking, i.e., on "the Word."

to signify wind, breath, and spirit. When in John 3:8 Jesus tells Nicodemus, "The wind blows where it will," he is speaking of invisible, irresistible power actively at work. So also in the famous vision of the Valley of
Dry Bones, where Ezekiel was commanded to prophesy to the wind
(Ezek. 37:1–10), wind, spirit, and the power of new and active life are all
combined in the one Hebrew word *ruach*.

When we turn to the statements in the First Epistle of John that God is
light and also love, we are still in the presence of irresistible power. Light
is a force moving at a speed which nothing else in the universe can surpass, and even before our present scientific knowledge light was thought
of as power, piercing the darkness, which cannot overcome it (John 1:5).
Similarly love can never be a passive emotion. It must issue forth continually in action, or it is not love at all. Spirit can thus be seen as that which
makes all things *cohere*, binding them together into one active and
meaningful existence, light as that which makes things *coherent*, revealing
their integrated meaning to the human mind, and love as that which makes
things *cohesive*, welding men and women of all races together indissolubly
in the true community.

To these Johannine statements we may perhaps dare to add three others;
that God is life, that God is mind, and that God is purpose. The word
Father, of course, claims that He is the initiator of life, but we need to go
further and say that life issues forth from Him, and that He is indeed life
itself. The universe is certainly not what we could call in any meaningful
sense alive, and for most of its existence our own planet seems to have
been lifeless. Once we have accepted the hypothesis that God is what the
universe is not, we must surely go further and say that life belongs to the
essence of God, since it apparently does not belong to the essence of the
universe, of which the greater part seems to be altogether without life.

That God is mind is a concept we owe to the scientists rather than the
theologians. We cannot, of course, say what lay behind the "big bang,"
with which most physicists believe the universe began, for any prior evidence must have been destroyed by the "bang" itself. We can do no more
than speculate. In fact, we cannot properly speak of "before the big bang"
at all, since time is a dimension of the universe and began at that point.[16]
Yet the fascinating patterns, structures, and developments which proceeded out of the bang and which unfold continually before our eyes as
our explorations of the universe extend further and further have suggested
to more than one thinker that mind and reason must somehow lie behind
and beyond the universe, though not all would go so far as to call this God.

But mind without purpose, without will and intention, seems a con-

16. One of the most remarkable features of the account of creation in Genesis 1, too little
noticed by commentators, is the statement that time began at creation—a very sophisticated concept for someone writing at the latest twenty-five hundred years ago.

tradition in terms. If we are right in arguing that God is most effectively revealed in activity and also right in speaking of God as "mind," then mind and activity must belong together, the second proceeding from the first, and we must think of God in terms of sheer will. This, of course, is thoroughly biblical, for in Genesis God creates the world by direct command, and in Isa. 55:10–11 His word rushes forth to fulfill His will, and does not return until this is done. But no less important is the impact of the Mind of God upon the minds of men and women, His direct self-disclosure, for apart from this impact God would have no meaning or reality for us. We cannot ourselves by searching find out God, for He completely transcends us. He must make Himself known.

Images and Idols

> You shall not make for yourself a graven image, or any likeness of anything that is in heaven above, or that is in the earth beneath, or that is in the water under the earth; you shall not bow down to them or serve them.
>
> Exodus 20:4–5

Man is not God, and God is not man.[17] All Christian belief, and indeed all three monotheistic religions, are built upon this assertion. Men and women are finite and mortal. We have a beginning and an end. We are limited in both time and space, and limited also in everything we do, say, or think. At no point at all is the human being, or even the whole human race, capable of the absolute or the infinite. Therefore, when we think or speak of the absolute and infinite, we are driven to use symbols, and in describing the activity of God to tell symbolic stories, for which the technical term is "myth."

This may seem quite obvious, but so incapable are men and women of comprehending, or even coming close to, the infinite that many forget again and again that the words they use are symbols, and they slip into thinking that these words are *factual* descriptions of God, and that the stories are literal accounts. Sometimes, it is true, men and women are aware that when they themselves speak of God, they are using only picture language, but believe that the biblical writers, being closer to God, were able to describe Him exactly.

What is forgotten is that there is literally *no* other way at all of speaking about God except by using symbols, and that all symbols are images. The making of images of God is, of course, forbidden in the Commandments, for the excellent reason that all images are inadequate, and therefore false and misleading, but we cannot avoid making images, even if we steer clear

---

17. A large number of contributors pointed out that Christians understand Jesus to be uniquely both God and man. This is true and will be discussed in chapter 5, but it in no way detracts from the basic assertion that human nature and divine nature are essentially different.

of wood and stone. We seem here to be in an impasse, compelled to do what is forbidden. The only way out is to be fully conscious that we are in fact making images, and conscious, therefore, that we must at all costs avoid turning the images into idols, ascribing to them an absolute value which they do not possess. We must not treat them as authoritative, bowing down to them and serving them, for "that way madness lies."

A strangely persistent and certainly false verbal image is the use of "a God" instead of "God." It is altogether false because it conveys the sense of one among many, just as "a glass" or "a stone" indicate single objects among a multitude of similar ones, whereas "glass" and "stone" are comprehensive terms. The expression "a God" belongs to the eighteenth-century belief in a Supreme Being, but God is not, and cannot be, an entity, a being. Some theologians have spoken of Him as Being itself, or the Ground of Being, and in this they speak the truth. Everything else exists, God alone is.

Yet this is a cold truth. We cannot do without our images, without such words as *light, life, spirit,* and *mind.* And above all, we cannot do without the image of *father* and *mother,* if we are to express the Christian experience of close personal relationship with God, and His intimate, unceasing care for us in our weakness. But we must not idolize these terms—they are still images.

ADDITIONAL NOTES

1. One contributor wrote, "A good statement, but 'external influence' includes also those preconceptions which guide a scientist in his search for relevant relationships. Louis Pasteur said that 'the illusions of an experimenter form a great part of his power. These are the preconceived ideas which serve to guide him. Many of these vanish in the long path which he must travel, but one fine day he discovers and proves that some of them are adequate to the truth.' (Garrett Hardin and Carl Bajema, ed., *Biology: Its Principles and Implications* [New York: W.H. Freeman, 1978], 7)." Another contributor disagreed to some extent with the argument put forward, saying: "I agree that 'science' as the search for truth and reality should never be rejected by Christians, and that science proper should not include the divine as part of its research, but science in actual practice is in no sense pure. False presuppositions, faulty assertions, pride in holding on to particular theories, are all things which lead Christians, as well as others, to talk disparagingly of science. I do not think that it is sheer folly to ascribe to science a secondary place. Science deals with the universe and how things work; religion deals with the purpose of life and why things are the way they are. If these are taken as acceptable definitions, then I see religion as being the more important of the two."

4. Some contributors objected to the inclusion here of the Hindu belief about Brahman and Atman, pointing out with perfect truth that Hinduism is well known for its multiplicity of gods. Nevertheless, the argument of the Bhagavad Gita, to give but one example, is that those who offer themselves sincerely to these different gods are in fact worshiping the One.

9. This section caused a great deal of discussion and some sharp criticism. The objection was largely to the idea that people who go sincerely to church on Sunday could be worshiping other gods during the rest of the week. This seemed to some a contradiction in terms, one contributor commenting: "The idea of a sun god is on a totally different level from a god of the political forum. You are comparing the actual belief in a particular god to a situation in which priorities step in front of God. There are no grounds for such a comparison. In the next paragraph you talk about how the early Christians had to deal with polytheistic people, but committed Christians are not polytheistic just because they succumb to the temptation of other priorities. Polytheism means many actual gods."

With all respect to this position, there does seem to be some misunderstanding here about what worshiping other gods means, both in the Old Testament and in the New. When David complained to Saul that being forced to live in another country meant his being forced to "serve other gods" (1 Sam. 26:19), he meant that in a foreign country he would have to accept foreign principles and methods of behavior. To obey another god does not just mean addressing one's prayers to something called Zeus or Astarte. It means being obedient to principles and priorities other than those of God Himself, as made known to us in the Bible. If anything is allowed to have priority, or take precedence, in relation to God, then we have allowed something which is not God to act as if it were God, which is idolatry. If we say about nuclear arms that the security of the United States must take precedence over all other considerations, or that in advertising the essential purpose is to ensure a profit for the company rather than tell the truth, then surely what we have done is to set up an idol, and say, "My future depends on this, and so this is what I will obey." This is well discussed by H. Richard Niebuhr in his short book, *Radical Monotheism and Western Culture* (New York: Harper & Brothers, 1943).

14. It is curious that before the development of modern physics so little attention should have been given to the question of whether God, being Himself infinite, could have created an infinite universe. Surely there cannot be two infinities, distinct from each other? Thoughtful Christians owe a great debt of gratitude to Einstein!

4

CREATOR AND
CREATION

And he showed me more, a little thing, the size of a hazelnut, on the palm of my
hand, round like a ball. I looked at it thoughtfully and wondered, "What is this?"
And the answer came, "It is all that is made." I marvelled that it continued to
exist and did not suddenly disintegrate; it was so small. And again my mind sup-
plied the answer, "It exists, both now and for ever, because God loves it."

Julian of Norwich, *Revelations of
Divine Love* (c. A.D. 1393)

In the Beginning

"In the beginning," we are told, "God created the heavens and the
earth" (Gen. 1:1). Beginnings and endings are powerful occasions in the
lives of individuals and communities. They may be sudden or gradual, and
they are seen as providing meaning about human life. We are finite beings
and we live in a world of beginnings and endings. Some we mark by
ceremonies and some by symbols, such as a college gateway or the threshold of a house. Each underscores our human experience of passage,
change, finality, and renewal. What we say about these beginnings and
endings can seldom be literal accounts. They are faith statements, and
therefore always open to rethinking and deeper understanding. In speaking
about origins, we speak about the nature of human existence and the
human condition, and in speaking of the end we speak of life's purpose
and our destiny. Such statements may be profoundly true, but they are
always pictures, symbolic language describing what no human being has
ever seen.

Throughout human history there has been a need to go beyond the confines of the present moment, beyond the here and now. This is not just
curiosity. We need to discover in these powerful events some sense of
energy and direction, so that we may understand and cope with the present. Some do so mathematically, constructing models on the basis of dig-
ital calculation to describe and predict our world. Other models are

analogical, visual, sensual, or linguistic. Perhaps the person most open to this understanding of human experience and knowledge may be the physicist, fully conscious that his work involves the making of constantly improving models. Certainly, a model is never the world, and yet it is only by making models that we can understand the world at all. Nor does one method of model building exhaust the possibilities of human experience. We are not more human if we see the world through the eyes of Einstein only, and not also of El Greco.

In modern society there are different ways of perceiving beginnings and endings, according to whether we see the universe as the source of its own meaning, or as dependent for meaning upon that which is not itself. Many see this as a conflict between science and religion—a dramatic but oversimplified view, which nevertheless illustrates the confusion we often feel when we try to relate religious faith to scientific research, or to any other aspect of secular culture. A way out of this difficulty has been suggested by Langdon Gilkey.[1] He points out that traditionally science, philosophy, and religion have asked distinct, but related, questions about the universe and have constructed their own worldviews, sometimes at variance with each other. Today this variance is more acute, since the modern scientific perception of the universe is no longer that of something finished and stable, but of incessant change. The scientist seeks to trace the cause and effect relationships of the physical world in order to learn about the origins of the universe. The philosopher asks a different question: Why is there anything at all; why is there something and not nothing? The religious question is different again. It probes the meaning of life and asks, Why am I here and what must I do?

Our concern in this chapter is with the religious question. This does not mean that religion is separate from culture in general, but rather that the Christian religion has something else significant to say about the world in which we live. We must not, of course, try to use the Christian creed or the Bible as a kind of textbook from which we can correct science, nor can we use science to prove the Christian faith. Our question is simply this: In what sense is it meaningful in today's world to speak of God as Maker of heaven and earth?

Creation in the Old Testament

For all early Christians the sacred Scriptures were the books of what today we call the Old Testament. It was from these writings that they drew their understanding of creation.[2] The two accounts at the beginning of Genesis are the most familiar to us today, but they by no means exhaust

---

1. Langdon Gilkey, *Maker of Heaven and Earth: The Christian Doctrine of Creation in the Light of Modern Knowledge* (Garden City, N.Y.: Doubleday & Co., 1959), 15-40.

2. The theme of this section is dealt with more fully in Denis Baly, *God and History in the*

the subject. The theme of creation comes up again in Genesis, and frequently in the Book of Psalms and in the writings of the Prophets.

In speaking of creation the Hebrew writers were not attempting a factual account of the beginning of the universe. They were concerned with the far more urgent and immediate question of its significance, and the meaning, therefore, of human life within it. To explain this they drew upon traditions older than their own, such as the myth of the destruction of the dragon of chaos in order to make the world.[3]

> Thou didst divide the sea by thy might;
>   thou didst break the heads of the dragons on the waters.
> Thou didst crush the heads of Leviathan,
>   thou didst give him as food for the creatures of
>   the wilderness.
>
> Psalm 74:13–14

They used these different images because the meaning of the universe cannot be expressed in a single statement. One concept, however, they completely rejected: the idea, most widespread in ancient Egypt, that the universe came into existence spontaneously, by generation and birth.

Israel's creation myths differed from those in surrounding cultures also in another way: they were concerned less with the renewal of natural cycles than with history. The Creation and the Exodus, i.e. the delivery from Egypt, followed by the preservation of the people in the desert and the beginning of the nation, were seen as parallel to each other.

> For the Lord is a great God,
>   and a great King above all gods.
> In his hand are the depths of the earth;
>   the heights of the mountains are his also.
> The sea is his, for he made it;
>   for his hands formed the dry land.
>
> He is our God,
>   and we are the people of his pasture,
>   and the sheep of his hand.
>
> O that today you would hearken to his voice!
>   Harden not your hearts, as at Meribah,[4]
>   as on the day of Massah in the wilderness,
> when your fathers tested me,
>   and put me to the proof.
>
> Psalm 95:3–5, 7–9
> See also Psalm 136

Old Testament, a book also written in close cooperation with Kenyon College students (New York: Harper & Row, 1976), chaps. 9–10. See also Claus Westermann, *Creation,* trans. J. J. Sullivan (Philadelphia: Fortress Press, 1974). An excellent short book on the subject.

3. The most celebrated example of this myth is the Babylonian *Enuma Elish.*

4. Meribah and Massah were the place where the Israelites rebelled against God as a result of their sufferings in the desert (Exod. 17:7).

It was in the historic experience of liberation from Egypt, the Exodus and the covenant, that a new perception of the world and of God was revealed. Israel, seeking to understand this new reality and their national identity, looked back at the origin of the world from the foot of Mt. Sinai. In American history also we are conscious of a somewhat parallel experience, of exodus from Europe and of delivery from oppression. We may be said to look back at the history of the world from Plymouth Rock.

The ancient Israelites were helplessly entangled in the endless power struggle between Egypt and Mesopotamia, and so for them the most urgent question about the meaning of the world was that of the meaning of historical events. "Pray, sir," said Gideon to the heavenly messenger, "if the Lord is with us, why then has all this befallen us?" (Judg. 6:13). As through the centuries the political situation grew worse, and first the kingdom of Israel, then the kingdom of Judah were overwhelmed by the great powers, their understanding of creation developed. They rejected the widespread idea that conflict had brought the world into existence, and was therefore an essential feature of human existence. There is no hint at all of superhuman conflict in the Genesis stories of creation. Conflict was for them the struggle of evil against good, and they were convinced that however long it took, good must ultimately be triumphant.

Rather than conflict, they perceived covenant or agreement as the fundamental feature of the universe. It was by covenant that order was restored after the chaos of the flood (Gen. 9:8–17), by covenant that God established the family of Abraham (Gen. 15:18–20), by convenant that the Israelite community was preserved in the wilderness (Deut. 5:1–21), and by covenant that the house of David was maintained on the throne in Jerusalem (2 Sam. 7:8–16; Ps. 89:19–37). Amos was the first of the prophets to teach that both exodus and covenant were universal, even the enemies of Israel having had an exodus (Amos 9:7), and both Jeremiah and Ezekiel taught that even after the refugee experience of the exile in Babylon covenant would once more be restored (Jer. 31:31–34; Ezek. 11:17–20; 34:25–31). After this dread punishment, this estrangement from God, there would be not only new covenant, but new creation and a new exodus.

Behold, I am doing a new thing;
   now it springs forth, do you not perceive it?
I will make a way in the wilderness,
   and rivers in the desert.
                    Isaiah 43:19

From this time forth I make you hear new things,
   hidden things which you have not known.
They are created now, not long ago;
   before today you have never heard of them.
                    Isaiah 48:6–7

For the mountains may depart
  and the hills be removed,
but my steadfast love shall not depart from you,
  and my covenant of peace shall not be removed.
                                    Isaiah 54:10

Creation, therefore, is not merely a past completed action. It is the continuing involvement of God in maintaining the universe, even the creatures that flourish for but an hour and the particles that exist for a mere fraction of a second. Those who have committed themselves to trusting implicitly in God, and have entered into covenant with Him, share in this creative power, and are made responsible for working toward its fulfillment. Creation, no less than covenant, is a constant. Here we encounter an essential feature of the human relationship with God. We live, as we have seen, within the confines of time and space, but God is in that realm where there is neither space nor time. What we think of as either present or absent, beginning or ending, God knows constantly and eternally. This truth is so little understood by the ordinary Christian that we shall have to return to it more than once. For the moment it is sufficient to say that the constancy of creation is the basis of all our hope. Every moment is a new beginning, and however dark the morning sky, every day, as G. K. Chesterton said so vividly, God says to the sun, "Get up, and do it again!"

It may well be that the biblical views of God as Creator have made possible the modern worldview and the whole scientific method. The oneness of God ensures the oneness of all truth about the world; there cannot be some other source of truth and meaning. The Bible insists that the world is not an emanation from or extension of God, nor the body of a god defeated in cosmic combat, nor yet itself a divine being. Since the universe is created by God, and there is no other ultimate power, we may study the universe altogether without fear. We may scour the heavens to their utmost limits, and peer into the most minute of all particles, but we shall never discover inherent evil. We may, of course, grossly and evilly misuse what we discover, as we have done again and again, but that is another matter. The universe itself remains untainted. It was made by God, and we have full biblical sanction for our studies, for our desire to know the world, and to find within it an arena for moral purpose and action. We have the right to claim, as did John F. Kennedy in his inaugural address, that "here on earth God's work must surely be our own."

New Testament and New Creation

Christians fully accepted the Old Testament, for they saw Jesus Christ as the fulfillment of all that the Scriptures had said. They accepted, therefore, without question the Old Testament understanding of creation. Yet in one sense they found it insufficient, as they found also the Hellenistic philosophies insufficient. They could affirm with the psalmist, "The heavens are telling the glory of God; and the firmament proclaims his handiwork" (Ps. 19:1), but that was not enough. The heavens and the firmament might speak about God, but they did not directly reveal God. They did not make Him manifest. In the glorious works of nature and the providential events of history He was still hidden.

This apparent contradiction, that God was at one and the same time proclaimed by His creation and yet obscure to human eyes, they saw resolved in the person and work of Jesus of Nazareth. The Scriptures had taught them that God's creation had a purpose and goal, for what had been begun in the beginning must have an ultimate goal, but what this goal was they had not known. In the work of Jesus this goal was at last apparent, for "God was in Christ, reconciling the world to himself" (2 Cor. 5:19). In Jesus God was seen to have disclosed Himself to human beings in terms that they could understand. In his life and teaching, his crucifixion and his resurrection, human life took on for them new and complete meaning. Their beginnings and their endings became coherent. They spoke of him, therefore, as "the Alpha and the Omega," i.e., the beginning and the end (Rev. 1:8). They saw him also as present and active in the very fact of creation, the divine production of meaningful existence.

> In the beginning was the Word, and the Word was with God, and the Word was God. He was in the beginning with God; all things were made through him, and without him was not anything made that was made. . . . And the Word became flesh and dwelt among us, full of grace and truth; we have beheld his glory.
>
> John 1:1-3, 14

> He is the image of the invisible God, the firstborn of all creation; for in him all things were created, in heaven and on earth, visible and invisible, whether thrones or dominions or principalities or authorities—all things were created through him and for him. He is before all things, and in him all things hold together.
>
> Colossians 1:15-17

Thus, for the early Christians, all that the Old Testament had proclaimed was now brought to fulfillment, and had reached an end in Christ, but since God is by His very nature Creator, all endings are also beginnings. If the old is complete in Christ, then in Christ the new takes its beginning. In him there is a new creation, "a new heaven and a new earth" (Rev. 21:1). The life, death, and resurrection of Christ, therefore, anticipate our collective future, just as the history of ancient Israel prefigured the destiny of the world. And so for the Christian, to talk about creation is to speak, not only about the old creation, but about constantly ongoing creation, and above all about the new creation in Jesus Christ, and about the coming of the kingdom, "prepared . . . from the foundation of the world" (Matt. 25:34).

This concept of the new creation, of the new heaven and the new earth, is at the heart of all New Testament writings, and therefore we shall have to discuss it again in later chapters. For the moment we can do no more than insist upon its enormous importance.

Creation and Redemption

The early Christian thinkers did not merely repeat the worldview they had learned from the Scriptures. They had to wrestle also with powerful ideas from the Hellenistic world. For them there could be only one God, who was not in any way part of the universe, but the Creator of it, and the Father of Jesus Christ. They rejected, therefore, not only all ideas of other gods, but also the pantheist belief that the universe was in some manner part of God, or an emanation from Him. They affirmed, as did much later the poet Gerard Manley Hopkins, that "the world is charged with the grandeur of God," but they refused absolutely to identify the cosmos with God. Their view was that the cosmos, no less than humankind, had become enslaved, bound by the effects of sin and alienated from its Creator.

Therefore, the basic unit of the redemptive power and purpose of God is the whole universe. Just as man is not the measure of creation, so too man is not the measure of redemption, which is the new creation. God saves the cosmos, not merely humankind or the individual alone. Humanity and nature are bound together in a longing for completion, for a fullness which they do not now possess. A simple return to nature is no guarantee of happiness, or of safety or salvation. Walden is not Eden. As Augustine wrote in his *Confessions*, "Our hearts are restless until they rest in thee, O God," so also Paul saw all created things straining toward a new birth:

> We know that the whole creation has been groaning in travail together until now; and not only the creation, but we ourselves . . . groan inwardly as we wait for adoption as sons, the redemption of our bodies.
>
> Romans 8:22–23

Christians also rejected dualism, the belief that there are really two absolute powers in the world, one good and one evil, and they rejected, as had the Old Testament, that creation came about as a result of combat between good and evil, or that it was the work of a "demiurge," a sort of lower, corrupt god beneath the level of the true, spiritual God. The danger in this conviction that God must be fully distinct from the created universe is that He could only too easily disappear into the infinite distance and become altogether too remote and unapproachable by desolate men and women. This indeed happened during the Enlightenment of the eighteenth century, when many thought of God as a supreme clockmaker, who had devised and wound up the universe, a fascinatingly complex mechanism, which then, under His infinitely distant gaze, ticks on remorselessly and will ultimately stop. God, the loving and caring Father, could not thus desert His creation.

Finally, they rejected monism, the idea of one all-encompassing system in which all are absorbed into the impersonal Absolute. Such a belief would render impossible any relationship to God as revealed in the Scriptures, and would nullify any real identity for the individual person, as well as all ideas of human free will and independent creativity. As Karl Barth has observed, human beings, who are made in the image of God, are responsible for imaging God to the world, and they cannot do this if they are not able to think and act freely and creatively. The resurrection of the body, upon which Paul insists so strongly in the fifteenth chapter of 1 Corinthians, means that human identity is never destroyed, not even by death.

Christians engaged these other worldviews essentially on the issue of *creatio ex nihilo*, creation out of nothing, from absolute nonexistence. As we have seen, they inherited this from the Jewish scriptures. It was already implicit in the oracles of the great prophet of the exile (Isaiah 40—55), and it is stated explicitly in 2 Macc. 7:28, where the mother urges her son to maintain his faith, even under torture:

> I beg you, child, look at the sky and the earth; see all that is in them and realize that God made them out of nothing, and that man comes into being in the same way.

The Christian community strongly reaffirmed this, asserting that there had been no primordial matter, that the universe was not eternal, as Aristotle had taught, that it had had a beginning and it would therefore have an end. Human methods of creation, having to begin with what is already in existence, provided no analogy. God alone created out of nothing.

But why did God create? What need, if any, was there for Him to do so? Was He not complete in Himself, being infinite? There could have been no external necessity which compelled Him to create, since before creation there was nothing else except God. There was no compulsion upon God to create, except the compulsion of His own nature. He created out of sheer love. "God is love" (1 John 4:8), and love absolutely alone is meaningless. There must also be the beloved. "God creates," said Irenaeus in the second century, "so as to have someone on whom to confer His goodness."[5]

---

5. Irenaeus, *Against Heresies*, 14.14.

The Concept of Creation in the Modern World

We live today in a world that is evidently on the move, changing and developing with ever-increasing momentum. It is a world characterized by rapid social change, intense technological development, and what has been called the knowledge explosion. Both Christian believers and non-believers alike are confronted by a world that not merely *is*, as earlier generations might have described it, but is constantly *becoming*, and it is this "becomingness" which they need to comprehend and interpret. Some have argued that this sense of a world in process is closer to the biblical concept of the dynamic activity of God in endless creation than traditional views of a more static world. But little, if anything, in the Bible has prepared us for the startling speed, not only of development, but of human activity. Before the invention of steam transport in the nineteenth century it still took fourteen days to travel from London to Rome, just as it had done in the time of the Roman Empire. Now we have the Concorde and super-high-speed trains.

It cannot be denied that the modern world is more than a little frightening, forcing us to cope ever more frequently with the unfamiliar, and holding over our heads threats of economic collapse, population explosion, germ warfare, or nuclear destruction. It is not in the least surprising that a large body of Christians have reacted against modern developments, and have seen what they rather loosely call science as an enemy. They are far from being without reasons for this attitude. It is an undoubted fact that in the technologically advanced and scientifically sophisticated Western countries the Christian community is losing members at the rate of seventy-six hundred every day. Africa, on the other hand, gains four thousand Christians a day by conversion and twelve thousand through the birth rate. White Christians are now the minority, and the center of gravity has moved to what we are apt to call the undeveloped or backward countries.[6] The extraordinary triumphs of science and technology have so far exalted human power over things that many wonder whether we need God any more, and many others have found it impossible to be obedient to what they understand to be the rules of Christian behavior in an increasingly secularized society. There can be no common day of worship in a city where machines have to be tended throughout the twenty-four hours, and public services maintained for seven days in the week.

---

6. These figures come from David B. Barrett, ed., *World Christian Encyclopedia* (New York and London: Oxford University Press, 1982). It should be noticed that Islam is spreading with almost equal speed in Africa, and elsewhere the undermining of Islamic faith is being caused not by Christian missionary efforts but by the challenge of scientific discovery and technological methods.

In this country the encounter between science and religious belief has taken dramatic form in the battle between creationism and evolutionism, which has boiled over into the law courts.[7] That both sides in the encounter are passionately convinced that they are right is quite evident, but we should be cautious about coming down rapidly on one side or the other, although our immediate reaction may be to say that it is obvious which side is right. "Isms" are always dangerous. Consider for a moment the distinction between such related pairs as nation and nationalism, community and communism, liberality and liberalism, conservative and conservatism, racial and racism, sex and sexism. "Isms" are usually derogatory terms, suggestive of closed minds and belligerent attitudes. They provoke passionate debates, in which each side is wholly convinced of the rightness of its cause, and neither side listens to the other. There is nothing Christian about these encounters.

Creationism is very different from belief in creation and the Creator, and evolutionism very different from the scientific understanding of evolution. Evolution is not a statement of scientifically proven facts, because we do not have the evidence with which to prove the past. It is a hypothesis, based on such evidence as is available to us, but it is undoubtedly the best working hypothesis that we have. Serious geology is not really possible without it. Moreover, the hypothesis of evolution in no way challenges the concept of creation, for the simple reason that it says nothing whatever about it. It neither affirms nor denies the activity of God, Creator of all that is.

Equally, "creation" is not in itself a scientific term. It is a statement about God, about what He did and what He does, and this is not available to the scientific method of inquiry. Science, as we have seen in an earlier chapter, has to leave God entirely outside its purview; it does not have the tools with which to conduct the research. Therefore, there cannot be, as some have claimed, "creation science." The two terms contradict each other. The very essence of the scientific method is that it is the study of all the investigable facts in the universe, a study which can be equally well conducted by scholars of every religious or philosophic persuasion, or even by those having none at all. It is on these matters altogether neutral. Creation is a wholeheartedly religious interpretation of the universe, and to believe in creation is at the same time to adore the Creator. Creation is not a statement about the facts of the universe; it is a statement about the profound meaning of those facts. There is no necessity at all that evolution and creation should be in conflict.

Why, then, are the creationists and the evolutionists so vehement in their

7. In its present form this is largely an American phenomenon. The debate hardly exists in Europe, although a recent article suggests that the problem is also present in Europe. See James B. Bates, "The Pastor and the Young Fundamentalist," *The Expository Times* (July 1983): 292–95.

debate? Why does the question have to be taken to court? What are they alarmed about? The evolutionists are anxious to protect the integrity of science, the right of scientific research to investigate anything, and to propound whatever theories the evidence suggests. The creationists are anxious to protect the uniqueness of human beings as a special creation, not merely things that have developed out of the so-called lower animals, and they are anxious also to preserve what they understand to be the integrity of the Bible, for if that is undermined, what then can we trust?

It is doubtful whether the fears of either are justified. The integrity of science is in no danger of being undermined by those who do not accept scientific evidence. The danger is much greater that evolutionists will extend the doctrine that everything is open to scientific inquiry to making the assertion that all methods are justified in the cause of scientific knowledge. Vivisection of animals strongly questions this assertion, and the abominable experiments conducted by Nazis upon human beings in the time of Hitler totally condemn it. The evolutionary hypothesis does not in the least undermine the unique quality of human beings, and the vast triumphs of scientific research by humans gloriously confirm it. Evolution fully recognizes that dramatic qualitative changes can take place, for it asserts that animate matter developed out of the inanimate, which in principle would seem to be a flat contradiction. The greater danger here is that creationists will impose upon Scripture a particular interpretation, and believe that God stands in need of their protection—a very arrogant conclusion.

The concept of creation cannot be divorced from questions about human responsibility, about the function of stewardship for creation, which in the biblical understanding is committed to men and women. "The LORD God took the man and put him in the garden of Eden to till it and keep it" (Gen. 2:15), to continue, that is, the work which God Himself had already begun. The command earlier in Genesis that men and women should "fill the earth and subdue it"(Gen. 1:28) does not mean that they should behave as autocratic and tyrannical rulers. It means rather that like governors and princes appointed by an emperor, they are responsible for maintaining peace and order, and for ensuring the welfare of all the inhabitants, and the well-being of the territory itself. They are answerable to the emperor, and if they fail to carry out his wishes, they are subject to dismissal and punishment.

Defenders of the doctrine of creation ought to be questioning the arms race, commercial exploitation of natural resources, pollution, and waste, and not be found silently observing the growing threats to the well-being, and even existence, of creation. In the recent celebrations of the eight hundredth anniversary of Francis of Assisi we see a symbolic expression of the concern to reassert the unity of all creatures with Brother Sun and

Sister Moon. St. Benedict, the founder of Western religious communities, may also provide us with a powerful example of such concern, since his disciples, though unavoidably interfering with the landscape, sought to conserve, recycle, and improve the earthly environment they inhabited. Not everyone can be a mystic like St. Francis, the sweet troubador of nature, but surely more could make St. Benedict's wise stewardship their model.

Finally, there is an aspect of the human understanding of creation which is the concern equally of science, philosophy, and religion. It is the sense of awe which all should feel when facing the universe around us, and its ultimate unity, which we still do but dimly perceive. The great Swedish botanist, Linnaeus, fell on his knees in adoration of the Creator when he first saw a gorse bush in full bloom,[8] and this deep, abiding sense of wonder that Aristotle said was the beginning of wisdom seems to be a constant in human experience. We may, and should as Christians, reject the system of pantheism, but nonetheless sense the appeal of matter, of the earth, and the cosmos, as reference points in the immense and fertile matrix of life. We experienced a communal sense of this nature mysticism when we saw the first photographs from space of the planet earth, a blue and green icon of the new age, and we sense it also in the disappearing flight of the condor, and the solemn songs of whales.

The priest and the poet in our culture have seen in this panorama the work of mind, will, and purpose: "He fathers-forth whose beauty is past change."[9] And they have seen an even greater mystery, as when William Blake contemplated the "fearful symmetry" of the tiger, and asked in wonder, "Did he who made the Lamb make thee?"[10] Mystery opens onto deeper mystery in the universe. Whether believing in a Greater or not, modern men and women are drawn by wonder at both the complexity and the simplicity of the cosmos. It is not just the fact of physical life, but the quality and energy of life, that lures us closer to the world in which we live. For the Christian, belief in the "Maker of heaven and earth" still retains its power to elicit awe and to open the human spirit to the world around us.

---

8. Carolus Linnaeus, 1707–1778, the founder of modern methods of classifying plants and animals.

9. Gerard Manley Hopkins (1844–1889), *Pied Beauty.*

10. William Blake (1757–1827), *Songs of Experience.*

5

JESUS OF NAZARETH—SON OF MAN
AND SON OF GOD

Jesus went on with his disciples, to the villages of Caesarea Philippi; and on the way he asked his disciples, "Who do men say that I am?" And they told him, "John the Baptist, and others say, Elijah; and others one of the prophets." And he asked them, "Who do you say that I am?" Peter answered him, "You are the Christ." And he charged them to tell no one about him.

Mark 8:27–30

How Much Can We Know
About Jesus?

Without Jesus of Nazareth there would be no Christian faith at all. But Jesus is a very elusive person. It would hardly be an exaggeration to say that there is no one in the ancient world about whom we know both so much and so little. Our main sources are the four Gospel accounts of his work and teaching, all written during the same century in which he lived, the earliest about A.D. 65. We also have some still earlier evidence from Paul's letters, for example, 1 Cor. 11:23–26 and 15:1–17. That Jesus lived, taught, and worked in Palestine, and that he was put to death by the Romans on a charge of sedition during the governorship of Pontius Pilate (A.D. 26–36) must be counted among the best-authenticated facts in ancient history.[1] For knowledge about the great figures in Greek and Roman history we often have to rely upon only one author writing long after the events that he describes. Moreover, the evidence for the accuracy of the New Testament texts is overwhelmingly stronger than it is for any other classical writing.[2]

However, the person and character of Jesus himself continually escapes

---

1. See additional notes.
2. See additional notes.

us. Throughout the centuries writers have struggled to define and describe him and they have arrived at the most varied answers. Prophet, revolutionary, pacifist, rabbi, opponent of the rabbis, wonderworker, philosopher, social reformer, dissenter, liberal, enemy of society—these labels and many others besides have been attached to him. But none has proved adequate and none has won general acceptance. Indeed, one might well apply to these attempts what Luke says of Jesus in a rather different context, "But he passing through the midst of them went on his way"(Luke 4:30 KJV).

Scholars have ranged between two extreme positions. In the late nineteenth and early twentieth centuries there was a strong tendency to treat at least the Synoptic Gospels (i.e., Matthew, Mark, and Luke) as essentially factual, and on this basis to write the "Life of Jesus." Some of these were of a high literary and spiritual quality. For instance, T. R. Glover's *The Jesus of History*, written in 1917, was constantly reprinted and had a profound influence upon the successive student generations between the wars. However, during the same period the so-called "form critics" made themselves more and more heard. They argued that the entire New Testament, Gospels included, reflects the teaching of the early Christian leaders, and that the stories, though often based upon valid memories, have been reworked and repolished in order to strengthen and spread abroad the postresurrection faith. They were seen as having small value for reconstructing the earthly life of Jesus, in which, these scholars claimed, the writers were little interested. R. H. Lightfoot in Britain went so far as to say, "The form of the earthly no less than of the heavenly Christ is for the most part hidden from us. For all the inestimable value of the Gospels, they yield us little more than a whisper of his voice; we trace in them but the outskirts of his ways."[3]

Modern students of the Gospel should be profoundly grateful for this debate, since it brings out into the open the problem that faces anyone who sits down to write about Jesus. From the beginning the Christian community has always maintained that Jesus has a double character: that of an actual historical person, Jesus, son of Mary, whose physical life, and especially his death, are fundamental and important facts, but also that of the Christ, Son of God, a person who completely transcends history, and that this transcendent character brilliantly illuminates and overwhelms the often painful earthly life. "Death," said Paul, "is swallowed up in victory" (1 Cor. 15:54).

We will discuss this second aspect of his character in chapter 7, but here and in the next chapter we are concerned with the Jesus of history. In con-

---

3. See additional notes.

sidering this we would be wise to steer a middle course between the two extremes of interpretation, as most scholars now do. Certainly, none of the four Gospel writers intended to write the biography of Jesus, and so it was not their purpose to arrange the stories in chronological order. We do not need, therefore, to argue about who was right: Mark, who places the cleansing of the Temple close to the end of Jesus' ministry, or John who puts it at the very beginning (Mark 11:15–19; John 2:13–22).[4] The primary purpose was to tell the stories in such a way as to bring out their profound meaning, and to arrange them accordingly. But this in no way means that they were inaccurate, or that they felt free to alter the stories just as they wished. On the contrary! They were writing about an actual person, who had been born and who had died within living memory. His work and his teaching they believed to be profoundly significant. Too much revising and repolishing of the stories would have defeated the writers' purpose. Moreover, accuracy of memory was strongly encouraged in the society of that time, when books were not available for everyone to own and read.

Certainly there are variations in the telling of the stories. Compare, for instance, the account of the healing of the paralytic, and especially its ending, as told first by Mark (2:1–12) and then in somewhat revised versions by Matthew (9:1–8) and Luke (5:17–26). Occasionally there is a story whose factual accuracy we may be permitted to doubt, for example, that of the coin in the fish's mouth (Matt. 17:24–27), since it is so unlike anything else that Jesus is said to have done. Yet, there is no reason why we should not have solid confidence in the greater part of the information, even if the details are not always certain. We have already seen that there can be little doubt that Jesus was put to death by the Romans as a dangerous rebel, and we may be equally sure that many of the religious leaders at the time viewed his behavior and teaching as seriously blasphemous and disruptive, and were glad to see the Romans get rid of him. Anyone who lived in Palestine during the British colonial administration could recognize exactly the same tensions at work. Religious and political beliefs cannot be kept separate from each other, as we may see today in Poland, Iran, and Northern Ireland.

But we can go much further. We may be sure that he grew up in Nazareth, that after his baptism by John he did most of his work around Capernaum on the Lake of Galilee, and that he called disciples and designated twelve of them to form an inner core, Peter, James, and John being

---

4. One contributor suggested that the action could have happened twice, and pointed out that the two stories are different. However, the parallels are more numerous than the differences, and it seems more probable that we have here one incident, which John has placed at the beginning because he wants to establish from the start that Jesus, as Son of God, is the new center of worship. See additional notes for a further comment.

the leaders. His work lasted only a short time, certainly not more than three years and perhaps (though this is much less certain) no more than one.[5] He was undoubtedly a charismatic person, exercising a profound influence on the people whom he met. Some were his passionate supporters, but others hated him, thinking that the already tormented country would be a great deal better off without him. Strange things certainly happened when he was present. All four Gospels see these "mighty works" (they do not speak of "miracles") as primary, and no serious study of Jesus can ever disregard them.[6] The people of the time did not know what to make of them. Some saw them as the activity of God (John 3:1–2) and others as diabolical and dangerous (Mark 3:22).

We may also be certain that Jesus was severely critical of the establishment of his day, and the establishment critical of him. He evidently ate and drank with disreputable people, and sat lightly to rules about the Sabbath. He taught people by means of parables and he proclaimed the coming of the kingdom of God. He urged people to love their enemies, refused to use methods of violence to further his cause,[7] and at his final meal with the Twelve he instituted what today we call the Eucharist, the Mass, the Communion, or the Lord's Supper. All four Gospels are also agreed that there was an evident break in his career, the second part being different from the first.[8]

What Jesus thought about himself is much more difficult to ascertain. He was evidently committed to doing the work of God and initiating the kingdom of heaven, which most of his parables sought to explain (Matt. 4:17; Mark 1:14–15). He saw himself also as the successor to John the Baptist, who had prepared the way by his preaching and by the sacred washing of people in the river Jordan (Luke 3:1–17; 7:18–28). That he perceived his function to be that of saving the people can hardly be doubted, and what we today call the temptations (Matt. 4:1–11; Mark 1:12–13; Luke 4:1–13) indicate that he was under intense social and internal pressure to do this in some other way than that to which he was committed and which, he was convinced, would lead to his own death. Certainly also, he saw his role as that of a servant, even a slave, rather than that of an autocratic ruler exerting power over people.

---

5. A considerable number of scholars have suggested that Jesus' ministry lasted only one year, on the grounds that the first three Gospels mention only one Passover feast, whereas John speaks of three. This argument, however, does not seem very persuasive.

6. The problem of miracles will be discussed in the next chapter.

7. Some contributors raised the question of Jesus' action in cleansing the Temple (Matt. 21:12–17; Mark 11:15–19; Luke 19:45–48; John 2:13–25). Two points, however, need to be noted: (1) the whip may have been intended for the animals rather than the men; and (2) the only time when Jesus may be said to have acted violently was when he did so on behalf of the hated and despised Gentiles.

8. See additional notes.

Son of Man

That Jesus during his lifetime often spoke of himself as the Son of man seems altogether beyond question, and no less certain that he accepted Peter's recognition that he was the Messiah, the Christ, the anointed one (Mark 8:29-30; see also Matt. 16:15-16; Luke 9:20-21). But the exact meaning of these two terms is difficult to determine. Both in Hebrew and in the closely related Aramaic, which is the language Jesus would have spoken, the phrase "son of man" normally means no more than "man" or "somebody." We find it in this sense in the psalms,

> O LORD, what is man that thou dost regard him,
>   or the son of man that thou dost think of him?
>   Psalm 144:3

and in the Book of Ezekiel the prophet is always addressed by God as "son of man," emphasizing his merely human character. It is used in the same sense by the writer of the Book of Daniel, where in 8:17 Daniel is called "son of man" by the angel Gabriel.

However, a little earlier in the book we find the oft-quoted passage:

> I saw in the night visions,
> and behold, with the clouds of heaven
>   there came one like a son of man,
> and he came to the Ancient of Days
>   and was presented before him.
> And to him was given dominion
>   and glory and kingdom,
> that all peoples, nations, and languages
>   should serve him;
> his dominion is an everlasting dominion
>   which shall not pass away,
> and his kingdom
>   one that shall not be destroyed.
>   Daniel 7:13-14

The writer here says only that the strange being who is to be given such overwhelming power has the appearance of a man, but later speculation on the passage greatly elaborated the picture, so that the phrase "the son of man" came to mean for many much more than a man. It meant instead a heavenly visitor, the chosen, righteous one, who would set God's people free from their domination by foreign and evil powers. We find this concept most fully developed in a book called *The Similitudes of Enoch*, part of a much longer work that was compiled between 150 and 80 B.C. We must recognize, therefore, a very wide range of meaning that Jesus' hearers could have attached to the phrase. Our problem is to decide whether Jesus himself intended any particular interpretation.

It is possible that he was quite intentionally ambiguous, since he apparently wanted the people to whom he spoke to make up their own minds, and he may have intended his use of son of man to cover the whole range. He certainly used it in the sense of a man, that is, a physical human being, as when he said, "The Son of man is betrayed into the hands of sinners" (Mark 14:41), or "Foxes have holes, and the birds of the air have nests, but the Son of man has nowhere to lay his head"(Luke 9:58).[9] Another possible meaning could be humankind in general, with Jesus seeing himself as the representative man, destined to carry out to the full the proper function of human beings on earth. Such sayings might perhaps include Mark 2:10, "That you may know that the Son of man has authority on earth to forgive sins," i.e., that all men and women have the power to forgive the sins committed against them, and should in fact do so.[10]

But in a large number of other passages Jesus speaks of the "coming" of the Son of man, both in the sense of someone who has already come and of someone whose coming is still in the future. In Luke 19:10 he says that "the Son of man came to seek and to save the lost," but he said also, "You will see the Son of man seated at the right hand of Power, and coming with the clouds of heaven" (Mark 14:62), and again, "You also must be ready: for the Son of man is coming at an unexpected hour" (Luke 12:40). Many scholars explain such predictions of the future as later interpretations made by the writers in the light of the resurrection experience. But this may well be too easy a way out of the complexity. That Jesus foresaw his own death must be taken as certain. Indeed, one might go so far as to say that only a very foolish person (and Jesus was certainly not that!) would have failed to recognize that the end result of his work, if persisted in, would be arrest and death, for the authorities clearly saw him as a troublemaker who would be a great deal better out of the way.[11] The Roman policy toward enemies of the state was perfectly clear. Crucifixion was not an uncommon punishment, but a fairly frequent and very public one. Sometimes whole groups of people were nailed up on trees or posts along the roadsides as a warning to others who might be tempted to act in opposition to Rome.[12]

We must, of course, consider all these possible meanings of "Son of man" in our efforts to understand what the Gospel writers had in mind as they recounted the works and words of Jesus, but over the centuries one particular meaning has come to stand out as primary. This is the insistence that Jesus of Nazareth was in every sense of the word a human being,

---

9. See additional notes.

10. See additional notes.

11. A revealing parallel is the prolonged efforts made by the FBI to get rid of Martin Luther King.

12. The best brief discussion of this subject is Martin Hengel, *Crucifixion* (Philadelphia: Fortress Press, 1977).

growing up as a child in the village of Nazareth, at times tired or hungry and thirsty (Mark 11:12; John 4:6-7), and subject to all the difficulties, frustrations, and temptations that beset a normal human life, "one who in every respect has been tempted as we are, yet without sin" (Heb. 4:15; see also 2:17-18).

"Yet without sin." This is for many a stumbling block. What does it mean? It cannot mean that he knew everything and therefore never made a mistake, because that would have meant that he did not share one of the basic features of human existence, which is to be strictly limited in knowledge. Not even the most brilliant mind is capable of knowing everything. Nor can it mean that he never broke the rules of society, for it is quite clear from the Gospel accounts that he both did so and permitted his disciples to do the same (Mark 2:15-28; 7:1-8). Probably the best interpretation is that he dedicated himself utterly to the service of God and not to any standards set up by the world, however exalted; that this was the constant orientation of his life and thoughts, and that from this he never allowed himself to be deflected.

The Messiah/The Christ

"Messiah" is another difficult term. Literally it means "anointed" and therefore set aside for the service of God. Priests were evidently anointed on the head with oil (Exod. 28:41; Lev. 8:12; Ps. 133:2), but the phrase "the Lord's Anointed" referred most commonly to the king (1 Sam. 12:2, 5; 2 Sam. 1:14, 19-21; 2 Kings 9:1-6, 11:12). After the destruction of Jerusalem and the end of the monarchy in 587 B.C., there was no longer any king who could be called the Lord's anointed (Lam. 4:20), and the phrase began to be used for some future ruler who would one day deliver the Jewish people. The prophet whom we call the Second Isaiah shocked and horrified the exiles in Babylon when he spoke of Cyrus, the foreign, and to them barbarian, ruler as the Lord's anointed, who would save them (Isa. 45:1). Cyrus did indeed enable them to return to rebuild Jerusalem and the Temple, but they remained continually under foreign rule, with only a temporary independence after the Maccabean revolt in 165 B.C.[13]

From the year 63 B.C., when the Roman general Pompey arrogantly forced his way into the most sacred part of the Temple, the subjugation and frustration of the people became more intense. No less intense, therefore, was their longing for a deliverer, someone coming with divine power and authority, able to thwart even the might of Rome, someone whom they could rightly call the Messiah, the anointed one. Whether Jesus was

---

13. The revolt actually began a few years earlier, but 165 was the year in which Judas Maccabeus recaptured and cleansed the Temple, which had been desecrated by the foreign Seleucid government.

indeed this long-awaited savior was apparently much debated (Mark 14:61; Luke 24:21; John 4:29; 7:26; 10:24). Jesus himself seems to have made no public claim to the title and his final response to the high priest's direct question is somewhat ambiguous (Matt. 26:63–64; Mark 14:61–62; Luke 22:66–71). When privately, in the remote pagan region of Caesarea Philippi,[14] Peter blurted out his conviction, "You are the Christ," Jesus accepted the title, but ordered the disciples to tell no one about him, and from that moment he began to teach them that the Messiah whom they so desperately wanted would be arrested and executed (Mark 8:27–33). The story of his temptations (Matt. 4:1–11; Luke 4:1–13) indicates that it was only after an agonizing struggle that he saw clearly what his task was to be and set himself wholeheartedly to perform it.

The Kingdom of God

A similar problem confronts us when we seek to probe the very heart of Jesus' teaching: the kingdom of God, or as Matthew would have it, the kingdom of heaven. The Greek word *basileia* defeats all attempts to find an exact translation into English, for it could mean: kingship, royal power, royal rule, the people or territory under the royal authority, or the reign of a particular king. Probably Jesus himself included all these meanings within his oft-repeated phrase "the kingdom of God," and even he had difficulty in finding the right words to explain it to the people who could not grasp what he was talking about: "And he said, 'With what can we compare the kingdom of God, or what parable shall we use for it?'" (Mark 4:30; cf. Luke 13:20). He spoke of it as something imminent (Mark 1:14–15), even already present (Luke 17:20–21), but also as something which could be long postponed (Luke 19:11ff.). It is also described as something into which men and women may enter (Matt. 5:20; 19:23), even as violently besieged and taken by storm (Matt. 11:12).

We must return here to the all-important fact that men and women and the phenomena of the entire universe are imprisoned within time, but that God is altogether beyond it, in no way constricted by the passage of time, which for us is inescapable. The kingdom of God, his rule, authority, and control, are therefore for human beings always (1) something which has existed from the very beginning of the universe, (2) something which is true at this actual moment of our lives, (3) something which is imminently about to happen, and (4) something which will remain forever in the future until the universe itself comes to an end and there is no more time. Every human experience of eternity is bound to have this complex and confusing character.

For all that we know at present, since we have as yet no evidence at all

---

14. See additional notes.

on the matter, the whole of the universe, apart from this little planet earth, may proceed upon its way in complete harmony with the rule and purpose of God.[15] But here, upon "the dark terrestrial ball," there has been a race of beings who have consciously sought to obtain and exercise power over the rest of creation, since at least their discovery of how to use fire for their own purposes about seventy thousand years ago. Ever since that date the kingdom of God has been opposed, and it is this opposition which renders the question for us so complex. The "kingdom," the power and authority of God, have always maintained the world; they are present to us at this very moment, because without them we should not be here at all; they are nevertheless imminent, because in this sphere where the divine authority is disregarded or opposed we never know when something will happen that may compel us to recognize that we do not have the power we thought we had; and they are far away in the unknown future because we have no idea at all how long this condition of confrontation will last. Indeed, in this nuclear age it seems that the end, and final judgment upon humankind, may come a great deal sooner than we would have thought possible fifty years ago.

It must continually be emphasized that what the universe is, God is not; what God is, the universe is not. This is no less true of men and women who form such an exceedingly minute part of the universe.[16] The power of God, therefore, is altogether other than human power, indeed other than any kind of power that exists in the universe, and the kingdom of God altogether different from what we mean when we speak of kingdoms, principalities, and governments. "And he said to them, 'The kings of the Gentiles exercise lordship over them; and those in authority over them are called benefactors [what withering sarcasm Jesus could use when he chose!]. But not so with you." (Luke 22:25–26).

This presents us with an interesting, and indeed disturbing, possibility. If the normal human understanding of power and authority is that of rule and control by some people over other people, then we may have to recognize that God's understanding of power could be exactly the opposite. Even the best intentioned and most benevolent use of power in the human realm is, almost without exception, directed toward the protection, prosperity, and well-being of our own society, for in the words of Walter Bagehot,[17] "the primary function of society is to preserve society." The use of power and authority for the preservation of power and authority, or of the status quo, or of the community within which the power resides, is explicitly rejected in the Gospels. "Do you know what I have done to you?" said Jesus to his disciples at the Last Supper. "You call me Teacher and Lord, and you are right, for so I am. If I then, your Lord and Teacher,

---

15. See additional notes.
16. See additional notes.
17. Walter Bagehot, English social scientist, 1826–1877.

have washed your feet, you also ought to wash one another's feet" (John 13:12-15; see also Luke 22:24-27).

It is easy, of course, to see this as indicating how human beings should exercise power, and this is how such passages have always been explained. Such explanations are entirely justified, although admittedly Christians in power have very often failed to use their power in this manner. But the writers of the Gospels did not see Jesus only as Son of man, in every sense a human being, but also as Son of God, by which they meant, at the very least, that the power which he exercised was the power of God working through him. Therefore, we are confronted with the possibility that God, whom we normally and rightly speak of as Lord, King, Judge, Master, and so on, does not perceive Himself in these terms, but rather as servant and slave, continually obedient to the needs of His creation, and on this planet earth obedient therefore to the needs of human beings.

> As the eyes of a slave follows his master's hand,
>   or the eyes of a slave-girl her mistress,
> so our eyes are turned to the Lord our God
>   waiting for kindness from him.
>   Psalm 123:2 NEB

So the psalmist rightly describes the proper attitude of human beings toward God, ever watchful for some gesture indicating the master's desire even before a word is spoken. But can it be that the Almighty God, dwelling in light unapproachable, stands obediently before us, watching our every gesture, so that He may fulfill our needs even before we have found words to express them? It seems almost blasphemous to suggest such a thing. But if God through Jesus of Nazareth acts in this manner, then we can hardly avoid such a conclusion, and with what awe and wonder we must ourselves then approach Him! "Who is like the Lord our God, that hath his dwelling so high, and yet humbleth himself to behold the things that are in heaven and earth? (Ps. 113:6 Coverdale).

Son of God

We must turn finally to the difficult question of what is meant by the expression "Son of God," which occurs nearly one hundred times in the New Testament. Christian writers could not possibly have meant anything physical, for the very idea would have been to them abhorrent. They were not, in fact, the first to use the term, for it appears in the Wisdom of Solomon, a book written about a century before any of the New Testament writings, and evidently known in early Christian circles.[18] There we find the ungodly accusing the righteous man of boasting that God is his father.

---

18. See additional notes.

"Let us see if his words are true," they say, "and let us test what will happen at the end of his life; for if the righteous man is God's son, he will help him, and will deliver him from the hand of his adversaries" (Wisd. of Sol. 2:17-18, but see the whole passage 2:12-24).

In our modern Western world we tend to think of a son as distinct from his father and, ever since Sigmund Freud taught us about the Oedipus complex, to see the two as often in opposition to each other, sometimes violently so. Nothing could be further from the ancient and traditional Jewish understanding. The true son remained with his father, working with him, gradually learning his trade until in due course he was able to carry on his father's work in his place. Only the disreputable and prodigal son left his father and went into a distant country (Luke 15:11-32). In John's Gospel, where the theme of the Father and Son is most fully developed, we should probably translate 5:19 without the usual capital letters, but as something entirely familiar to Jesus' audience, "In very truth I tell you, the son can do nothing by himself; what the father does, the son does." None of his hearers would have wished to dispute this, and from this the rest of the argument develops. Therefore, in the first place the New Testament use of the phrase "Son of God" means that here is someone who watches carefully what God is doing, listens to his instructions, and then dutifully carries on the same work.

But the early Christian teachers and writers, struggling to find words to express the impact of Jesus on the world, were unable to stop there. The description, though they would have accepted it as true, was for them inadequate, and they were driven to plunge deeper. In striving to explain these depths they spoke of the "virgin birth" and the "incarnation," both very difficult concepts to explain.

The story of how Jesus, by the power of the Holy Spirit, was born from a virgin mother, without the participation of a human father, is clearly not an essential part of a gospel, for two of the four Gospels are written without any mention of it. Those that tell the story, Matthew and Luke, do so in strikingly different ways (Matt. 1:18-25; Luke 1:26—2:40). To understand the lesson they were teaching by means of this story we must return once again to the understanding at that time of the father-mother-son relationship and try, without intruding modern ideas, to look at it in the same way. For them, as we have already seen in chapter 3, the mother endowed the child with its physical identity, and therefore, when early Christian writers said that Jesus was the son of Mary, they were insisting that Jesus was a human being like every other human being, for he was born of a human mother.

But they thought of the will, purpose, work, and activity in life as being bestowed by the father, for, as we have seen, the proper function of the true son was to watch what his father was doing and carry on his work.

Consequently, when writers like Matthew and Luke denied Joseph any part in bringing the baby Jesus into the world, they were arguing that the will, purpose, work, and activity of Jesus came to him wholly from God, and were not determined for him in advance by any human source. That Jesus as a boy must have learned Joseph's trade as a carpenter is probably true, but for Matthew and Luke it was irrelevant. For them, as for all the Gospel writers, the true work of Jesus began when he came to be baptized by John (Matt. 3:1-2; Mark 1:1-8, Luke 3:1-18; John 1:25-34).

It must be left to each individual person to decide how literally, or how symbolically, to take these birth stories, remembering, of course, that "symbolic" does not mean less true than "literal." The Christian faith does not stand or fall upon debates of this nature, nor is it likely that questions will be asked about them at the Last Judgment. The essential is to understand the lesson that those who told the story were seeking to convey.

They were trying to put into words what we speak of today as "incarnation," the taking of physical form, from the Latin *caro* (genitive *carnis*) meaning "flesh." This had its first precise statement in the prologue to the Gospel of John, where it is said that "the Word became flesh (*verbum caro factum est*) and dwelt among us, full of grace and truth; and we have beheld his glory, glory as the only Son from the Father" (John 1:14), but the idea was already there in Paul's letter to the Colossians, written very much earlier: "In Christ the whole fullness of deity dwells bodily" (Col. 2:9).

Probably the best way of understanding incarnation is in terms of what C. S. Lewis called "transposition."[19] By this he meant that whenever something from a greater dimension is expressed and given shape in a lesser dimension, as when an orchestral piece is transposed to a piano arrangement, things in the lesser dimension have to take on a double, or even multiple, character. This is inevitable because the lesser dimension has a more limited number of things with which to work. Consequently, to continue with C. S. Lewis's example, for someone playing the piano version of an orchestral piece a G major chord is both the sound made by the hammers striking the strings of the piano and also the sound made by a whole group of different instruments in the orchestra. Or, to put it another way around, it is the much grander and more glorious orchestral sound taking recognizable shape in the more limited world of pianos and pianists. So, in speaking of Jesus of Nazareth as the incarnation of God, we are saying that all the majesty of God, His love, power, authority, have taken recognizable shape in the very limited world of men and women.

---

19. C. S. Lewis, *The Weight of Glory and Other Addresses*, rev. ed. (New York: Macmillan Co., 1980).

When we come to examine the question of the Trinity, we shall see that the Christian writers who first spelled out the idea of the incarnation were careful to distinguish between God the Father, infinite and immortal, and God the Son, who was on earth the limited and thoroughly mortal Jesus of Nazareth.

But why should such a complicated process be necessary? Could not the teaching be given in a simpler fashion? No, it could not, for teaching and learning about God are very different from coming to know God. Knowing about is very much less than knowing. For this reason a child born in a foreign country of American parents is required by American law to come back and live in the United States, and to know American life directly, if he or she is to keep the right of citizenship. But human beings cannot go and live with God; God must in some way come and be present with them, living and working within their limits.

We must remember that God belongs to the realm of otherness, where space and time do not exist, whereas we are human beings, always limited by time and space, and limited even more by the fact that we cannot be anything else except human beings, and that it is only as human beings that we can perceive and know anything at all. The infinite, therefore, can be understood by us only when it is expressed in terms of the finite realm, and God can be known by us only when He is transposed, and works within the very limited framework of human life and human understanding. All else that God may be or do lies totally beyond human comprehension. It is this expression of God in human terms, this manifestation in the only form that human beings can perceive, that we speak of as incarnation.

It has always been the Christian conviction that the most complete incarnation must be in the form of an actual human life, for nothing can pierce more directly to the heart of humanity. This complete incarnation, Christians insist, did indeed take place in the person of Jesus of Nazareth. But could it happen again? The answer is both no and yes. It is no because to be human is to be unique. No human being, no human life, is ever repeated. Even so-called identical twins are different; they do not, for instance, have the same fingerprints. There cannot, therefore, be another and separate Jesus Christ.

But the answer is also yes, because what we see expressed in the framework of time, that is, at a particular moment in history, God always is. We speak of creation as something that happened at what we call the beginning, at the moment of the big bang, of God giving Torah (the Law) on Mt. Sinai in about 1250 B.C., and of his judgment coming upon Jerusalem when it was destroyed by the Babylonians in 587 B.C. But these are manifestations of the eternal; they are constants expressed in terms of limited, temporal existence. Whenever we encounter God, we encounter the Creator, the Lawgiver, the Judge. Incarnation, therefore, must also be a constant, for God encountered is always God expressed in human terms.

Theologians have used the phrase "the preexistent Christ" to describe the eternal character of God expressed in terms of Jesus of Nazareth, but it is an unfortunate phrase because it means "existing before," and it is exactly this sense of "before and after" that we must eradicate from our minds when we try to think about God. God made known to us is always incarnate, not in the literal sense of actual flesh but in the sense of humanness. He takes shape in human minds when His will is revealed, in books written by human beings when His purposes and actions are recorded, in very human deeds when His love or His wrath make themselves known. We must never try to put limits to God, or to determine in advance how His shattering power, what the biblical writers so often call His Word, will explode into the world, for to erect these barriers is to make an image and claim that it is absolute. We cannot, therefore, speak of the incarnation of God as being ended, never to happen again. We can say no more than that that particular incarnation of the Word, the manifestation of God's purpose and activity in the very human Jesus of Nazareth, was complete in itself. How else God may manifest Himself in the world of human beings always remains open.

There remains one final question. At what point did it first become clear to anybody that in meeting Jesus men and women were being confronted, not merely by the "one who should come," the expected savior, but by the direct power of God Himself? The answer is: at that moment when he was nailed up for public display, naked, helpless, humiliated, condemned, and dying in agony. That was the moment when he was both most human and least human. Most human because he was sharing the fate of thousands similarly condemned, helpless within the all-too-human structures of political and social power, but also least human because at that moment the tremendous work of the Father was brought to fruition. *Tetelestai*, "it is finished, complete, accomplished," he cried out on the cross just before he died (John 19:30), and in John's Gospel this moment is the glory of Jesus, illuminating with radiant light everything that he had done and said before. Mark entirely agrees with him that this was the moment of supreme revelation, but records also that the only person to recognize this was not one of Jesus' disciples, nor someone learned in the Scriptures and *Torah*, but a complete foreigner, an officer in the hated colonial army. "When the centurion, who was standing face to face with him, saw that he died in this way, he said, 'This man was indeed Son of God'" (Mark 15:39).[20]

---

20. See additional notes.

ADDITIONAL NOTES

1. Apart from the united witness of the four Gospels, there is evidence from two non-Christian authors, neither of whom seems to have drawn his knowledge from Christian sources. Josephus, the Jewish historian writing toward the end of the first century A.D., says "Now, there was about this time Jesus, a wise man . . . for he was a doer of wonderful works, a teacher of such men as receive the truth with pleasure. He drew over to him many of the Jews and many of the Gentiles. And when Pilate, at the suggestion of the principal men among us, had condemned him to the cross, those that loved him at the first did not forsake him. . . . And the tribe of Christians, so named from him, are not extinct to this day." (*Jewish Antiquities*, 18.3.3).

The Roman historian Tacitus, writing in about the year A.D. 115 of Nero's persecution of the Christians in A.D. 64, says, "To scotch the rumors, Nero substituted as culprits, and punished with the utmost cruelty, a class of men loathed for their vices, whom the crowd called 'Christians.' Christus, the founder of the name, had undergone the death penalty in the reign of Tiberius, by sentence of the procurator Pontius Pilate, and the pernicious superstition was checked for a while, only to break out once more, not merely in Judaea, the home of the disease, but in the capital itself, where all things horrible or shameful in the world collect and find a vogue" (*Annals*, 15.144). The evidence is summarized conveniently in Roderic Dunkerly, *Beyond the Gospels* (New York: Penguin Books, 1967), and W. D. Davies, *Invitation to the New Testament* (Garden City, N.Y.: Doubleday & Co., 1969), chap. 6.

2. It is worth quoting in this connection the statement of Herbert G. May and Bruce M. Metzger in their notes to *The New Oxford Annotated Bible with the Apocrypha: Revised Standard Version* (New York and London: Oxford University Press, 1973), 1168–69:

> Three sources of information exist today for our knowledge of the text of the New Testament. They are the Greek manuscripts, early translations into other languages (primarily Syriac, Latin, and Coptic), and quotations from the New Testament made by early ecclesiastical writers. The total number of Greek manuscripts of all or parts of the New Testament is close to five thousand. Of this number the most important are, in general, the oldest; more than three hundred, written on papyrus or parchment, date from the second to the eighth century. In evaluating the significance of this rich store of manuscripts, it should be recalled that the writings of many ancient classical authors have survived in only a few copies (or even in only one) and that not infrequently these copies date from the late Middle Ages, separated from the time of the composition of the originals by more than a thousand years.

3. These were the closing words of his Bampton Lectures given at the University of Oxford in 1934 and 1935, and subsequently published under the title *History and Interpretation in the Gospels*. He was a very gentle and devout man and later softened this statement, expressing surprise that his critics had not recognized that he was quoting from Job 26:14.

4. One contributor commented: You might want to raise here the argument that G. S. Stanton makes in *Jesus of Nazareth in New Testament Preaching* (New York: Cambridge University Press, 1975), "The Gospels must be read against the background, not of modern biographical writings, but of their own times. . . . For if the modern preoccupation with chronological precision, historical background, personal appearance and character development is largely missing in ancient biographical writing with its strong literary tradition, the absence of these is even less surprising in the gospels, which can scarcely be described as literary productions" (p. 125). In view of their

extraordinary impact on later literature, some readers may want to take exception to the final clause!

8. In the Synoptic Gospels the break is described as occurring when Peter at Caesarea Philippi recognized Jesus as the Messiah, after which Jesus began to teach his disciples that he would have to be arrested and put to death (Mark 8:27–33; cf. Matt. 16:13–23; Luke 9:18–22). In John's Gospel the crisis comes after the Feeding of the Five Thousand and the subsequent discussion, which provoked most of Jesus' followers to desert him (John 6:66–71).

9. One contributor disagreed, saying, "Rather, I think that it seems to refer to his special status. That the Son of man is betrayed into the hands of sinners seems to contrast his sinless nature with that of the others. And if the Son of man refers to his uniqueness, Luke 9:58 shows the irony of his having nowhere to lay his head."

10. A few contributors called this interpretation "*very* misleading" and said that all sins are against God and cannot be forgiven by men and women, although at a lower level human beings should forgive each other.

14. Caesarea Philippi had earlier been called Paneas, i.e., the place of the god Pan, and the modern name, Banias, is derived from this. It was a pagan sanctuary where one of the chief sources of the river Jordan gushes out of the base of Mount Hermon, and the niches for statues of Pan may still be seen today. It was here, in an altogether Gentile and pagan environment, that Jesus confronted the Twelve with his question.

15. One contributor pointed out that research by Jane Goodall into aggression and social structure of chimpanzees indicates that the struggle for power is an innate tendency. It is true that what Tennyson called "nature red in tooth and claw" characterizes this planet and must, therefore, be in some sense in accord with the purposes of God. What distinguishes human beings, however, is their willful misuse of power.

16. One contributor commented: "What? I thought that men and women were created in the likeness of God" (Gen. 1:27). This is certainly a valid point. Yet, the interpretation of the Genesis passage is notoriously difficult. It seems probable that it refers not to human nature but to the human function, which is defined in the following verse. This is to "subdue" the earth, i.e., to produce order wherever there may be disorder. All biblical writers preserve the absolute distinction between human beings and God.

18. The Wisdom of Solomon is one of the books found in the Septuagint, or Greek translation of the Old Testament made in Alexandria in about the middle of the third century B.C., but not found in the Massoretic Text, i.e., the Hebrew version which was established many centuries later. The Septuagint was the version used by the New Testament writers.

20. The exclamation of the centurion is difficult to translate exactly. The normal translation is "This man was the Son of God," as in the RSV, but in Greek there is no definite article in front of the title, and so it could equally well mean "a son of a god," which a pagan observer might exclaim. However, it is highly unlikely that Mark intended his readers to understand it in a pagan sense, and so it seems best to adhere to the Greek and put no definite article, but to use capital letters for "Son" and "God" so as to avoid any suggestion of a pagan interpretation. The exclamation would then mean something like "the essential quality of this man was the quality of God Himself," or we might paraphrase it as "here, in the death of this man, we are confronted directly by God."

6

THE WORKS AND WORDS
OF JESUS

Since the incarnation of God in the person of Jesus of Nazareth is fundamental to Christian belief, it is not surprising that Christians should always have been interested in his earthly life. What is perhaps surprising is that the first Christians were interested in only a small part of it. Apart from the birth narratives and a brief account of the visit to the Temple when he was twelve years old (Luke 2:41–51), the Gospels speak only of the brief period between his baptism by John when he was about thirty years of age (Luke 3:23) and his death and resurrection three years later. We would today dearly love to know more about these "hidden years,"[1] but for the writers of the four Gospels the essential facts were all to be found in his active ministry, and not in his formative period.

Also somewhat surprising to many modern readers is the fact that all four writers saw the teachings of Jesus as secondary and his actions as primary. Mark, the first Gospel to be written, says very little about the teachings of Jesus and concentrates upon his "mighty works." The other three Gospels contain a great deal more of the teaching, but they present it as dependent upon his work. Both Matthew and John always precede any block of teaching by a preparatory account of Jesus' actions. The Gospel of Luke does not have such a clear structure, but it is significant that in the introduction to this second book, *The Acts of the Apostles*, the author describes the first as dealing with "all that Jesus began to do and teach" (Acts 1:1). For all these writers the authority for what Jesus taught derived from who he was, and this was made evident by what he did.

Innumerable books, sometimes of great length, have been written about

---

1. The "hidden years" were the subject of a great deal of later speculation and legend, some of which appears in the so-called apocryphal gospels. None of this, however, can be considered trustworthy biographical material.

the ministry of Jesus, and quite evidently in a book of this kind we are compelled to be selective. This chapter, therefore, will deal with only three subjects: miracles, parables, and the Sermon on the Mount.[2]

The Miracles of Jesus

What exactly are we talking about? Do we mean "interferences with the course of nature," as in most dictionaries?[3] This does not seem to be the intention of the New Testament writers. The biblical words are (the Hebrew being given first, and the Greek second):

geburoth, dunameis = mighty works, acts of power, strong deeds.
oth, semeion = a sign, or signal.
mophet, teras = a wonder. This is often combined with the previous term as *semeia kai terata* (signs and wonders), e.g., Exod. 7:3; Deut. 4:34; 6:22; Neh. 9:10; Isa. 8:18; and in the New Testament, Matt. 24:24; Mark 13:22; John 4:48; Acts 2:43; 4:30; 7:36; 14:3; Rom. 15:19; 2 Cor. 12:12; Heb. 2:4. The phrase occurs less commonly in the New Testament than in the Old, where it usually refers to the delivery from Egypt.

Macbeth, when confronted by the ghost of Banquo, exclaimed:

Can such things be,
and overcome us like a summer's cloud,
without our special wonder?
> Shakespeare,
> *Macbeth*, 3.4.110-2

We are certainly concerned, when talking about miracle, with things that excite our special wonder, but overemphasis upon the wonderful is specifically rejected in the Gospels. "Except you see signs and wonders, you will in no wise believe," said Jesus in rebuke to the royal official (John 4:48), and in the Synoptic Gospels the term "sign" is used almost always for something which only the corrupt and willfully blind demand (Matt. 12:38-9; 16:4; Mark 8:11-12; Luke 11:16, 29), although it can sometimes mean a portent indicating future catastrophe (Matt. 24:24; Mark 13:22; Luke 11:30). John, however, uses the word in a more favorable sense. Everything that Jesus does, his *erga* or "works" are, for those with eyes to see and understand, *semeia* or "signs" of who Jesus is.

2. A list of the parables and the miracles recorded in the four Gospels is appended at the end of this chapter.

3. Webster defines "miracle" as "an event or effect that apparently contradicts known scientific laws and hence is thought to be due to supernatural causes."

Miracle concerns the activity of God, not only through men and women by healing, but also through things. Fundamental to any understanding of this is the recognition that either *all* things are created or nothing is. There cannot be a universe in which some things have been created by God and other things have not. Consequently, either everything that is, every event that happens, reveals in some manner the Ultimate Reality, or nothing does. There cannot be a special class of God-given things or God-produced events. In the Christian understanding, therefore, the growth of every blade of grass is a miracle.

"Miracle," it should be noted, is a human word, a human description. It is probable that there is no such thing as something which by itself is a miracle, something which would be miraculous upon an uninhabited planet. One might compare the concept that the clock does not tick if there is no one to hear it. Certainly the action of the clock causes sound waves, but the ticking is the effect of these waves upon the human ear. For the completely deaf person there can be no tick.

Nevertheless, the question remains: are there what might be called swellings, events more fully charged with the power of the Ultimate? Probably we ought to say yes, just as there are men and women more fully charged with power, with intelligence, with strength, with sanctity, and so on. But we should be very careful not to be too hasty in saying "Lo here!" or "Lo there!" about miracles.

> If anyone says to you, "Look, here is the Christ!" or "Look, there he is!" do not believe it. False Christs and false prophets will arise and show signs and wonders, to lead astray, if possible, the elect.
>
> Mark 13:21–22

On the other hand, we need to be no less on our guard against failing to perceive the activity of God. The fourth chapter of Amos contains a list of what his hearers evidently thought of as natural disasters, requiring no change of heart on their part, but which Amos insisted should be understood as God Himself confronting His people, and demanding from them a complete reexamination of their society.

It is common among modern biblical scholars to divide the miracles into healing miracles (curing the blind, lame, deaf, dumb, paralyzed, epileptic, insane, and leprous, and raising the dead) and nature miracles (feeding the multitude, stilling the storm, walking on water, turning water into wine) and to suggest that on the whole the former are easier to explain. Certainly, we now know a great deal more than the ancient world did about psychosomatic problems and the close relationship between mental states and physical disease, and about the validity of much of what is loosely called faith healing. But this is not how the ancient world looked at the question.

They were not necessarily more credulous, but they had different questions in mind.[4] We have, therefore, to consider what the writers of the Gospels expected their readers to understand by the stories. What significance did these stories have so that they were worth recording? The ancient world was always conscious of powers at work, forces beyond their control, which might bring either good or evil results for human beings. Disease and death were understood in these terms, as dangerous and evil powers at work in the world, in conflict with the forces that were working for the good of the human race. Sick people were consequently spoken of as inhabited or possessed, in the merciless grip of something stronger than themselves. Widespread sickness was evidence of the apparent triumph of evil, and therefore widespread recovery from sickness must portend the triumph of the powers of good. The Gospel writers tell so many stories of healing, since for them and for their readers this was clear evidence of the new aeon, the new world breaking into the old, reality overcoming the artificial and fallacious, order prevailing over disorder. "Go and tell John," said Jesus, "the things you have seen and heard: the blind receive their sight and the lame walk; lepers are cleansed and the deaf hear, and the dead are raised up, and the poor have the good news given to them" (Matt. 11:2-6; Luke 7:19-23).

In the Old Testament the phrase "signs and wonders" is most commonly used in relation to the Exodus from Egypt and the delivery from slavery and bondage. Therefore, it is important for readers of the New Testament to grasp how many of the Gospel miracles refer back directly to that experience. This is particularly true of the feeding of the multitude, a story told no less than six times (Matt. 14:13-21; 15:32-39; Mark 6:30-44; 8:1-10; Luke 9:10-17; John 6:1-13). It happened in a "desert place," in the wilderness (an essential point that is obscured in many modern translations), and so the story is a vivid portrayal of the fact that God is once more performing his constant work of saving His people from tyranny and bondage.

All the miracles are *dunameis*, acts of power. Power is present, often secretly, underground, as indicated by the parables in the fourth chapter of Mark. These acts are always what, according to the ancient Scriptures, God does. It is God who walks upon the waters (Job 38:16), and who is able to say to the tempestuous sea,

Thus far shall you come, and no farther,
and here shall your proud waves be stayed.
Job 38:11

---

4. Hans Küng, in his book *On Being a Christian* (London: William Collins Sons, 1974), has an excellent short section entitled "miracles" (pp. 226–38), but he is surely wrong in describing the stories as "simply unsophisticated popular narratives which are meant to call forth admiring belief" (p. 229).

Mark 4:35—5:20 is a direct reflection of the "dread deeds" of God spoken of in Ps. 65:5-8, where He stills the roaring of the seas and causes those who dwell at the farthest bounds to be afraid at His signs. In reading this passage from Mark it is essential to remember that the farther side of the Sea of Galilee was pagan territory beyond the frontier, and understood, therefore, to be no less disorderly than the wind and the sea.

The miracles are also the work of the Creator, forever making things new, so that those who learn of them are compelled to recognize that this is indeed a new world, no longer constricted by the rigid structures of the past. Once again, this is most dramatically expressed by Mark, though the other evangelists would fully agree with him. Toward the conclusion of the section of his Gospel in which Jesus is in pagan territory (7:24—8:10) he tells the story of the healing of the deaf-mute (Mark 7:31-37) in language which refers directly to Isaiah 35. In the concluding sentence the exclamation, "He has done all things well," calls immediately to mind the statement in Gen. 1:31, "And God saw everything that he had made, and behold it was very good."[5] In other words, there is now a new world in which the Gentiles are to be thought of no longer as people incapable of hearing the good news and incapable also of making it known. They are fully members of this new world, and in the subsequent story, the Feeding of the Four Thousand, they share the Exodus experience and the delivery from bondage.[6]

Finally, the miracles portray also what was expected to happen in the Messianic age. This is already apparent from the parallel with Isaiah 35, but the "Banquet of the Messiah" was a common feature of the messianic expectations of that time, and the mention of a banquet in more than one parable is related to this expectation. However, the popular thinking of the day saw the pagans as completely excluded, or if they were present, as performing the part of the slaves. The wholehearted admission of the Gentiles to the Messiah's feast is an essential feature of the good news.

> More important than the number and extent of the cures, expulsions of devils and wonderful deeds is the fact that Jesus turns with sympathy and compassion to all those *to whom no one else turns:* the weak, sick, neglected, social rejects. People were always glad to pass these by. Weaklings and invalids are burdensome. Everyone keeps his distance from lepers and "possessed." And the devout monks of Qumran (and similarly up to a point the rabbis), faithful to their rule, excluded from the very beginning certain groups of men: *No madman, or lunatic, or sim-*

---

5. The parallels are clearer in the Greek than can be reproduced in English translations.

6. Mark is not the only gospel to insist on this. John tells only of the Feeding of the Five Thousand, but he understands it to have happened on the Gentile side of the lake so that those fed were both Gentile and Jewish (John 6:1-14). Matthew also places the Feeding of the Four Thousand east of the lake (Matt. 15:32-39).

pleton, or fool, no blind man, or maimed, or lame, or deaf man, and no minor,
shall enter into the Community, for the Angels of Holiness are with them.
                                                        Hans Küng,
                                    On Being a Christian, 235 (Küng's italics)[7]

The Parables of Jesus

The Greek word is *parabole*, meaning a "parable," or "similitude." It
is used only in the Synoptic Gospels. John never uses the word, but he
speaks four times of a *paroimia* (an obscure saying, or proverb), once
about the Good Shepherd (10:6), and three times concerning the teaching
after the resurrection (16:25–30). It seems clear that the use of parables
was a very characteristic feature of Jesus' teaching, and Matthew goes so
far as to say, "All this Jesus said to the crowds in parables; indeed, he said
nothing to them without a parable" (Matt. 13:34). He apparently saw this
as the fulfillment of Ps. 78:1–4, believed at that time to have been written
by Asaph the Seer (2 Chron. 29:30):

Give ear, O my people, to my teaching;
   incline your ears to the words of my mouth!
I will open my mouth in a parable;
   I will utter dark sayings from of old,
things that we have heard and known,
   that our fathers have told us.
We will not hide them from their children,
   but tell to the coming generation
the glorious deeds of the Lord, and his might,
   and the wonders which he has wrought.
                                                        Psalm 78:1–4

Parables are essentially stories, intended to illustrate by pictorial language what could not be easily understood by ordinary men and women.
Mark says that to the ordinary people "everything comes by parables," and
explains that this is "so that they may indeed see but not perceive, and may
indeed hear but not understand" (Mark 4:11–12). He had in mind Isaiah's
great vision in the Temple, when the prophet was told,

Go and say to this people:
  "Hear and hear, but do not understand;
   see and see, but do not perceive."
Make the heart of this people fat,
   and their ears heavy,
   and shut their eyes;

---

7. The blind and the lame were forbidden to enter the Temple, on the basis of 2 Sam. 5:8;
hence the importance of stories about lame people who were healed outside the Temple and
thereby enabled to go in (John 5:2–14; Acts 3:1–10). The effect of Jesus' teaching and example
may be seen in the fact that from very early days Christian monasteries, in both the Eastern and
Western church, did not exclude the blind and deformed, but welcomed and took care of them.

> lest they see with their eyes,
>   and hear with their ears,
> and understand with their hearts,
>   and turn and be healed.
>
> Isaiah 6:9–10[8]

A large number of scholars have taken Mark to task, saying that obviously the parables were meant for clarity, not confusion, and that therefore he has misunderstood them. But these scholars are surely wrong and Mark is right. A modern parallel might be the explanation commonly used in popular books on science that atoms are like billiard balls knocking up against each other. This certainly helps the ignorant reader to know something of the subject, but it also leads to misunderstanding because the picture gets in the way of the reader's perceiving the true nature of atoms.

Closely related to parables are *similes*, for example, "You are like whitewashed tombs, which outwardly appear beautiful, but within they are full of dead men's bones and all uncleanness" (Matt. 23:27), and *metaphors*, for example, "Give and it will be given to you, good measure, pressed down, shaken together, and running over, will men give into your bosom" (Luke 6:38). All reveal to us the vividness and liveliness of Jesus' teaching. He did not, however, originate this method of instruction, which was, in fact, very common at that time and much used by the rabbis, but the evidence of the centuries since his day demonstrates how powerfully his parables have worked upon the minds of men and women, even in translation. In the Old Testament parables are hardly to be found, Jotham's parable about the trees (Judg. 9:7–15) being the best example, but the wisdom teachers certainly used similitudes, for a man of understanding should acquire skill

> to understand a proverb and figure,
>   the words of the wise and their riddles.
>
> Proverbs 1:6;
> see also 7:6–26

In both Matthew and Mark the parables are collected in blocks. Mark in fact has very few, all but two gathered together in 4:1–34. They are all concerned with the mysterious but irresistible power of God, which has been driven underground by the antagonism of the establishment of Jesus' day (see especially Mark 3:6). There, unperceived by men and women, it germinates and grows, forcing its way out into the open, and producing in the end a rich harvest (4:26–29).[9] The smallness of the beginning bears no relation to the greatness of the final result (4:30–32). The seeds are

---

8. This command to Isaiah is intensely ironical, saying the opposite of what is meant in order to compel the hearers in Jerusalem to stop and think seriously about the warning which comes in the following verses. It does not mean that God does not want to heal His people.

9. This is the only parable peculiar to Mark.

scattered freely, for before the use of machinery the sower threw them out of a bag by hand, and they do not take effective root everywhere, but where the words about the kingdom, spoken freely to all and sundry, are able to find fertile soil, the outcome transcends any normal earthly harvest (4:3–20). The only parable in this group which does not concern seed is that of the lamp, which is not "brought in to be put under a bushel, or under a bed" (4:21, literally, "does not come in"). Although for a time driven underground, "the kingdom," the power and majesty of God, is not what we might call an underground movement, surreptitious and secret by nature, but brilliant light, dispelling the darkness that envelops humanity.[10]

A very large number of the parables concerns the *basileia tou theou*, normally translated "kingdom of God" (in Matthew "kingdom of heaven"), but *basileia* means more than kingdom. It includes also the concepts of "kingship," "realm" "society," "commonwealth." In a world where the normal political structure was that of a country under the authority of a king or emperor, and administered through his appointed representatives, "kingdom" comprised all that we have in mind when we think of our nation, by which we are protected and in which we are at home, although, of course, it did not include any idea of representative government and popular choice. Nor can the "kingdom of God" include that idea for us today. God does not run for office.

The essential feature is that within this realm God is the supreme authority, His will prevailing unchallenged, but without any hint of tyranny, for His whole purpose is the well-being of His people. The whole order of society is according to His wishes, and therefore in every sense harmonious. In this kingdom all proceeds without violence, without power struggles, without class distinction, without poverty, discrimination, and degradation. The concept of this kingdom of heaven is the foundation of Jesus' proclamation, and is by no means confined to the parables. The imminence of the kingdom was his first recorded teaching (Mark 1:14), and was the subject of his final conversation with his disciples at the Last Supper (Luke 22:16). This kingdom is the new age, the new world, the new society, with a completely new structure and requiring entirely new behavior.

It is new, and yet not new, because God has been king from all eternity. Therefore, the "new commandment" (John 13:34) is also not a new commandment, "because the darkness is passing away, and the true light is already shining" (1 John 1:7–8). The kingdom is not new also, because it is that of which Moses and the prophets spoke. It has already come; it is

---

10. In Matthew the blocks of parables are in the last four out of his five sections on the teaching of Jesus, the first being the Sermon on the Mount. They are: 13:1–52; 21:28–41; 22:1–14; 24:32–33 plus 25:1–46. Luke has the parables scattered throughout his Gospel.

"near to you" (Luke 10:9–11), even "within you," or perhaps "amongst you" (Luke 17:21). It has come and yet is still to come. In Mark 4 and Matthew 13 it has already begun, but in Matthew 25 it is still in the future. We live, therefore, between the times, as it were in enemy-occupied territory, but where the ultimate victor has already established a beachhead, a situation similar to that of occupied France after D-day. It is an inestimable treasure, worth selling every scrap of one's property in order to obtain (Matt. 13:44–46).

How easy it is to write these words, and probably no less easy to read them, but how profoundly difficult it is to understand them and make them one's own. Living in enemy-occupied territory involves all the pressures to accept enemy rule for the sake of food to eat and escaping the danger of arrest at four in the morning, and the grim punishments earthly rulers can inflict upon those whom they suspect of disobedience. More than half the governments in this world today interrogate prisoners by torture as a matter of course, and international conferences are held to discuss the most effective methods of torture. Our own government is in close political alliance with totalitarian and brutal regimes.[11] Jesus was speaking to people who knew well the pressures of political and military power, and how desperately difficult it was to scrape a living if one did not conform. He himself underwent torture and execution, and, if the New Testament is telling us the truth and the Christian argument is sound, he knew full well the pressures to conform, which we in our own society find so imperious, so very difficult to disobey.

There are, of course, parables on other themes, though they are all related to the one central theme. There are parables of judgment and the Last Day in Matt. 21:28–41; 22:1–14; and chapter 25; and parables of divine forgiveness in Luke 15. There are also, especially in Luke's Gospel, parables of right behavior, for example, the Good Samaritan (10:25–37), the Rich Fool (12:13–21), the Watchful Servants and the faithful and wise steward (12:35–48), behavior at a marriage feast (14:7–11), the Unjust Steward and those who love money (16:1–15), and parables about temptations and true faith (17:1–10), as well as about how to pray (18:1–14).

The Sermon on the Mount

It is best to keep this title, instead of "mountain, mountainside, hill," as in almost all modern translations, since undoubtedly Matthew had in mind Mt. Sinai, and the giving to the people of Israel the divine Torah, the Law or Teaching. This Torah, though given to his disciples (not merely

---

11. Notorious examples are the Philippines, South Korea, and South Africa. South Africa, in principle a Christian country, is the only country in the world where it is actually against the law not to practice racism.

the Twelve, for they have not yet been chosen), is universal and the introduction to the sermon in 5:1–2 should be compared closely with 15:29–31. There Jesus, traveling among the pagans,[12] went up once again onto "the mount," and healed these outsiders, so that they were all able both to hear the teachings and to teach other people, and able also to walk in the right way, according to the word of the Teacher, having cast away their idols (Isa. 30:20–22). They all then "glorified the God of Israel," about whom until then they had known nothing.

The teaching of the Sermon on the Mount, therefore, is delivered to all among humankind who are prepared to listen, and to learn about the life that must be lived within the realm of God. Unquestionably it is addressed to the Christian community of Matthew's own day, but unquestionably also it is teaching addressed to the Jewish community, to whom Torah and the Prophets had been given in the first place, and addressed also with equal authority to the entire world.[13]

Since the sermon portrays life within the kingdom, it represents the absolute standard of God, by which all things are measured. "You, therefore, must be perfect, as your heavenly Father is perfect" echoes the commandment in Lev. 19:1–2, "You shall be holy, for I the Lord your God am holy." Torah and the teaching of the prophets remain, and must remain until the end of the world, altogether true, but the transcendent purity of God renders every human interpretation of the standards and pattern of His commonwealth inadequate, and demands that all men and women must forever strive to go beyond these human patterns and structures, however exalted. This is the standard by which all that human beings do or say must be measured, especially if they consider themselves to be in any sense an elite, a "chosen people," citizens of "God's own country." Because of its unattainable perfection, this standard cannot be used as a basis for practical politics, but it is, nevertheless, the standard by which all political activities are ultimately judged.

When studying the Sermon on the Mount, it is important to compare it with the so-called Sermon on the Plain (Luke 6:17–49), with which it has very many parallels. Luke's version is probably the earlier and is decidedly down to earth in comparison with the exalted transcendence of Matthew's account. This does not mean that one is more valid than the other. Luke's account seems to be more factual, preserving more of the

---

12. Matthew in chapter 15 is using Mark 7:1—8:10, where the authoritative definition of "uncleanness" (Mark 7:1–23; Matt. 15:1–20) is followed immediately by Jesus' departure to the land of the Gentiles, i.e., the "unclean people" (Matt. 16:21; Mark 7:24). Everything until the return across the Lake of Galilee (Matt. 15:39; Mark 8:10) takes place in Gentile territory.

13. One contributor objected: "Is not 'Blessed are you when men revile you and persecute you and utter all kinds of evil against you on my account' said only to Christians?" Certainly, it is addressed in the first instance to Christians suffering persecution, but it must apply also to all who are "persecuted for righteousness' sake."

actual words of Jesus, and Matthew's to owe more to the activity of the *paracletos*, "the Holy Spirit, whom the Father will send in my name," and who "will teach you all things, and bring to remembrance all that I have said to you" (John 14:26).[14]

The sermon is divided into three distinct parts represented by three chapters, Matthew 5, 6, and 7, each ending with a summary statement.

The first section contains the Beatitudes (5:1–12), the teaching about salt and light (13–16), the continuing validity of "the law and the prophets," already discussed (17–20), and finally the true fulfillment of Torah.

In Luke those who are blessed, or truly happy, are the destitute beggars (*ptōchoi*) in the streets, the starving and thirsty, the miserable, for it is they who will be cared for when the kingdom of God truly comes, but in Matthew the blessed are those who beg for the Spirit, who "hunger and thirst for righteousness," the "meek," the gentle, considerate, and unassuming (*praeis*), the "pure in heart," literally cleansed, single-minded, and sincere (*katharoi*), and those who strive for peace. The only place where the two lists of Beatitudes come close together is at the end where both affirm that the followers of Jesus should count themselves blessed and be joyful when they are persecuted, since this is what happens to those who adhere resolutely to the truth in a hostile society.

5:13–16. Light and salt represent the function of the minority within the whole community, working gradually to enlighten and purify the society as a whole. There are, of course, dangers here that there may develop a double standard for those inside and those outside the minority, and also that the "righteous minority" may succumb to the temptations of arrogance and separatism, and that, if they ever become the dominant group, as often happened in Christian history, they may misuse their power and persecute others in their turn.

5:17–48. This section deals with the meaning of Torah. It cannot be abolished, for the true path can never become the false path. There is, properly speaking, no "new religion," since every reformer, every prophet who makes known the truth, and who calls men and women to adhere to the truth, calls them to recognize and adhere to what has been true since the beginning of the world, though he may, of course, enlarge and deepen their understanding of the truth. The section ends with the insistence that the goal must always be recognition of the character of God Himself, and complete identification with that character (*teleioi*, normally translated "perfect," can also mean "complete").

This command to strive for perfection again raises the problem of a double standard, one standard for the inner community and another for the community at large. Is it possible to be perfect while participating in

---

14. See chapter 8.

the everyday life of the world at large, or is it necessary to form a separate community which by its perfection sets an example to the world? It also raises the question of whether moral standards can provide a basis for political policy. Is it possible to make people good by act of Congress? Should the United States set up moral standards by which other countries, notably the communist countries, are judged? Or should high moral standards be seen as setting limits for human behavior, as providing restraints, rather than as making positive political demands? Should the "righteous," those who are striving to right the wrongs of society, seek to attain political power, whether by election or by forming resistance movements, so as to achieve a better society? How true is Lord Acton's dictum, "All power tends to corrupt; absolute power corrupts absolutely; great men are almost always bad men"?[15]

The second section of the Sermon on the Mount in chapter 6 is concerned with the rituals of religion, as exemplified by almsgiving, prayer, and fasting—first, care for and protection of the community and especially the *personae miserabiles*, the widows, orphans, and destitute; second, constant communication with the Source of all life and power; third, the training and education of oneself, by self-control and self-discipline, for life in a strenuous and possibly hostile world.

Ritual in any religion is necessary. It gives the members of the community a common pattern of life, and holds them together, strengthening them to live through times of stress. It provides a refuge, and enables them to feel at home in a foreign world. Ritual, however, is not without its dangers, and hence the insistence that it be done discreetly. It can too easily become "mere ritual," actions performed and words repeated without serious thought behind them. There is also the danger of equating the familiar patterns of behavior with right behavior, and consequently the rejection of less familiar patterns as false. It is fatally easy to become so concerned with the correct methods of worship that we "trust in ourselves that we are righteous and despise others" (Luke 18:9-14).

The section concludes with the discussion of "treasures on earth" and "treasures in heaven." Again and again in the Gospels, Jesus insists on the dangers of wealth and material well-being. This raises very serious questions for us who live in what is still an affluent society, despite the present high unemployment rate. What we define as "poverty," that is, an income of less than $9000 a year for one person, would be affluence for a huge section of the world's population who live in countries where the average income can be as low as $750 a year or even less. Our churches and their members, though there are notable exceptions, are insufficiently con-

---

15. From his correspondence with Bishop Creighton of London concerning the medieval papacy.

cerned with the poverty of those outside. White people are too little troubled by the staggering unemployment rate among young blacks. The country as a whole pays too little attention to the appalling destitution in the so-called Third World, and is a great deal more troubled by the East-West struggle than by what has come to be known as the North-South problem, the enormous difference between the affluent countries and the disadvantaged.

The crisis for Christians is exacerbated today by modern advertising techniques, commanding us to think of ourselves to the exclusion of all others. The constant media pressure is on being a "conspicuous success," and they create for us false images, such as the "Aqua-Velva Man" or the woman who uses Oil of Olay. We are all urged to regard our own careers as primary, and so powerful is this constant battering by the world that even those whose profession should in some sense give them protection, for example, clergy and teachers, succumb to the temptations. They demand higher salaries, reckon success by the numbers of those who attend their church or classes, and tailor their teaching or preaching to popular demand. It is quite desperately difficult to swim against the monstrous tide of modern values.

> Compassion, solidarity, and self-interest all call for the urgent abolition of hunger. Yet progress has been stumbling and slow. Eight hundred millions are estimated to be "destitute" in the Third World today . . . Millions will either die from lack of food or have their physical development impaired. It is an intolerable situation.
>
> *North-South* (Brandt Report)

The third and final section of the Sermon on the Mount concerns judgment and judging. The Greek word used is *krinein*, which means to "separate, distinguish; select, prefer; judge, think, consider, look upon; reach a decision, decide, propose, intend; judge, hale before a court, condemn."[16] All these meanings should be borne in mind. It is also worth considering certain other English words that come from the same root: criticize, criticism, crisis, crime, criminal, discriminate. Thus, in verse 1 we find the command, "Do not judge," that is, adversely or critically, but in verses 6 and 15–20: "Do discriminate and judge impartially between one thing and another." Also in verses 13–14, 21–23, and 24–27 comes the repeated warning: "Remember that you yourselves will be judged."

7:7–12. The Golden Rule is by no means unique to the teaching of Jesus, and we find it in other religious traditions as well, though usually in the form of "Do not do to others what you do not want them to do to you," for example, in the *Analects* of Confucius and in the teaching of the great Jewish Rabbi Hillel, who lived in the century before Jesus. The verses

---

16. William F. Arndt and F. Wilbur Gingrich, *A Greek-English Lexicon of the New Testament and Other Early Christian Literature* (Chicago: University of Chicago Press, 1952).

preceding it form a connecting link between the instruction that we must be discriminating in what we ask for and the giving of a principle of discrimination for our own behavior.

The Golden Rule is often quoted, but it is in fact very difficult to carry out, since the things we want for ourselves are not necessarily what other people want, and it is easy to succumb to the temptation to impose our own pattern of thinking upon other people, with often disastrous results. To fulfill this command faithfully demands much consideration, sympathy, and empathy.

Throughout the Sermon on the Mount we are given standards for human behavior, but the setting of standards always poses a problem, since any consideration of standards involves the necessity of judging, and therefore the danger of being judgmental. It is well-nigh impossible to be truly just, and human justice is therefore always approximate; it is never absolute justice and must, therefore, be continually tempered with mercy. It is altogether impossible to be just politically, where we deal inevitably with large bodies of people, and so the belief that we can by wise political means establish a "just and durable peace" is a dangerous will-o'-the-wisp. We must strive for both justice and peace, but not deceive ourselves about the constant and inevitable frailty of human beings.

Finally, there is very little indeed that is new in the teaching of Jesus. Almost the whole of it can be paralleled in the teaching given by the rabbis and in other religious traditions. Christians must avoid making arrogant claims for Christianity. What does, perhaps, approach uniqueness is the command to love one's enemies, a command that Christians throughout the centuries have obeyed only intermittently, and very often not at all. It forms only a small part of established liturgies and is sometimes completely absent. But even this commandment is just as much Buddhist as it is Christian.

THE MIRACLES OF JESUS

	Matthew	Mark	Luke	John
Turning Water into Wine				2:1–12
Man with the Unclean Spirit		1:21–28	4:31–37	
Peter's Mother-in-Law	8:14–15	1:29–31	4:38–39	
Miraculous Catch of Fish			5:1–11	21:1–6
Healing of a Leper	8:1–4	1:4–45	5:12–16	
Centurion's Servant (Nobleman's Son)	8:5–13		7:1–10	4:46–53
Stilling the Storm	8:23–27	4:35–41	8:22–25	
Gadarene Demoniac	8:28–34	5:1–20	8:26–39	
Paralytic Let Down Through Roof	9:1–8	2:1–12	15:17–26	
Paralytic at Pool of Bethesda				5:1–14
Man with the Withered Hand	12:9–14	3:1–6	6:6:11	
Raising of Widow's Son at Nain			7:11–17	
Raising of Jairus's Daughter and the Woman with a Hemorrhage	9:18–26	5:21–43	8:40–56	
Feeding of the Five Thousand	14:13–21	6:30–44	9:10–17	6:1–13
Walking on the Water	14:22–33	6:45–52		6:15–21
Syrophoenician Woman's Daughter	15:21–28	7:24–30		
The Deaf-Mute		7:31–37		
Feeding of the Four Thousand	15:32–39	8:1–10		
Blind Man of Bethsaida		8:22–26		
The Man Born Blind				9:1–12
Two Blind Men	9:27–31			
Epileptic Boy	17:14–21	9:14–29	9:37–43a	
Coin in the Fish's Mouth	17:24–27			
Woman with Spirit of Infirmity			13:10–17	
Man with Dropsy			14:1–6	
Healing of Ten Lepers			17:11–19	
Raising of Lazarus				11:1–43
Blind Bartemaeus	20:29–34	10:46–52	18:35–43	
Cursing of the Fig Tree	21:18–22	11:12–14, 20–25		
Healing of Slave's Ear	(26:47–54)	(14:43–47)	22:47–51	
General healing of the sick	4:23–25	1:32–34, 39	4:40–41	
	8:16–17 12:15–21 14:34–36 15:29–31	3:7–12 6:53–56	6:17–19	

THE PARABLES OF JESUS

	Matthew	Mark	Luke
The Sower	13:1–9	4:1–9	8:4–8
The Lamp		4:21–25	8:16–18
Seed Growing Secretly		4:26–29	
The Tares or Weeds	13:24–30		
Mustard Seed	13:31–32	4:30–32	13:18–19
Leaven	13:3		13:20–21
Hidden Treasure	13:44		
Pearl of Great Price	13:45–46		
The Net	13:47–50		
The Householder	13:50–52		
The Lost Sheep	18:10–14		15:3–7
Unmerciful Servant	18:23–35		
The Good Samaritan			10:29–37
The Friend at Midnight			11:5–8
Return of the Evil Spirit	12:43–45		11:24–26
The Rich Fool			12:13–21
The Servant's Wages (a)			12:47–48
Invitation to Supper			14:7–14
The Great Supper	22:1–10		14:15–24
The Lost Coin			15:8–10
The Prodigal Son			15:11–32
The Unjust Steward			16:1–13
The Rich Man and Lazarus			16:19–31
The Servant's Wages (b)			17:7–10
The Unjust Judge			18:1–8
The Pharisee and Publican			18:9–14
Laborers in the Vineyard	20:1–16		
The Pounds, or Talents	25:14–30		19:11–27
The Two Sons	21:28–32		
The Wicked Tenants	21:33–46	12:1–12	20:9–19
The Fig Tree	24:32–33	13:28–29	
Watchful Householder	24:42-44		
Faithful and Wise Servant	24:45–51		12:42–46
The Ten Virgins	25:1–13		
Jesus' Use of Parables	13:34–35	4:33–34	

7

RESURRECTION

If death and hasty burial in a borrowed tomb had been the last episode in the story of Jesus, then Christianity would probably have faded out and died as a peculiar sect in Judaism, as other messianic movements had done. But something else happened, so that the death of Jesus was not the end. Instead, it was seen as the vindication of his life and teachings, and the special power of his small circle of followers. The early Christian community based its new life, and the power and authority of its message, on the conviction that God had raised Jesus from the dead. So central to their life was this conviction that one may say that the Christian faith stands or falls with the resurrection of Jesus. If there is no Easter, there is no Christianity.

"If Christ was not raised, then our gospel is null and void, and so is your faith; and we turn out to be lying witnesses for God" (1 Cor. 15:14–15 NEB). This is the first written testimony about the resurrection that we have, since Paul's letters were written before the Gospels.[1] Behind both, however, there is still earlier evidence: the reports of the empty tomb and the repeated assertions that Jesus had more than once appeared alive after his death.

All the evidence that we possess is that the tomb in which Jesus had been buried on Friday was empty on the following Sunday morning. This is a strange and striking fact. The assertion that God had raised Jesus from the dead could have been refuted by producing the body but, as far as we know, no one in ancient times ever tried to show that the Christian message was false because the body was still there.[2]

---

1. We do not know the exact dates, but Jesus was crucified in about A.D. 30. Paul's letters belong to the period between A.D. 52 and 62. Mark's Gospel, believed by most scholars to be the first, appears to have been written in about A.D. 65.

2. There are some stories belonging to a rather later period which claim that Jesus' body had never left the tomb. Earlier, the accusation had been that the tomb was empty because the disciples had hidden the body.

The Gospel accounts of the empty tomb are varied, but share a number of common elements. The most striking of these is the statement that women, always including Mary Magdalene, made the discovery (Matt. 27:61—28:8; Mark 15:47—16:8; Luke 23:55—24:11; John 20:1-18). This is remarkable because in those days the unsupported testimony of a woman would not be accepted in a court of law as admissible evidence. It is clear, therefore, that the Gospels were not written in a way that would win easy approval. What the women witnessed to was an empty tomb. That is all. There is no foundation in any of the four Gospels for the later legends about Jesus leaving the tomb, or how the resurrection actually happened —stories that became popular in medieval art.

The Gospels vary in the details of their accounts of what these women saw. In Mark a young man, or in Luke two young men, sit inside the tomb; in Matthew an angel sits outside; and in John, Mary Magdalene sees two angels inside the tomb after Peter and "the disciple whom Jesus loved" (probably John) had seen only the grave cloths (Mark 16:5; Luke 24:4; Matt. 28:2; John 20:11-12).[3] The first three Gospels agree in stressing the bewilderment, awe, and terror of people suddenly confronted by the empty tomb. According to Mark, the women "went out and fled from the tomb; for trembling and astonishment had come upon them; they said nothing to anyone, for they were afraid" (Mark 16:8). Matthew speaks of a great earthquake and of an angel with a face like lightning, so that "for fear of him the guards trembled and became like dead men" (Matt. 28:2-4). Luke says that "the women were frightened and bowed their faces to the ground" at the sight of "two men in dazzling apparel" (Luke 24:4-5).

This sense of terror, fear, and helplessness, present also later when the disciples were confronted by the risen Jesus, demonstrates the reaction of human creatures when face to face with God's mysterious power at work in the world (Luke 24:36). It becomes even more vivid when compared to the quiet manner and gentle reassurance of Jesus himself when speaking to the confused Mary Magdalene, or walking alongside the two men on their way to Emmaus (John 20:16; Luke 24:13-15). The earlier psychological state of the disciples, who had all fled in panic when Jesus was arrested (Matt. 26:56; Mark 14:50), provides no explanation for the hope, joy, and more profound understanding apparent after the discovery of the empty tomb and the events that followed.

It was not, however, the empty tomb but the appearances of Jesus to his disciples and his conversations with them which really convinced them that God had indeed raised him from the dead. The accounts in the Gospels and the Book of Acts vary as to the duration of these appearances

---

3. The fact that the early disciples not only accepted the women's testimony, but went so far as to base the fundamental tenet of the Christian faith, i.e., the resurrection, upon this testimony, may well reflect their response to Jesus' own close relationship with his women followers.

(one day or many days), the location (Jerusalem alone or also in Galilee), and also the people present. In the earliest written account that we have Paul cites a list of such appearances as evidence for the resurrection, and as the fundamental authority for his preaching:

> For I delivered to you as of first importance what I also received, that Christ died for our sins in accordance with the scriptures, that he was buried, that he was raised on the third day in accordance with the scriptures, and that he appeared to Cephas [Peter], then to the twelve. Then he appeared to more than five hundred brethren at one time, most of whom are still alive, though some have fallen asleep. Then he appeared to James, then to all the apostles. Last of all . . . he appeared also to me.
>
> 1 Corinthians 15:3–8[4]

Here Paul claims to have seen Jesus in the same way as the other privileged witnesses had done. But he had seen him in a vision (Acts 9:1–22), not physically as in the Gospel accounts. In his letter to the Galatians (1:16) he insists that "God was pleased to reveal his son" to him, and that therefore what he teaches is not based merely upon other people's reports.

Peter also, in his response to Cornelius, insists upon the appearances of Jesus, rather than the empty tomb, as evidence for the resurrection:

> God raised him on the third day, and made him manifest; not to all the people but to us who were chosen by God as witnesses, who ate and drank with him after he rose from the dead.
>
> Acts 10:40–41

Paul, writing to the Corinthians, who had doubts about the resurrection because they knew that corpses decay and perish, did not focus upon the earthly body, its disposition, or its final resting place. The resurrection of Jesus, he maintained, was that of an imperishable "spiritual body." The appearances demonstrated for him that Jesus is "the first fruits of the harvest of the dead" (1 Cor. 15:20 NEB). So too Luke, who certainly knew about the empty tomb, since he speaks of it in his Gospel, does not mention it in describing Peter's address to Cornelius (Acts 10:34–43). It is the appearances of the living Jesus that confirm the resurrection faith, while the empty tomb makes clear that he who appeared was no phantom.

We need to ask what these early Christians were affirming when they spoke of the resurrection appearances. Certainly, they intended a sense of dramatic change, for they had experienced a newness in Jesus. He was no longer exactly what he had been before. This is evident from the strange fact that those to whom Jesus appeared often did not recognize him at first. Mary mistook him for a gardener, the two men going to Emmaus thought he was a stranger, and those in the boat on the Lake of Galilee did not at

---

4. The accounts of the appearance to Paul are in Acts 9:1–22; 22:4–16; 26:9–18. The Gospel accounts of postresurrection appearances are in Matt. 28:9–20; Luke 24:13–49; John 20:11–21:22. See also Acts 1:3–11.

first grasp who he was (John 20:11–18; 21:1–14; Luke 24:13–43). The accounts of Jesus breaking bread with his followers (Luke 24:28–35), or of Thomas touching his wounded side (John 20:24–29), emphasize that this was no mere ghostly apparition. Yet, at the same time these accounts demonstrate that the body was different. He could appear and disappear, and even enter a locked room. But seen or not seen, the insistence is that Jesus continues to be present and to be recognized at those moments when the Scriptures are explained and the disciples are fed. The dramatic change they experienced was for them evidence of that new creation which began when Jesus cried out in agony on the cross, a cry like that of a woman in childbirth, bringing new life into the world.

This creation of a new, imperishable body demonstrates that a new power is now at work. Just as in the first creation "God formed man of dust from the ground, and breathed into his nostrils the breath of life" (Gen. 2:7), so now the power of God as Spirit raises from the dusty grave a spiritual body:

> Thus it is written, "The first man Adam became a living being"; the last Adam [i.e., Christ] became a life-giving spirit.
>
> 1 Corinthians 15:45

Those who belong to the new creation must therefore be "born from spirit." Just as the seed has to fall into the ground and die as a seed before it can have the power of new life (a favorite image in the Gospels; see Matt. 13:24–30; Mark 4:26–29; John 12:24), so too the perishable body of Jesus had to die in order that the imperishable, spirit-giving body might live. The risen Christ, partaking of a new mode of being in and with God, bestowed upon his followers the power of the Spirit, together with the authority to forgive sins, and so restore the relationship with God which had been lost in the first creation (John 20:22–23; see Genesis 3).

> All authority in heaven and on earth has been given to me. Go therefore and make disciples of all nations, baptizing them in the name of the Father and of the Son and of the Holy Spirit, teaching them to observe all that I have commanded you; and lo, I am with you always, to the close of the age.
>
> Matthew 28:18–20

As in almost all accounts of Jesus appearing after his resurrection, there is here a command to the listeners to go out and make known the truth. Those who heard it realized in their own lives the ultimate meaning of Jesus and his message; and this experience compelled their missionary activity, preaching, as Jesus had done, with authority about the coming kingdom and the need for repentance, demonstrated by the sacred washing of baptism.

The preaching of the apostles was that in the life of Jesus the presence and the mighty deeds of God are visible. Belief in the meaning and the possibility of resurrection is therefore dependent on belief in the power of God. They perceived the resurrection of Jesus as an especially significant manifestation of God's power, for it was not something natural, or worked for, nor, indeed, something which could have been foreseen ahead of time from the life and teaching, or even the death of Jesus. It took them completely by surprise. Resurrection, therefore, completely transcends the normal processes of life and death, processes that bound Jesus of Nazareth, and also bind us, to this world of space and time. The language they used to express resurrection demonstrates this. "Glorified body" and transcendent light cannot be understood within the confines of the world as we know it. Something new, something dynamic and powerful was here proclaimed.

The resurrected Christ, therefore, was evidently regarded as alive in the lives of his disciples. This was no mere subjective experience of faith, "born out of reflection on the completed life of Jesus."[5] Jesus for them was much more than a great teacher or rabbi. His life after death transcended the literary and moral example of Socrates, whose own unjust death for the sake of others has seemed to many so parallel. Any impressive teacher or leader lives on after death, but this was not the kind of living that Christians thought of when they spoke of Jesus. He was more to them than the remembered and cherished personification of his teachings, nor was his resurrection merely a resuscitated corpse. As Simone Weil sharply pointed out, Adolf Hitler could rise from the dead a thousand times and she would never believe that he was the Son of God.[6]

It is certainly possible to believe that Jesus rose from the dead and yet still not believe that he was the promised Messiah, the Anointed One. The two are not necessarily synonymous. Yet the preaching of the early apostles demonstrates their certainty that with the death and resurrection of Jesus the age of the Messiah had in fact dawned, unleashing power to speak in tongues, heal the sick, cast out demons, and forgive sins. A mighty act of God can be perceived only by those for whom "God" has meaning, and who can therefore discern and judge the event. No historical or physical fact is by itself sufficient to cause anyone to change his or her mind. It is the perception and interpretation of the event that compels the change. Jesus, therefore, made no appearance after his resurrection to the Romans or the high priest and the scribes. The event may have been before their eyes, but their perception and their mind set could not apprehend it. Resurrection belongs to that realm beyond both birth and death which in chapter 1 we called "the realm of the absolutely transcendent, where there are no discernible 'facts.'" Therefore, Jesus appeared, and could appear,

---

5. See Don Cupitt, "The Resurrection: A Disagreement" (with C. F. D. Moule), *Theology* 75 (October 1972): 509, 516

6. Quoted by John Garvey in "The Reality of Easter," *Commonweal* 109 (no. 7): 200.

only to those able to perceive him, those with eyes of faith, though they may have been at first uncertain, like the two men at Emmaus, or cautious and doubtful like Thomas, who in the end made the greatest acclamation of all: "My Lord and my God!" (John 20:28).

If, as Christians assert, there is now after the resurrection of Christ a new creation at work in the world, then a new perception, a new dimension of faith, is necessary to perceive and comprehend it. The story of Thomas and Jesus' response to him was a great consolation to those early Christians who had not seen Jesus during his life on earth, nor yet by some special vision, for the story affirms that faith far transcends physical sight: "Have you believed because you have seen me? Blessed are those who have not seen, and yet believe"(John 20:29). Only those prepared to believe can truly see the power at work. Using the image of Abraham, the Father of Faith, of whom it had been written, "He believed the Lord, and he reckoned it to him as righteousness" (Gen. 15:6), Jesus himself had told his followers, "If they do not hear Moses and the prophets, neither will they be convinced if someone should rise from the dead" (Luke 16:31).

Resurrection Is for All

If the resurrection affected only the Son of God, now exalted at the Father's right hand, then we would need to ask why it should be the central focus of the Christian message. What gospel, what good news, for humankind would such a divine drama convey? It is precisely this question that Paul deals with in 1 Corinthians 15. He was writing to people who were evidently Gentile Greeks, and who had grave doubts about whether resurrection would really happen to everyone.

> Now if this is what we proclaim, that Christ was raised from the dead, how can some of you say that there is no resurrection of the dead? If there be no resurrection, then Christ was not raised; and if Christ was not raised, then our gospel is null and void, and so is your faith. . . . If it is for this life only that Christ has given us hope, we are of all men the most to be pitied.
>
> 1 Corinthians 15:12–14, 19 NEB

"But," Paul continues, "the truth is, Christ was raised to life—the first fruits of the harvest of the dead," not the end but the beginning. If the grave is the final statement about human life, if there is nothing at all for us on the further side of birth and death, then life itself is but a melancholy shadow of future annihilation. "If the dead are never raised to life, 'let us eat and drink, for tomorrow we die'" (1 Cor. 15:32; Paul was quoting Isa. 22:13). But Christ is risen indeed, and we have an antidote to the mortal fear of both death and life. Christians therefore proclaim in their worship,

"By thy dying thou hast destroyed our death, and by thy rising thou hast
restored our life."

But it is not enough to say only that resurrection shows that death is not
irrational, not something to be postponed as long as possible, or to be
avoided by denying that it happens. It is much more than this. Death is
a constant, and in fact we "die daily," and "all our lives begin to die."
What we call "life" is a kind of living death, for which the moment of
death itself provides a final and inescapable conclusion.

Paul argued that life and death have these qualities because of sin. "The
sting of death is sin, and sin gains its power from the law" (1 Cor. 15:56
NEB). This does not mean that Torah, the sacred law and teaching, is
itself evil. "The law is holy," he said in Rom. 7:12, "and the commandment is holy and just and good." But the tragedy of human life is that
while we know perfectly well what is right and just, we continually fail
to do it. "I can will what is right, but I cannot do it. For I do not do the
good I want, but the evil I do not want is what I do. . . . Sin dwells within
me" (Rom. 7:18–20). It is the essential goodness of Torah that makes so
abundantly clear the corruption of human life, and demonstrates also what
would be the appalling tragedy of death, if life were indeed to come to an
abrupt end at that point. But "death is swallowed up in victory" (1 Cor.
15:54). The resurrection demonstrates that the power of sin, and the disaster of unfulfilled Torah, are annulled. Men and women need no longer
be in the grip of the old state of sin, for by the power of resurrection Christ
has rescued them, and given them an imperishable body (1 Cor. 15:42ff).

These early Christians saw the resurrection as "the immediate prelude
to the redemption of man and nature, the final overthrow of Satan. It is
not an isolated event but part of God's final new creation."[7] Had this not
happened, we would indeed have been "of all men most to be pitied."

The Achievement of Christ

But how could the death of Jesus, even though followed by the resurrection, redeem men and women? Why did he have to die at all for this purpose? To have been born, but not to have died, would have made him
irrelevant to human existence, for death, no less than life, is an inescapable fact of humanity. The self must die, if there is to be a new creation.
Both in society and in personal relationships we see death and life producing new situations, which must in their turn confront the inevitability of
change and end.

But given that he had to die, why did it have to be such a wretched
death? It is not a paradox that the Messiah, the Savior and Redeemer,

7. Amos Wilder, *Otherworldliness and the New Testament* (New York: Harper & Brothers,
1954), 97.

should be nailed to a cross, jeered at, forsaken, and in helpless agony? Again the answer is that the Savior of humanity must share to the uttermost humanity's torments, and allow the powers of evil to do their worst. A savior who had been spared these savageries would have little to say to blacks in South Africa, and to all victims of torture and police brutality. Nor would he be able to speak from the depths of experience to the torturers. God was at work through Jesus, participating in a manner beyond human comprehension in the appalling human suffering that results from the no less appalling human sin. At the same time the death and resurrection of Jesus demonstrate that other divine power, the forgiveness of sin. Perceiving this, the early Christians began to use new and divine titles for Jesus, titles drawn from Judaism and also the wider Hellenistic culture, such as Son of God, God Incarnate, the Word of God (*Logos*), and Exalted Lord (*Kyrios*).

The concept of resurrection was already there in the Scriptures, where there were stories of how God had raised the dead (1 Kings 17:17–24; 2 Kings 4:32–37). In the time of Jesus the Pharisees firmly believed in resurrection, although the more conservative sect of the Sadducees did not (Matt. 22:23–33; Mark 12:18–23; Luke 20:27–40; Acts 23:6–9). Just as God could create a world out of nothing, so He must surely have the power to resurrect, to create a new world for the Jewish people enduring persecution and martyrdom under foreign rule. But resurrection was for them something in the future, something that would happen on the Last Day. But for the early Christians it had suddenly become present and immediate, demanding a response from them with the same urgency that compels us to respond to the inescapable fact of death.

The death and resurrection of Jesus were redemptive, since he was, as we have already seen, "without sin."

> Since then we have a great high priest who has passed through the heavens, Jesus, the Son of God, let us hold fast our confession. For we have not a high priest who is unable to sympathize with our weaknesses, but one who in every respect has been tempted as we are, yet without sin. Let us then with confidence draw near to the throne of grace, that we may receive mercy and find grace to help in time of need.
>
> Hebrews 4:14–16

As the early Christian writers meditated upon the sinlessness of Jesus, they saw in him the model, the archetype, the fulfillment of human possibilities. As Irenaeus wrote in the second century, "He presented *man* to man in a new light," adding, "He also presented God to man in a new light."

But the more exalted these views of Christ's sinlessness became, the more acute was the question posed by Augustine, and others after him: What terrible crime must humankind have committed to require so great a sacrifice from so sinless a person? They turned to ponder the third chapter of Genesis, and

> Man's first disobedience, and the fruit
> Of that forbidden tree, whose mortal taste
> Brought death into the world, and all our woe.
> John Milton,
> *Paradise Lost*, 1.1–3

For so vast a burden of cruelty and corruption it would seem that no less a price would have to be paid to set us free. For this reason

> God so loved the world that he gave his only Son, that whoever believes in him should not perish but have eternal life. For God sent the Son into the world, not to condemn the world, but that the world might be saved through him.
> John 3:16–17

Resurrection and the Modern World

So far in this chapter we have been talking about resurrection and the power of God as Creator and Redeemer largely in terms of the thinking of early and medieval Christians. Now, however, we must ask how valid their ideas are in our modern scientific and increasingly technological culture. Is it not possible that their thinking was altogether too simplistic, and therefore unacceptable to us today?

We need here to distinguish between their concepts and the symbols they used to express them, being careful not to imagine that because the symbols, and therefore the language, at their disposal may have been limited, their thinking was consequently superficial. The Gospel of John is written in extremely simple language, and with a very limited vocabulary, using everyday symbols like father, son, word, wind, bread, water. The uneducated peasant can read the book and have it speak to him, and yet the greatest scholars admit that they never come to the end of plumbing its depths. "If heaven were nothing more than being allowed to read and to reflect and meditate quietly on this gospel, then I should be more than happy."[8] Our task is that of transposition, but this time not of transposing down, but transposing up. We have, as it were, to take a rich and complex fugue by J. S. Bach, written originally for the harpsichord, and score it for a large modern orchestra containing instruments quite unknown in the early eighteenth century. The sounds will be richer and more diverse, but the whole wealth of meaning was already there in the delicate notes of the original.

---

8. Said by Père Lagrange, the founder of the Ecole Biblique in Jerusalem, during the lectures on St. John's Gospel given in his old age. Luc H. Grollenberg, *Interpreting the Bible* (New York: Paulist Press, 1966), 93.

It is, for instance, hardly possible for us today to lay all the blame for human sin upon Adam and Eve, because we have difficulty in taking this story so literally. Even more impossible is it for any thoughtful person in the modern world to lay the whole blame for the crucifixion of Jesus on the Jewish people. Yet by our greater knowledge of history and of human behavior we are better equipped to be appalled when we consider the totality of evil committed since the first emergence of human beings as recognizably different from other animals, the immeasurable cruelties of our own still-unfinished century, and the terrible crimes men and women may commit in the future with all the dread technology at their disposal. We can no longer think of ransom being paid by God to the devil, but we cannot hide from ourselves the fact that for so vast a burden of brutality a vast price will somehow have to be paid. We do not need to ask, as did the medieval theologians, to whom the price must be paid, because we are well aware that those who pay the price of our sin—Jews in the Holocaust, tortured and ravaged prisoners at the mercy of secret police, sick and starving refugees—give nothing to anyone, for they have nothing at all to give.

They have nothing to give except their lives, and these are not so much given as stolen from them. We know now, in a manner that no earlier generation could have known, that the end of the world, and the death of all humanity, is a scientific possibility. In such an event all men, women, and children would pay with their lives, and it would gain them nothing. Left to themselves, there is nothing more that they could do on the further side of death. If for humanity there is truly nothingness beyond the limits of time and space, then indeed we are without hope.

If we are true to the New Testament concepts, rather than just the language, then it is a complete misapprehension to speak, as many do, of "immortality," or "life after death." There are ample examples of contemporary concern for immortality, this urge to preserve intact some aspect of humanity. We see it in the public notoriety of an assassin, the cult of folk heroes such as Elvis Presley, or the attempt to establish contact with the dead through spiritualism. Such concerns as cloning, freezing dead persons for later resuscitation, long-term sperm banks, and so on, are all in their own way attempts to escape the physical limits of death and preserve the continuity of the mortal body.

Immortality in itself does not necessarily imply a body of any kind, for it includes the concept of a wholly disembodied spirit, a ghost or phantom, lingering on endlessly and without purpose. The New Testament writers insisted upon the "resurrection of the body," and rejected the spiritualizing views of Greek philosophers, who tended to see matter as earthy and defiling, something from which pure spirit sought release. In the Hebrew understanding there was no distinct and separate entity called "spirit," for the human being was a unity. Mind, spirit, and body were one and indivisible, created as such by God. All was His creation, and therefore part of His purpose. To separate out the spirit and eliminate the body would render meaningless the human being, and therefore in the resurrection there must be body and complete identity, although, as Paul said to the Corinthians, it would be a "spiritual body" (1 Cor. 15:44). What exactly he meant by this is far from certain, for he did not explain, but he undoubtedly had in mind a body not subject to change, disintegration, and decay, yet still part of the creation, not vanishing into the Creator. There is no suggestion that human beings will someday, if they are good, become God, but what they will become cannot be expressed in terms of our present existence.

Modern science, biology as well as psychology, also insists that the human being is a unity, even while saying that there is dynamic interchange of the body with its environment, in which some five hundred million cells change or are lost in a single day. This conjunction is necessary for the full expression of the self, its mind, purpose, and will. The human being cannot be reduced merely to its chemical or atomic components without ceasing to be human, and for the same reason existence apart from a body is neither conceivable nor desirable. This is reflected in both traditional and contemporary ghost stories, where the disembodied spirits are portrayed as either bored and ineffective or frustrated and malevolent, or perhaps as the soulless "zombie," the living dead. All are presented as horrific, something to make the reader shudder. Thus does popular imagery confirm religious belief: spirit and body are one being and any disunity or dualism of mind and matter is destructive and inhuman.

Both New Testament and medieval Christians might well have spoken of a "life after death," for they had no other language available to them, but in the modern age we would be wrong to do so. "Life after death" suggests a continuation of time, and we now know time to be a dimension of the universe, part of the creation. Eternity is not an endless extension of time, but, as we have seen, either a complete absence of time, or else a dimension which includes time, but altogether surpasses it. Eternity is what we mean when we speak of the realm of God, for whom everything is "now" and everywhere is "here." Resurrection, therefore, if it is, as Christians believe, a translation to the realm of God, is not so much after death as beyond death, transcending death, reducing death to insignificance. Eternity is without corruption, whether this be corruption of the minds of men and women, so that they are swift to do evil, or of their frail flesh, or corruption of the body politic, for corruption is a consequence of time, and where there is no time there can be no decay. There and only there "the wicked cease from troubling, and the weary are at rest" (Job 3:17), and there "sorrow and sighing shall flee away" (Isa. 35:10).

But "there" is where? It cannot be nowhere, for that would mean that it had no existence at all, and it cannot be somewhere, for then it would be part of the universe and subject to all "the changes and chances of this mortal world."[9] Heaven, which is the realm of resurrection, altogether transcends, and is beyond, other than, the nature of this finite universe. We are at a loss for words to describe it, for words are but human inventions. Yet we may not be far wrong if we speak of resurrection as a condition, a mode of being, and heaven as a realm, a situation rather than a place. In these terms heaven is the realm of God, the situation in which the will and purposes of God prevail absolutely, and are in no way opposed or disregarded. Resurrection is the participation in, the belonging to, this realm.

We can no longer speak of either heaven or hell as a place, since "place" means some aspect of space and time, but we might well not be wrong in thinking that death is for everyone a transposition to the same mode of being. For those who have striven here, in this mortal and finite existence, to live according to the Truth, according to the will and purposes of God, the experience of finding themselves participants in a situation where this is done naturally, with none of the earthly antagonism, opposition, persecution, and frustration, will be pure bliss, the culmination and fulfillment of all their hopes. But for those whose life on earth has been directed toward strictly finite ends, who have seen wealth, a successful career, political or military power, as the dominant factors in life, or who have placed self above all things, whether the personal self of "me," or the corporate self of "my country, my business, my political views, my department in college or university," the complete disappearance of all this, the total inability to live in this manner, could well be described as "sheer hell." Even for such people there is in the Christian understanding still hope. God is merciful, and "eternity" does not mean "forever."[10]

That for God everything is "now" and everywhere is "here," whereas we still remain within the absolute bounds of time and space, means that although death is an event in time, resurrection is a constant, just as we have seen creation and incarnation to be constants. In other words, although we cannot avoid thinking of resurrection as what happens "after death," and of the resurrection of Jesus as having initiated a new era, resurrection did not begin on the first Easter morning, nor do we have to wait until the grave to experience resurrection. We can in great measure partake of it already, for life within life is now possible.

When Martha said of her recently dead brother Lazarus, "I know that he will rise again in the resurrection at the last day," she was speaking of the general resurrection that was believed would come at the close of his-

---

9. *Anglican Book of Common Prayer*, Collects after the Offertory.

10. An interesting short book on this subject is C. S. Lewis, *The Great Divorce* (New York: Macmillan Company, 1946).

tory. Jesus corrected her: "I am the resurrection and the life; he who believes in me, though he die, yet shall he live, and whoever lives and believes in me shall never die." In other words, resurrection is here at this moment, confronting you and demanding a response from you, no less certainly than death does (John 11:25–26). The stress is on the here and now; eternal life is already present. There is a new qualitative dimension to human living that is not confined within the normal limits of physical birth and death. It is possible now to be born again, and possible now to die to death. Resurrection to newness of life is the experience of everyone who truly believes. "This is eternal life, that they know thee the only true God, and Jesus Christ whom thou hast sent" (John 17:3).

This is symbolized for Christians in the ceremony of baptism, the beginning of a new kind of life, in which "we have been born anew to a living hope through the resurrection of Jesus Christ from the dead" (1 Pet. 1:3). Moreover, it is not only we who can do so, for all the men and women who lived before the days of Jesus are likewise included. This is what is meant by the statement that "the gospel was preached even to the dead, that though judged in the flesh like men, they might live in the spirit like God" (1 Pet. 4:6)[11] and by the strange statement of Jesus to his opponents, "Truly, truly, I say to you, before Abraham was, I am" (John 8:58).

Christian understanding of the goodness of creation, and of the resurrection as the new creation, affirms both the goodness of the material world as God created and redeemed it, and also the difference between the physical body of this world and the resurrection body of eternity. It is not the body as such that maintains the continuity between creation and new creation. It is the dynamic power of God, the Creator. All that our language can do, and indeed must do, is to convey our wonder and amazement at such marvelous power at work in the world. Like the women at the empty tomb, Christians behold with awe this power, about whose work still to come they can say nothing. Before this terrifying and fascinating mystery

Let all mortal flesh keep silence,
And in fear and trembling stand.

---

11. In the symbolism of the time this preaching of Jesus to the dead was thought of as having taken place during the time that he was in the tomb. The conviction that resurrection must apply also to people who had died before the days of Jesus is demonstrated by the Corinthian practice (unknown elsewhere) of being baptized on behalf of the dead (1 Cor. 15:29).

8

THE HOLY SPIRIT

Where the Church is, there is the Spirit of God, and where the Spirit of God is, there is the Church and all grace.

Irenaeus, *Against Heresies*, 3.24.1

The Power of the Spirit

It is surprising that the Gospels have very little to say about the Holy Spirit. When they speak of "spirit," it is usually of evil or unclean spirits, those unseen powers that were believed to cause disease and mental disorders (e.g., Matt. 10:1; 12:43; Mark 1:23; 3:30; 5:2; Luke 7:21). They mention the Spirit of God, or the Holy Spirit, only about twenty times, whereas in Acts, the epistles, and the Book of Revelation, the Spirit is an active agent in the development of the Christian community, and appears over 130 times. Evidently between the death of Jesus on the cross and the dynamic outward movement of his early followers something more than the resurrection had happened. Certainly the resurrection convinced them that Jesus was alive and not dead, but it did not send them out into the streets of Jerusalem, and far beyond its walls into strange and foreign countries. This, they insisted, was the work of the "Spirit."

They could describe what had happened only as an explosion of power, a howling storm of wind and blazing fire, so great that the house itself was shaken (Acts 4:31). Then, and apparently not until then, were they able, "with great power," to speak publicly about the resurrection of Jesus (Acts 2:22-24; 4:33). They insisted that both the resurrection and what had suddenly happened to them fifty days later[1] brought to fulfillment all that had been proclaimed in the Scriptures. "This is what was spoken by the prophet Joel," said Peter.

---

1. The occasion was the Jewish feast of Shevuoth, seven weeks after the Passover, and therefore for Christians seven weeks, or fifty days, after Jesus' crucifixion and resurrection. "Pentecost" is the Greek word for "fifty."

And in the last days it shall be, God declares,
that I will pour out my Spirit upon all flesh,
and your sons and your daughters shall prophesy,
and your young men shall see visions,
and your old men shall dream dreams;
yea, upon my menservants and my maidservants in those days
I will pour out my Spirit: and they shall prophesy.

Acts 2:17–18; see Joel 2:28–32

Therefore, we must turn first to the Old Testament.

Spirit in the Old Testament

The Hebrew word for spirit, *ruach*, occurs in the very first verse of the Bible, where it is said that the *ruach* of God was moving (or perhaps hovering or brooding) above the dark waters of chaos and meaninglessness, and thereafter we encounter it more than 230 times. It is a rich and powerful word, meaning also "wind" and "breath," the air by which we breathe and live (Gen. 6:17; 7:15; Ps. 33:6; Job 4:9; 9:18; 27:3, etc.). When it is taken away, we die (Ps. 104:29). Sometimes the movement of the air is only a gentle zephyr, but sometimes the raging and destructive storm, savage and furious, whipping the sea into a tempest (Ps. 107:25), and serving as a chariot for God (Ps. 18:6–15; esp. v. 10). In the famous vision of the Valley of Dry Bones (Ezek. 37:1–14) it is difficult to know whether the *ruach* to which Ezekiel must cry aloud before the dead bones can come to life should be translated "breath" or "wind" or "spirit."

But the power is not only the power of life. It is the power of bringing into existence out of nothing, the power of creation, the power of establishing order in place of chaos and meaninglessness, the power of wisdom to discern the truth, to distinguish things that differ, and to "give to airy nothing a local habitation and a name."[2] The whole of this is already there and waiting in the pregnant statement of Gen. 1:1 that the *ruach* of God hovered over the grim and deadly waters of chaos.

The suggestion that *ruach* means order in place of disorder may seem strange in light of the terrible destruction wrought by a hurricane, or the apparently crazy behavior of Saul and some of the early prophets (1 Sam. 10:9–13; 19:18–24). The prophet who annointed Jehu to be king was described as a "mad fellow" (2 Kings 9:11), and Hosea said bluntly, "The man of *ruach* is mad, because of your great iniquity and great hatred" (Hos. 9:7), and he meant by this not that he had been driven insane by their behavior, but that the ecstatic prophets acted like madmen when they were seized by the *ruach* and were compelled to warn the people (Hos. 9:8). The power of God is such that the structures of this world, and the all-too-human limitations of men and women, are likely to be shaken, and

---

2. Shakespeare, *A Midsummer Night's Dream*, 5.1.17.

even shattered, when the *ruach* of God blows open the door, just as trees are shaken and overthrown in a storm.

That the Hebrews thought of the *ruach* of God as being the power of creation is evident from their using the word to indicate wisdom, understanding, and technical skill. Bezalel, who was in charge of making the Tabernacle,[3] was filled "with the *ruach* of God, with ability and intelligence, with knowledge and all craftsmanship, to devise artistic designs, to work in gold, silver, and bronze, in cutting stones for setting, and in carving wood, for work in every craft" (Exod. 31:3-6; 35:30-33). It is not surprising, therefore, that wisdom would have been identified with the act of creation:

> The LORD by wisdom founded the earth;
> > by understanding he established the heavens;
> by his knowledge the deeps broke forth,
> > and the clouds drop down dew.
> > > > > Proverbs 3:19-20

In the second and first centuries B.C., as Greek thought, with its emphasis upon wisdom, influenced the Jewish people, they began to speak of Wisdom as the divine agent of creation, strongly personal and always female, for both in Hebrew and in Greek the word for "wisdom" is a feminine noun (Hebrew *hochmah;* Greek *sophia*).

> The Lord created me [i.e., Wisdom] at the beginning of his work,
> > the first of his acts of old.
> Ages ago I was set up,
> > at the first, before the beginning of the earth.
>
> When he established the heavens, I was there,
> > when he drew a circle on the face of the deep,
>
> When he marked out the foundations of the earth,
> > then I was beside him like a master workman;
> I was daily his delight,
> > rejoicing before him always.
> > > > > Proverbs 8:22-23; 28-30

Wisdom, said an unnamed writer about fifty years before Jesus was born,

> is a breath of the power of God,
> and a pure emanation of the glory of the Almighty;
> therefore nothing defiled gains entry into her.
> For she is a reflection of eternal light,
> > a spotless mirror of the working of God,
> > and an image of his goodness.
> Though she is but one, she can do all things.

---

3. I.e., the "Tent of Meeting," which was the place of Israelite worship before the Temple at Jerusalem was built.

Compared with light, she is found to be superior,
for it is succeeded by the night,
but against wisdom evil does not prevail.
> Wisdom of Solomon 7:25–27; 29–30

O God of my fathers [he added] and Lord of mercy,
who hast made all things by thy word . . .

give me the wisdom that sits by thy throne.
> Wisdom of Solomon 9:1, 4

Such passages almost certainly lie behind the prologue to the Gospel of John (John 1:1–18), and Jesus himself, at least on one occasion, used the same concept: "Therefore also the Wisdom of God said, 'I will send them prophets and apostles, some of whom they will kill and persecute'" (Luke 11:49).

But in addition to wisdom and the power of creation, the devastating word of the prophet is also the *ruach* of God.

But as for me, I am filled with power,
with the spirit of the LORD,
and with justice and might;
to declare to Jacob his transgression
and to Israel his sin.
> Micah 3:8

Behold my servant, whom I uphold,
my chosen, in whom my soul delights;
I have put my Spirit upon him,
and he will bring forth justice to the nations.
> Isaiah 42:1

And just as the prophet must proclaim judgment, justice, punishment, mercy, and truth, so also it is the function of the true king to be obedient to the *ruach*.

And the spirit of the LORD shall rest upon him,
the spirit of wisdom and understanding,
the spirit of counsel and might,
the spirit of knowledge and the fear of the Lord.

He shall not judge by what his eyes see,
or decide by what his ears hear;
but with righteousness he shall judge the poor,
and decide with equity for the meek of the earth.
> Isaiah 11:2–4

The Holy Spirit in the Gospels

All four Gospels agree that when Jesus was baptized by John the Spirit descended on him in the form of a dove (Matt. 3:16; Mark 1:10; Luke 3:22; John 1:32). It is from this that we derive our concept of the Spirit as gentle and peaceful. Mark, however, turns at once to a sterner image, saying that "the Spirit immediately *drove* him out into the wilderness" (Mark 1:12), and Luke speaks more fully of the Spirit, both before and after the temptations: "And Jesus, full of the Holy Spirit, returned from the Jordan, and was led by the Spirit for forty days in the wilderness. . . . And Jesus returned in the power of the Spirit into Galilee" (Luke 4:1–2, 14). Both Matthew and Luke describe the work of Jesus as being the fulfillment of the descent of the Spirit in Isa. 42:1, already mentioned (Matt. 12:17–21; Luke 4:16–21, see Isa. 61:1–2). Matthew also has the promise that the disciples should have no fear when compelled to defend themselves before hostile judges, "for it is not you who speak, but the Spirit of the Father speaking through you" (Matt. 10:20). Also in Matthew is Jesus' response to the accusation that he cast out demons by Beelzebub, prince of demons: "If it is by the Spirit of God that I cast out demons . . ." (Matt. 12:28). Finally, in Luke there is the promise, "If you then, who are evil, know how to give good gifts to your children, how much more will the heavenly Father give the Holy Spirit to those who ask him!" (Luke 11:13). These are all the passages in the first three Gospels that speak of the Holy Spirit before the resurrection of Jesus. They do not tell us much. They speak mainly of the Spirit working through Jesus in fulfillment of the Old Testament promises. Only three times, once in Luke and twice in Matthew, do they speak of the Spirit given to, or working through, his disciples.

In the Gospel of John, however, a somewhat different picture emerges. This, the last of the Gospels to be written, has behind it "the Church's continuous experience of the Holy Spirit in the apostolic age. . . . It presupposes a Christianity which is lively, creative, and able to move fearlessly into new cultural environments."[4] It is also the work of a profound thinker, certainly Jewish and immersed in the Scriptures, but equally at home in Hellenistic thought. Fundamental to his Gospel is the understanding that the work of Jesus, and especially his death, has made clear to us that we do not live in a static world, but in one characterized all the time by newness, by creation, and resurrection. The dynamic activity of God is such that both creation and resurrection are existential facts, confronting us every day, as death does also. Even at this very moment the restless Spirit is shaking the foundations and causing a commotion, the results of which we cannot yet foresee (John 3:8; like the Hebrew *ruach*, so the Greek word *pneuma* means both "wind" and "spirit"). For this reason we must be ready to start all over again, like a tiny baby entering a new world and having, little by little, to come to terms with it.[5]

---

4. Michael Ramsey, *Holy Spirit* (London: SPCK, 1977), 89.

5. This is possibly the meaning of Jesus' statement to Nicodemus, "You must be born again," and Nicodemus's completely honest reply that he could not now divest himself of all that had made him into the kind of person he was (John 3:3–4).

"The time is coming," said Jesus to the Samaritan woman, "when you will no longer dispute whether Jerusalem or Mt. Gerizim provides the right form of worshiping the Father. The time is coming, indeed it is already here, when true worshipers will worship the Father in spirit and in truth, for the Father is searching for people like that to worship Him." "God is spirit, and those who worship him *must* worship him in spirit and in truth" (John 4:21-24).[6]

Spirit, the thinking, active power, which brings into being and makes all things new—this is God, this is ultimate Reality, this is the fundamental Truth, which gives meaning to our existence. But Spirit is more. This is the power that annuls all differences, destroys all barriers, and renders altogether irrelevant the bitter enmities and quarrels of the human race. Spirit must, therefore, also challenge and even shatter our most dearly held beliefs, by which we affirm our identity and distinguish ourselves from those who follow not with us. Spirit is the giver and essence of life. Nothing in this world, however "alive" in our terms, is of any avail. Already the words of Jesus are evidence of this (John 6:63).

But "the Spirit was not yet, for Jesus was not yet glorified" (John 7:39). By this strange phrase, which is smoothed over in almost all translations, John indicates the enormous gulf which divides the time before and the time after Jesus' crucifixion, when he cried aloud *Tetelestai* (it is accomplished), and "handed over the Spirit."[7]

In the final conversation of Jesus with his disciples, as reported by John (13:31—16:33), we meet for the first time the strongly personal Spirit, so evident in the Book of Acts and the epistles, although here spoken as of someone still to come. He is called the *Paracletos* (John 14:16, 26; 15:26; 16:7), an impossible word to translate fully. Literally, it is someone who stands beside you, especially if you have to appear before a judge, and who both advises and encourages you. Therefore, translators have spoken of the Comforter, the Counselor, the Advocate, the Strengthener, and some realizing that all these meanings ought to be included, have given up altogether and have said merely "the Paraclete."

In these discussions Jesus speaks of the Spirit as "another *Paracletos*," similar to himself, the "Spirit of Truth, whom the world cannot receive," because it cannot see him (John 14:17). He is also the "Holy Spirit," who "will teach you all things, and bring to your remembrance" all that Jesus has said (John 14:26). He will guide Christians into all the truth, and will make abundantly clear to the world the true nature of sin, and of righteousness, and of sound and valid judgment (John 16:13, 7-11).

---

6. This is obviously a paraphrase in an attempt to bring out the meaning.

7. John 19:30. The RSV has "gave up his spirit," but *paradoken* seems to indicate that he gave to his followers his very being. The water and the blood in v. 34, together with the Spirit, comprise life in its most complete sense.

After Pentecost

After that first extraordinary eruption of power, which had sent the apostles out into the streets, bubbling over with enthusiasm and crying out as if they were drunk, and had annulled the curse of Babel and the confusion of human languages,[8] the Spirit assumed control and directed their affairs. "We are witnesses" of the resurrection, they said to those who rebuked them, "and so is the Holy Spirit whom God has given to those who obey him" (Acts 5:32).

When the deacon Philip went down toward Gaza to preach, he met a distinguished Ethiopian returning from Jerusalem, and "the Spirit said to Philip, 'Go up and join this chariot' " (Acts 8:29). He did so and the result of this meeting was the Ethiopian's request for baptism.[9] Some time later, at Joppa, when Peter was wondering what his strange vision on the roof had meant, "the Spirit said to him, 'Behold, three men are looking for you.' " Peter went with them to the house of Cornelius in Caesarea, and after "the Holy Spirit fell on all who heard the word," he baptized all the household, the first Gentiles to be accepted into the Christian community. He was later taken to task for exceeding his authority, but replied, "The Spirit told me to go with them, making no distinction," and his critics were silenced (Acts 10:19, 44; 11:12, 18).

The first missionary work overseas began because "the Holy Spirit said, 'Set apart for me Barnabas and Saul for the work to which I have called them,' " and so, "being sent out by the Holy Spirit . . . they sailed to Cyprus" (Acts 13:2, 4). On their second journey into Gentile territory they "were forbidden by the Holy Spirit to speak the word in Asia"[10] and "when they attempted to go into Bithynia," certainly with the best intentions, "the Spirit of Jesus did not allow them" (Acts 16:6–7).

Therefore, it is not surprising that Paul should speak of the Spirit in the same strongly personal manner: "The Spirit helps us in our weakness; for we do not know how to pray as we ought, but the Spirit himself intercedes for us with sighs too deep for words" (Rom. 8:26). He says even that "the Spirit searches everything, even the depths of God" (1 Cor. 2:10).[11] But for him, surpassing even this sense of personal direction, is the unceasing work of the Spirit, the endless thrusting forth of energy, cleansing,

---

8. This binding together into one of previously scattered and separated communities has, in many commentaries, been given less attention than the "speaking with tongues." Yet the thrust of the story is not confusion, but that all these diverse peoples could understand what was being proclaimed.

9. It is not clear whether the Ethiopian official was a Jew or a Gentile, but since he was a eunuch, he would have been forbidden to take a full part in Jewish worship (Deut. 23:1).

10. "Asia" here means what we today would call central and eastern Turkey. No explanation of the prohibition is given in the Bible.

11. See additional notes.

bestowing gifts of wisdom and power, alive and producing fruit in abundance.

> There are varieties of gifts, but the same Spirit; and there are varieties of service, but the same Lord; and there are varieties of working, but it is the same God who inspires them all in every one. To each is given the manifestation of the Spirit for the common good. To one is given through the Spirit the utterance of wisdom, and to another the utterance of knowledge by the same Spirit, to another faith by the same Spirit, to another gifts of healing by the same Spirit, to another the working of miracles, to another prophecy, to another the ability to distinguish between spirits, to another various kinds of tongues, to another the interpretation of tongues. All these are inspired by one and the same Spirit, who apportions to each one individually as he wills.
>
> 1 Corinthians 12:4–11

> The fruit of the Spirit is love, joy, peace, patience, kindness, goodness, faithfulness, gentleness, self-control; against such there is no law.
>
> Galatians 5:22

The Holy Spirit in the World of Today

Within the Churches

In our modern, sophisticated world of space travel, nuclear fission, computers, and robots, there seems little place for the Spirit we meet in the Bible, save only in terms of the individual and our corporate worship in church. We will begin with these, therefore, but we should make a great mistake if we thought that in so doing we had exhausted the wisdom and driving energy of God.[12]

Wisdom, power, purpose, judgment, mercy, truth—these are the attributes of God Himself. They *belong* to God, but they are *entrusted* to us, for every day of our lives we are called upon to exercise them. But since they do not belong to us, we need to be in continual conversation with their true owner, lest we misuse and maltreat them. Here is part of the vast importance of the Spirit, the Wisdom of God, as Person. We can speak to her and she to us (let us never forget that in both Hebrew and Greek "wisdom" is feminine!), and she can do more. As Paul said, in the passage above, she can speak for us when we are feebly groping for words. By the activity of the Spirit in us God converses with Himself.

But how do we speak to the Wisdom of God, and how do we know her response? We speak by placing ourselves unreservedly in her hands. Whether we find it easier to speak to the Father, or the Son, or the Spirit is immaterial, for God is One, but before we embark on any task we

---

12. "The Spirit works in individuals and also in the Church; the Church exists for individuals, not individuals for the Church, and the Church was founded by Christ." Spencer Leeson, *A Study in the Gospel of Christ* (London: SCM Press, 1941), 104.

need to say simply, "Take me and use me. Use my mind, my tongue, and my hands, as a person would use a tool. I cannot do this job by myself." But then we have to trust absolutely that the Energy and Wisdom are indeed working, and proceed vigorously to the task confronting us. But how easy it is to slip into thinking, "Well, the work is going pretty well now. I can carry on from here!" Most of us do not normally enjoy using the words of the old prayer, "O God, who seest that we have no power of ourselves to help ourselves," and we cling to the hope that some of the power, some of the wisdom, some of the action can be our own, not bestowed on us by God. But it is by God's mercy that "the Spirit helps us in our weakness," and "intercedes for us with sighs too deep for words."

We have begun with the individual, but all true Christian work, indeed all truly human work, is corporate and communal, done, not for ourselves, but with and on behalf of others. We are never merely individuals, separate and alone, but each of us parts of a body, and "just as the body is one and has many members, and all the members of the body, though many, are one body, so it is with Christ. For by one Spirit we were all baptized into one body—Jews or Greeks, slaves or free—and all were made to drink of one Spirit" (1 Cor. 12:12–13).[13]

This body is the Church, the Communion of Saints, the Blessed Company of all Believers, but is it indeed in the Church that the dynamic activity of the Spirit is most evidently at work? Alas, the Church is invisible; we see only the churches, often cooperating, but only too often also divided and opposed. "How can Christians who have any regard for their Master's plain and unmistakable will continue in the wasteful sin of division?"[14] Certainly there is today much groping toward greater unity and remarkable progress has been made in the last eighty years, but very many divisions and much blindness still remain.

Then there is the problem of silence. This is twofold. First, why do the churches seem to take so long to speak out against social and political corruption, against the glorification of earthly desires so evident in the media advertising, against all malice, envy, pride, and uncharitableness? Why is there so little penitence, so little self-examination, so much money reserved for the churches at home and so little by comparison given to the poorer nations? Why is there so little knowledge of the Scriptures, little even among the clergy and abysmal ignorance among the laity?[15] Why has

---

13. See additional notes.

14. F. A. Cockin, *God in Action: A Study in the Holy Spirit* (Harmondsworth, Eng.: Penguin Books, 1961), 39.

15. In a recent examination of more than seven hundred candidates for ordination in the Episcopal Church, only 52 percent recognized the opening words of St. John's Gospel, and that was the best answered question in the whole examination!

there been so much simplistic misuse of scientific knowledge, which has alienated many from the churches?

Of course, we must not exaggerate, for the United States would be a sorry place without the churches. As well as asking these questions we need to remember—to remember the work of the Society of Friends and of such dedicated people as Dorothy Day and Mother Teresa, the admirable service performed by Mennonites among refugees, the solid and serious biblical instruction given in Baptist churches, and the recent protest by Roman Catholic bishops against nuclear weapons. Nevertheless, when we have remembered all this, and much more besides, the questions still remain.

Then there is the problem, not of silence *by* the churches, but of silence *in* them. The Wisdom of God does not lift up her voice or shout; she is most distinctly heard when the discordant noises of the world are hushed. The world, and especially the modern world, is very afraid of silence, and tries to dispel and suppress it by Muzak, record players at full blast, portable radios on the beach, and earphones for those who work or play. This is the world's way, and it may have reason for its fear, but it is suprising to find it also in the churches. "The LORD is in His holy Temple; let the whole earth keep silence before Him!" (Hab. 2:20) proclaims the minister at the beginning of worship, but far too often from that moment until the end of the service there is no silence at all, every gap being filled by a hymn or organ voluntary. This is not to decry making "a joyful noise unto the Lord," but no less necessary are times of silence, times to think about the Scripture reading, to meditate upon the sacrament, to recollect those for whom to pray and give thanks, times certainly for penitence, and times just to sit still and await the inward voice. How can the Spirit be heard if we are doing all the speaking?[16]

Outside the Churches

"Where the Spirit of God is, there is the Church and all grace" is the second part of Irenaeus's statement quoted at the beginning of this chapter. The Church does not define the Spirit; the Spirit defines the Church, and wherever the power and wisdom of the Spirit are at work, there, whether confessed Christians recognize it or no, is the Church, the people of God. They may be in our eyes, and perhaps in their own, thoroughly secular, even contemptuous of "religion." But "by their fruits you shall know them; a corrupt tree does not bring forth good fruit" (Matt. 7:18–20). If they produce harmony instead of discord, if they care for the needy and distressed, if they speak out openly against oppression and struggle to do

16. See additional notes.

something about it, if they reject the techniques of the marketplace and of mass persuasion, if they are aware of their own weaknesses, then there is the Church, and there the Wisdom of God is powerfully at work.

The activity of the Spirit is most evident where men and women have been born again, not merely in the popular sense of "born-again Christians," but because they recognize that at this very moment we are moving into a new world, which will certainly not have the old familiar shape and pattern. Such people recognize that the new world will not be built according to Western political and economic models, nor founded upon Western traditions of civilization, perhaps not even upon traditions of Western Christianity.[17] All these things are mortal, though we may speak of them as "eternal values," and the truly born again recognize this, and are not ashamed to ask even childish questions in their eagerness to learn about the world in which, whether we like it or no, we shall all shortly find ourselves. This coming world will certainly be strongly scientific and technological, but the United States will no longer be the dominant cultural power. Perhaps the heritage of the new world will be Chinese, perhaps Muslim, perhaps some other. "The wind blows where it wants to. We do not know where it comes from, or where it is going" (John 3:8). Of course, it may be objected that Jesus was talking about the heavenly kingdom, but if we are not already in this world the kind of people who are able to begin all over again, how shall we do so in a heavenly realm, where our heritage may play little part? "If I have told you earthly things and you do not believe," said Jesus to Nicodemus, "how can you believe if I tell you heavenly things?" (John 3:12).[18]

Among the fruits of the Spirit are joy and peace, but they do not ripen immediately. "This is the judgment: that light has come into the world and men prefer darkness, because their deeds are evil" (John 3:19). Wherever society is selfish, power-hungry, and corrupt, the winds of change will be resisted by lies and by force. The immediate effect of the coming of the Spirit, therefore, will often be violence, "distress of nations in perplexity . . . men fainting with fear and with foreboding of what is coming on the world" (Luke 21:25–26). But the *purpose* of the Spirit cannot be brutality and division; it must be harmony and the righting of wrongs. The function of men and women of the Spirit is therefore to minimize the violence, to be alert to the first stirrings of the air which presage the coming storm,

---

17. Less than half the Christians in the world today are white. In Africa, every day there are sixteen thousand new Christians, four thousand by conversion and twelve thousand by natural increase. See David B. Barrett, ed., *World Christian Encyclopedia* (New York and London: Oxford University Press, 1982). At the same time it should be noticed that Islam is spreading equally rapidly in Africa. Western Christianity loses seventy-six hundred members every day.

18. See additional notes.

and to prepare for it. They must, of course, make public the evils and warn the world of what will happen if they are not righted. They will not in self-righteousness condemn resistance movements because of their violence. They may sympathize with them, but never praise them, nor should they turn their backs on the oppressors. The oppressed are, unfortunately, no less selfish, no less anxious to get power into their own hands, than those who deny them that power. It was a people made desperate by colonial rule, a people, as we would say, "rightly struggling to be free," that handed over Jesus to be crucified, and they were no more wicked than other men and women.

Of all our pressing needs in the world today, the greatest is surely the breaking down of barriers, the dissolution of conflicts, the reconciliation of sundered peoples, and this can never be done by those who have identified themselves wholly with only one side.

> At present each of the two superpowers fears the other and resents the very existence of the other. Moscow would not feel truly secure unless the US went out of the power business. The US cannot feel truly secure so long as the Soviet Union continues to be a massively armed world power. Neither one truly accepts the right of the other to exist as a great power. Each likes to dream of a world without the other.[19]

This disastrous situation is why Christ was born in Bethlehem and the Spirit came down at Pentecost. Christ came and the Spirit was given so that men and women might be saved from the appalling results of their own economic selfishness, their political blindness, their cultural arrogance—in other words, their sin.[20]

But what of the science and technology characteristic of this strange new world? They are also the work of the Spirit. First, they proclaim by their very nature the divine Wisdom, ever present in creation, manifesting herself in the minds and skills of men and women, themselves made "in the image of God." All knowledge is divine knowledge expressed in human terms. Second, they know no social, political, or racial frontiers. They are no less at home in China or Peru than they are in Saudi Arabia, Japan, or the United States. Since the work of the Spirit is the breaking down of all barriers and inequalities between male and female, Gentiles and Jews, slaves and free, Christians should recognize gratefully that this is equally a feature of scientific inquiry and technological skill.

But science and technology are the power and wisdom of the absolute God freely handed over to the brains and hands of very human men and women to do with them as they think fit. So also was the Word of God in Jesus entrusted to men and women to do with as they thought fit, and

---

19. Joseph C. Harsch, "An Improved Relationship?" *The Christian Science Monitor* (23 November 1982).

20. See additional notes.

what they thought right to do was to make use of him for their own purposes. When they found that he could not be used, "they were urgent, demanding with loud cries that he should be crucified" (Luke 23:23). So is it likely to be with the Spirit, for human nature does not change, and in this sense the world is no different from what it was two thousand years ago. In such tragic misuse of modern knowledge as nuclear weapons, germ warfare, and toxic waste, we may see already the brutal crucifixion of the Spirit. The tragedy is that "without adequate guidance systems, the social consequences of technology come without advance warning and in a form in which effects are all too often irreversible."[21]

Therefore, the urgent question today for Christians, who proclaim their belief in "the Holy Spirit, the Lord, the Giver of Life," is whether they will truly acknowledge the Spirit. Will they seek seriously to annul the barriers between the Soviet Union and the West, freely welcome all knowledge, however apparently disturbing to Scripture, and accept unconcerned the passing of their own, familiar, comfortable world? Will they begin with the stumbling steps of children to explore the strange, perhaps alarming, world that the Wisdom of God is even now creating? Above all, will they accept for themselves the task of the Spirit, and in every sphere strive for reconciliation? It will be neither easy nor popular, even among those whom they meet in the churches.

> This I command you, to love one another. If the world hates you, know that it has hated me before it hated you. If you were of the world, the world would love its own; but because you are not of the world, but I chose you out of the world, therefore the world hates you. Remember the word that I said to you, "A servant is not greater than his master." If they persecuted me, they will persecute you.
>
> John 15:17–20

ADDITIONAL NOTES

11. One contributor commented: "A problem I have throughout the chapter is the need to remember that the Holy Spirit and Wisdom are aspects of God. God embodies both these, but I can easily slip into the idea that they are different entities." This is a very real problem, and it is not easy to write about the Holy Spirit without inadvertently suggesting such a separation. No separation of the Spirit from God is intended here, for God is Spirit. This will be dealt with more fully in the next chapter.

13. Some contributors wished to give a much more definite place to the individual and to the self. One wrote: "I disagree with this section. We must need a sense of 'self' in order to survive. As R. D. Laing points out in *The Divided Self* (New York: Pantheon Books, 1969), a sense of self is necessary in order to understand our sense of separateness and relatedness to the rest of the world. A sense of separateness is necessary for any corporate or communal work."

21. Sheldon Krinsky, "Social Responsibility in an Age of Synthetic Biology," *Environment* 24 (July 1982): 9.

Another wrote: "Without the feeling of personal satisfaction or personal gain society would move forward much more slowly. If a person worried more about other people's well-being, when would he or she have time for personal growth? Also biologically this altruistic society would not be possible. Altruism is linked to the continuation of one's genes. Therefore, only immediate relatives would receive this altruistic behavior. . . . This society, or God, of Christianity seems to parallel the Marxist idea of the final communist society, and as is evident in the Soviet Union, or any communist society, this fond ideal society is unattainable."

16. Despite much discussion, this paragraph has been left as it was in the original draft, since it had the approval of the majority. A number, however, were markedly critical. "Silent meditation," they said, "is right and proper for private prayer at home, but not in corporate worship. There Christians should manifest their joy to the doubting world."

18. One contributor wrote concerning the first two paragraphs of this section: "This is a completely biased, one-sided opinion. It has nothing to do with the biblical understanding and historical interpretations of born-again Christians throughout the ages. This extreme minority and far-out interpretation has no place in a book trying to explain what the faith of Christians is all about. You have the right to your own opinion, and even the right to express your own valuable ideas in this book, but you have no right to impose scriptural support for an opinion of your own making."

20. One contributor objected strongly to this section: "How can we say this? Jesus said, 'I have come not to bring peace, but a sword' (Matt. 10:34). The only way to bring peace in this world is for all people individually and personally to identify themselves with Jesus."

9

HOLY AND UNDIVIDED TRINITY

Firmly I believe and truly
God is Three and God is One
John Henry Newman,
The Dream of Gerontius

Christians affirm that God is one, absolute, and indivisible, and yet at the same time a Trinity: Father, Son and Holy Spirit. To many this suggests that Christians in fact worship three gods, and have inadvertently transformed the monotheism of the Jewish scriptures into polytheism. Muslims claim that by speaking of the Son of God Christians commit the worst of all sins, that of making something equal to God:

In the name of God, the Merciful Lord of Mercy:
Say: He is God, the One!
God, the eternally sought of all.
He does not beget, nor was He begotten,
And there is nothing at all comparable to Him.
The Qur'an,
Sura 112, often spoken of
as the essence of the Qur'an

Christians themselves throughout the centuries have often been puzzled and troubled by this seeming contradiction.

We need, therefore, to ask in what sense God is one, and in what sense also He is at the same time three. We must recognize at the outset that the complex Christian expression of the Trinity did not spring from learned and intellectual debate among theologians. It arose instead from the transformation of life experienced by Christian believers, and their profound convictions about the human condition and the mystery of God's revelation of Himself. "Thus the doctrine of the Trinity is a revealed doctrine

115

in the sense that it is the doctrine of God implied by that divine activity in history which is the Christian revelation."[1] Christians were convinced that at the same time as insisting upon the absolute oneness of God, they must proclaim their own experience of God as the Creator, as the One who had rescued them from the stranglehold of sin, and as actively at work in their midst. It is this deep sense of deliverance from human helplessness, this awareness of a new beginning, this consciousness of dynamic power at work, that provides the context wherein Christians have testified to the oneness of God. They hold these facets of human experience to be so vital that they must be reflected in any statements made about the nature of God, and His relationship to men and women.

Many Christians see the doctrine of the Trinity as dealing with divine relationship alone, and as having, therefore, no direct concern for us. But this is certainly not the picture we see when we trace the prolonged struggles to formulate and express the concept. Instead, we discover that the doctrine of the Trinity issued from the developing understanding of the divine purpose in history and a valiant effort to

> assert eternal providence,
> And justify the ways of God to man.
>   John Milton,
>   *Paradise Lost*, 1.22–3

The Biblical View

The word "Trinity" was first used in the second century A.D. It is not a biblical term, and in the Old Testament the concept nowhere directly appears. The early Christians maintained, of course, that the God they worshiped was identical with the God revealed to Israel, and they searched the Scriptures to discover foreshadowings of the Triune God, now so gloriously apparent to them. For instance, they perceived a strong indication of the Trinity in the story of how, at the oaks of Mamre, the Lord appeared to Abraham, who lifed up his eyes to see three strangers standing before his tent (Gen. 18:1–2).[2] They found a similar indication in the fact that when God created man and woman He spoke of Himself in the plural, as "Us," not "Me" (Gen. 1:26). They observed also that the Hebrew word for God, *Elohim*, is a plural noun, and that in Isaiah's great vision in the Temple, the seraphim praised God in threefold terms: "Holy, Holy, Holy, is the Lord of Hosts!" (Isa. 6:1–3). They explained the absence of more explicit references by the necessity for Israel, surrounded as it was by polytheistic neighbors, to be first of all established in a clear and unambig-

---

1. Leonard Hodgson, *The Doctrine of the Trinity* (London: James Nisbet & Co., 1943).

2. This scene is a favorite one for representing the Trinity in the iconography of the Eastern Orthodox church.

uous monotheistic faith. The full revelation could come only later in the person of Jesus Christ.

Few Christians today would adopt this method of interpreting the Old Testament, even while sympathizing with what lay behind it: the deep desire to bind into one the old revelation and the new. Methods of biblical research and interpretation have inevitably changed in two thousand years, and the questions we ask are no longer the same. We may not use their methods, but we can, and should, try to understand their purpose and seek to learn from their conclusions. In any age, however, it is an error to impose on ancient texts a doctrine which they do not state explicitly, and we may be forgiven for wondering whether the early Christian writers did not push their case too far.[3]

The New Testament also speaks of only one God, as in the Old Testament, but the doctrine of the Trinity seems here more evident. Paul's use in his letters of the distinct terms "God," "Lord," and "Spirit" provides an evident basis for the later theological statements. At the end of his second letter to the Corinthians he salutes his readers: "The grace of our Lord Jesus Christ, and the love of God, and the fellowship of the Holy Spirit be with you all" (2 Cor. 13:14). In his first letter also he suggests an evident distinction: "Now there are varieties of gifts, but the same Spirit; there are varieties of service, but the same Lord; and varieties of working, but it is the same God who inspires them all in everyone" (1 Cor. 12:4–6). But neither here or anywhere else does he specify the exact relationship. He indicates only that all the three share the power of the one, and only, God. Later Christians saw in such texts the self-communication of God to the world in both the Son and the Spirit, and they saw also an indication of how human beings are elevated by such gifts to participate in the divine life of Father, Son, and Spirit. It is this threefold understanding of God that marks the life of Christians, "chosen and destined by God the Father and sanctified by the Spirit for obedience to Jesus Christ" (1 Pet. 1:2).

In the Gospels the most explicit text and the most influential for later development is Matthew's description of Christ's command after his resurrection: "Go, therefore, and make disciples of all nations, baptizing them in the name of the Father, and of the Son, and of the Holy Spirit" (Matt. 28:19). There is but one "name" into which the faithful are baptized, but it represents three persons. This was seen, therefore, as an explicit indication of the unity in trinity. It is evident from the Book of Acts that people were consecrated into the Christian community by baptism from the very beginning.[4] But the use of more than one name laid

---

3. See additional notes.

4. See the account of Pentecost in Acts 2:1–42, especially v. 41. Although in the early baptisms the phrase is simply "in the name of Jesus," consecration by the Holy Spirit was evidently no less essential (Acts 18:14–17; 10:44–48).

Christians open to the accusation of polytheism from their opponents, a charge that would have horrified them, for they believed firmly in one God. Jesus, they insisted, is not another God, but one in divinity with the Father.

As Christianity spread and developed in the markedly polytheistic Gentile world, the problem confronting Christian thinkers and teachers was this: How can we put our experience as Christians into words? How can we make clear our complete commitment to monotheism, to the One God, Creator of the universe, and at the same time our no less complete commitment to Jesus Christ, by whose death and resurrection we have been saved, and to the Spirit whom we know to be powerfully at work in our midst? All the New Testament books had been written by the end of the first century, only sixty years after the time of Jesus, and it was therefore to these that they turned for help.

They saw the accounts of the Spirit descending upon Jesus at his baptism (Matt. 3:13–17; Mark 1:9–11; Luke 3:21–22; John 1:32–34) and the message of the angel Gabriel to Mary before his birth as undeveloped statements about the Trinity. Elsewhere, and particularly in the Gospel of John, they found more material about the mutual relations of Father, Son and Holy Spirit. The Father is there depicted as being "in the Son," and the Son in the Father (John 14:11). Jesus speaks of the Father and the Son as acting together to strengthen those who keep his words: "We will come to him and make our home with him," and says that the Father will send the Holy Spirit in the name of the Son (John 14:23, 26). Later in the same Gospel the Spirit is spoken of as being given through the Son: "But when your Advocate has come, whom I will send you from the Father—the Spirit of truth that issues from the Father—he will bear witness to me" (John 15:26 NEB). So also Paul told the Galatians, "God has sent the Spirit of his Son into our hearts, crying 'Abba! Father!' " (Gal. 4:6).

On the basis of such texts the early Christians developed clearer statements about the coequal divinity of Christ, the Spirit, and the Father. They began at the same time to put into words the self-communication of the Father through the Son and the Spirit, not only in terms of God's external work in the world, but as a true depiction of the inner life of God. These writers argued that God's action in creating, redeeming, and sanctifying indicated something profoundly true about His nature. If God is love, then how was this love expressed before the Creation? It was, and is, they said, expressed in the eternally active love between Father, Son, and Spirit.[5] No less important, the stress on the equality of Father, Son,

---

5. "Such a dogma found in the Trinity suggests that 'God' is no bare monad, but an eternal fellowship. It is exciting to realize that God did not exist in solitary aloneness from all eternity, prior to the creation of the world and men, but in blessed communion," Carl F. H. Henry, *Basic Christian Dogmas* (Grand Rapids: Baker Book House, 1971), 40.

and Spirit emphasized that whenever God is perceived and understood as active in the world, what is encountered is the fullness of the divine nature, the total power of God.[6]

The Way of Nicaea

In A.D. 312 Constantine the Great was established as emperor, and very shortly afterward Christianity became the dominant faith of the Roman Empire. Constantine was anxious to relate the Christian church to the secular state as closely as possible, and in the furtherance of this aim he called together in 325 the Council of Nicaea to resolve the fierce arguments which were dividing the church. Out of that council came the statement of faith that we know today as the Nicene Creed, although it did not take its final forms until the Council of Constantinople in 381. In this creed systematic and authoritative answers were given to the problem of how God is at one and the same time both one and three.

By the time of the Council of Nicaea the New Testament statements discussed in the last section had become part of the church's confessions and hymns of praise, but without any concerted effort to sort out or settle the theological problems involved. Even when Christian writers did discuss these problems, their language tended to be indefinite, and in the eyes of some thinkers, was apt to confuse the issues and lead to heresy. Previously the uncertainty was a matter mainly of scholarly debate, but now Christianity had become the imperial religion. What had earlier been tentatively put forward for discussion was now proclaimed by ministers of state and church leaders as official doctrine, normative and state enforced. But these authorities did not always see the questions from the same point of view. Loud were the accusations of heresy.

The Council of Nicaea laid the foundation for later doctrines, but by no means did it settle the disputes. Indeed, so heated were the debates during the next half century, and so emotionally involved were even the shopkeepers and laborers, that one observer said that the Christian community was suffering from "councilitis."

The situation arrived at by the Council was to affirm that God is one "substance" (*ousia*, which we might interpret today as one being, or one center of energy) in three divine "persons" (*hypostases*). By this they did not mean what we understand by "person," an independent and separate individual with a will of his or her own. They were convinced that in God there could be only one will, not three wills in possible conflict with each other, and only one power, one center of self-reflection. *Hypostasis* meant

---

6. The external work of God was formulated in terms of the so-called *economic Trinity*, because it was a description of how divine activity was apportioned, or economically arranged. The internal relationship was known as the *immanent Trinity*. Western Christians tended to concentrate their attention on the first, Eastern Christians on the second.

"substantial nature, essence, being, reality."[7] The council, therefore, was confirming the absolute monotheism of their heritage from Israel, but they found that this could be done only by asserting at the same time that in the Lord Jesus Christ, "who had taken away the sin of the world," men and women were confronted by the full power and essence of God Himself.

Not everyone accepted this formulation. The Arians[8] in particular argued that only the Father could properly be called "God," since He alone is the source of His own existence. The very term "Son," and the fact that the Father had "sent" the Spirit, they maintained, meant that despite their divine glory both Son and Spirit must in the last resort be "creatures," that is, they must have been made by God. They could not be "of the same substance" as the Father *(homo-ousios)*, for that would be blasphemy, but only "of similar substance" *(homoi-ousios)*.[9] That so prolonged and bitter a dispute should take place over a single letter has led to much derision among more recent writers,[10] but at the time it was desperately serious. The Arians were like Elijah, "very jealous for the Lord, the God of Hosts" (1 Kings 19:10), but those who resisted them were jealous for the salvation of men and women. Jesus Christ took upon himself human nature "that through death he might destroy him who has the power of death, that is, the devil" (Heb. 2:14), and only God can do that. The verdict of history has been that those who resisted the Arians were right.

The importance of Nicaea is that it preserved for humankind profound revelation about the inner nature of God and the affirmation that through Jesus and the Spirit men and women have come to know the transcendent God more directly. "No man has seen God at any time" (1 John 4:12), and yet God who creates, sustains, redeems, and gives eternal life is not infinitely remote, but has come to us in the flesh, in history, and in the depths of our existence. As did Isaiah (Isa. 6:1–9), so now every human being may look upon the King, the Lord of Hosts, and live, and in the work of the community of faith, and its saints and martyrs, the Spirit is manifest and active.

"Father, Son, and Spirit" are not interchangeable titles, or merely external features of God's action, as if in performing his work He put on differ-

---

7. William F. Arndt and F. Wilbur Gingrich, *A Greek-English Lexicon of the New Testament and Other Early Christian Literature* (Chicago: University of Chicago Press, 1952). Our English word "person" as a translation of "hypostasis" comes from the Latin *persona.*

8. I.e., the followers of Arius, a priest from Alexandria in Egypt.

9. Strictly speaking, this is a semi-Arian position, proposed as a compromise in the course of decades of debate. The strict Arians were more absolute.

10. Notably Edward Gibbon in his six-volume *History of the Decline and Fall of the Roman Empire*, published between 1776 and 1778.

ent "masks," so as to play different parts in the drama, but never disclosed the inner relationship. Such an interpretation is called Modalism, and though it maintains the undeniable unity of God, it reduces Him to an impersonal oneness, in which He Himself is unknowable. Like the Deism of seventeenth-century philosophy, it suggests that God is little more than the grounding place for the moral imperative. This is not God as Christians throughout history have known Him.

Understanding the Trinity Today

So far we have been concerned with the thinking and ideas of ancient centuries. This was essential, since the events of those distant days are for Christians the foundation of present faith and present decisions. Yet their thought forms and their culture are not ours, and every age must find its own language to express eternal truths. For us the term "three persons" is bound to be a stumbling block, since in our culture "person" denotes separateness and independence, and the maintenance of distinct personal rights. Speaking of God as comprising three persons inevitably conjures up in the modern mind a picture of division, even dispute and opposition. Such an emphasis upon separate personalities cannot be reconciled with the absolute oneness of God, and we are therefore left confused.

In *The Mind of the Maker*[11] Dorothy L. Sayers has suggested that the writing of a book provides a very helpful parallel. Every major piece of writing—a play by Shakespeare, a poem by Milton, a novel by Dickens, a modern work of scholarship—exists in three forms: (1) the book or poem as it is complete in the mind of its creator, complete yet unperceived by others; (2) the "incarnate" book, written, printed, and published, taking definite and limited shape, and subject to criticism, misrepresentation, and even to being banned by an oppressive government; (3) the power of the book as its influence spreads throughout the world, triumphant over any efforts by dictators and tyrants to suppress it. The Gospel of Mark, Magna Carta, Analects of Confucius, and the Communist Manifesto are all exceedingly short, yet each is a unity, complete in itself, and the power and influence of each is beyond measure.

There is, as we have already seen, a fundamental distinction between Reality as it reveals itself, and Reality as we perceive it, just as there is an evident difference between the book as the author conceives it and the book as understood by the reader, who interprets it in terms of his own experience. The revelation is always manifestation, self-disclosure, of the total Reality, the undivided substance. "He who has seen me," said Jesus, "has seen the Father" (John 14:9). It was not merely part of God that con-

---

11. Dorothy L. Sayers, *The Mind of the Maker* (New York: Harcourt Brace Jovanovich, 1941).

fronted and appalled the Israelites on Mt. Sinai, nor was it part of God
that rescued them from exile in Babylon, or spoke to the disciples in
Galilee, but always God in His absolute oneness and wholeness. Yet we
never perceive the whole, because our minds cannot comprehend it. "We
know in part, and we prophesy in part" (1 Cor. 13:9 KJV).

If we have at all "known the Father," then we have glimpsed something
of the truth, something of the reality of the universe, of the nature of space
and time, of the earth on which we live. However, the thing that we perceive is not itself the truth, but only what our eyes and ears have appre-
hended about the truth. A map of the world, despite all the skills of
surveyor and cartographer, is always both partial and misleading. A globe
cannot be accurately drawn on a flat piece of paper. Its otherness can be
no more than suggested.

There is always an otherness about our relation to anything that is not
ourselves. When we encounter the transcendent God, we are even more
conscious that we are confronted by the "absolutely Other," terrifying and
mysterious. "Moses hid his face, for he was afraid to look at God" (Exod.
3:6). The finite cannot comprehend, encompass, gaze upon the infinite
without ceasing to exist as it is, a finite being. "No one has ever seen God;
the only Son, who is in the bosom of the Father, he has made him known"
(John 1:18). Through the mediation of the Son of God, the Word made
flesh, the infinite is truly communicated, and in the Son we perceive, but
only as far as we are able to perceive, the truth about the human condition,
the mysterious phenomenon of humanness.

Finally, in speaking of the Spirit we are talking about the meaning of
meaning itself, about coherence and fundamental relationship. This, as we
have seen in an earlier chapter, is experienced as power, energy, dynamism, holding everything together. Human beings are social animals,
unable to exist in isolation from each other, and entirely dependent for
existence upon their relation with things on the earth and beyond. They
could not live without the sun, the moon, and the stars. Yet human beings
do not cohere naturally. They quarrel with each other, are jealous and mis-
trustful; they misuse and exploit anything within their reach. The unity
that they so desperately need requires power that in themselves they do
not possess, forthright and honest communication, concern for other part-
ners in the relationship—all that is summed up in the single word, *agape*,
or "love."

Special problems about the doctrine of the Trinity exist for people living
in the twentieth century, not because it is more difficult for us to *believe*,
but because it has become more difficult for us to *understand*. Our training and culture lay heavy emphasis upon isolation of the thing to be studied, and upon careful and detailed analysis, far beyond anything demanded
before. This does not mean, of course, that analytical studies were not

done in the past. The ancient Babylonians were expert analysts, and the human mind has always needed to separate out things to be studied, if they were to be understood. Nevertheless, the assumption was that the world could be understood as a whole, and brilliant minds were expected to achieve this.

Today the universe has become for us so enormous, and human knowledge so abundantly rich, that such polymaths are clearly impossible. Moreover, such wide-ranging minds, though sometimes admired, are seldom encouraged. Compartmentalization of knowledge and specialization have become the norm in academic studies. Even at liberal arts colleges, which in their catalogs lay great emphasis upon the broad view, freshmen and sophomores are frequently urged to "get your diversification behind you." We are therefore conditioned to see separation and analysis as the gateway to knowledge and understanding. This has become for us the "right way" to study and understand anything, and so this is how we approach the problem of God.

We can understand in principle how there can be only one God, and we can understand about distinguishing three persons and studying them separately. What our analytical minds reject is that anything, even God, could be *both* one *and* three. We tend to think that He must be one or the other. We also have difficulty in comprehending how in purely human affairs every person is both an individual and not an individual, completely unable to exist, in fact, as an individual. Modern thinking tends to emphasize, even insist upon, the individual and the rights of the individual. More traditional societies found it much easier to perceive the individual as distinct and yet as also completely merged into the community as a whole. For them "community" meant what it says: "co-unity."

Another difficulty imposed upon us is the unexamined belief that size and greatness belong together, and that infinite greatness, such as we believe to characterize God, must in some way involve infinite size. In part this happens because we are dazzled by the unimagined vastness of the universe, and in part also because we live in a world in which size and significance seem to belong to each other. For the first time in history the great powers are countries of enormous size,[12] and vast multinational companies dominate the market place. Consequently, though there are books to assure us that "small is beautiful," and though our lives are more and more influenced by the silicon chip, the general public does not grasp this, nor is it encouraged to do so by the mass media.

On the other hand, the idea that size and significance are necessarily related conflicts with the principle that sound knowledge and learning

---

12. In the nineteenth century the most powerful country was Britain, which is only half the size of France and one-fifth that of Spain. The ancient Roman Empire was also governed from a very small power base.

come by analysis. The physicist is aware of the tremendous importance of smallness, and works upon the principle that identification of the smallest possible particle is an essential key to unlocking the secrets of the entire universe. But the public mind does not think along these lines. It equates smallness with insignificance and irrelevance. Minds so conditioned inevitably misunderstand infinity, which for them connotes immeasurable bigness. God is perceived, therefore, as immeasurably great and immeasurably distant from us. But God must be also infinitely small, infinitely near to us.[13]

Understood in terms of infinity, Trinity makes complete sense because in the realm of infinity there are no measurements of any kind, large or small, and consequently no numbers and no numerical contradictions. The numbers and the contradictions creep in only when we struggle to interpret infinity in terms of our very far from infinite human experience and human language. The oneness expresses the absolute transcendence of God, since two infinities are by definition impossible. The threeness expresses not only the threefold revelation in time of creation, salvation, and new, more abundant life, but also the three-dimensional nature of relationship as the essence of coherence in the universe. Where there is only one there is no relationship; where there are two there is beginning of relationship; where the two reach out to include the outsider so that there are three fully equal to each other, there is the solid foundation of relationship, human or otherwise.[14]

Nevertheless, however we choose to express our understanding, we must still confess that we begin and end in mystery. The word "Trinity," the concept of "three persons in one God," remains a human construction. It struggles to express the infinity of God in finite, inadequate human words. God transcends any description, and therefore, in speaking of the "mystery" of God, the Christian is not indulging in mystification or pious obscurantism. Many people, it is true, dislike the idea of religious mystery, and want religion to be plain and simple. Yet we live with mystery every day. We are a mystery to ourselves, for we cannot know ourselves as others know us, and we are a mystery to others, because they cannot know what we choose not to disclose. We do not know the universe because we never come near the end of explaining it. We live, as it were, in an ever-expanding balloon of knowledge, and the skin of the balloon is therefore the ever-expanding frontier of our ignorance, the boundary that lies between us and all the things we do not know. Our questions become constantly more complex. The ever-receding horizon of the known is an integral part of the scientific method of inquiry. We pursue

13. See Chapter 2.

14. This is well illustrated by a great deal of Islamic decorative art, where the triangle forms the basis of an almost infinite variety of patterns.

our studies in faith, trusting that we will find unity beyond the multiplicity of experience, and some day transcend the multiplicity without denying its reality or goodness.

This element of mystery reminds us with what caution we should speak about God, never seeking to define Him exactly. We have no words with which to do this. We can use only the language of worship and adoration, acknowledging the ultimate mystery of the One God, wholly beyond our control. But acknowledging in our praises the oneness of God means that God is not our God alone, not merely God for Christians. It proclaims to the world that God's disclosure of Himself must have been, and is now being, encountered in different realms of knowledge, and in experiences far beyond the Christian sanctuary.[15]

> In future interpretations of the works of God, however, we are bound to take into account the all-inclusive love of the transcendent One, dimly perceived by us as Father, Son, and Holy Spirit, but ultimately making himself known to all men in religious languages which they can understand.[16]

ADDITIONAL NOTES

3. One contributor commented: "Good. This enforces the idea that this doctrine came out of experience. Christians today should learn something from this. C. S. Lewis in *Mere Christianity* (New York: Macmillan, 1964), 136, comments that such doctrines are often needed because vague religions often become just emotionalism. The Hansons also tell us (*Reasonable Belief,* pp. 183–84) that a doctrine should not hinder our belief, but help it. Of course, these writers also know that we have from time to time to examine how such doctrines affect our beliefs and explore their implications. Otherwise all aspects of our belief become mere recitations drawn from memory. We need to study the Bible to see how our beliefs drawn from it may change, and whether they are still viable today. We cannot blindly accept what these early believers tell us, because they may have had different reasons for studying the Scriptures, or they may have imposed their own preconceptions."

Another contributor held a different point of view: "You are wrong! Many Christians consider both Old and New Testaments to be equally inspired by God. Thus, that the Trinity would be perceivable in the Old Testament, however discretely, only makes sense. I think it is very wrong to take your understanding of Scripture and put it forth as that which most Christians hold. It simply is not true."

15. One contributor commented: "This contradicts what was just said. If our God is the true one God, and God for all people, then our experience of our God is a Christian experience, because God does not change from one culture to another. So no experience of God is 'beyond the Christian sanctuary.' "

---

15. See additional notes.

16. Robert M. Grant, *The Early Christian Doctrine of God* (Charlottesville, Va.: University Press of Virginia, 1966), 100.

10

SIN, SALVATION, AND REDEMPTION

Salvation

"Sirs, what must I do to be saved?" cried the terrified jailer when the prison doors had been broken open by an earthquake.[1] By this he probably meant safe from the danger of being put to death for negligence, and in that case his question was entirely secular. But the reply of Paul and Silas, who were among the prisoners, was not secular at all. "Believe in the Lord Jesus," they said, "and you will be saved, you and your household." Similarly, in modern English one may speak of someone being saved from drowning or from a burning house, and also of being saved in a religious sense, that is, delivered from the power of sin.

It is useful to begin with the everyday, secular meaning, for it is a guide to the religious meaning. In the days of the New Testament the problem of safety and security was an everyday one. Certainly, the creation of the huge Roman Empire and the establishment of the Pax Romana (Roman peace) had given men and women a measure of security quite unknown before. But much insecurity remained. Poverty was widespread, and ordinary people lived from hand to mouth, far from certain that in the months to come they would be able to feed their families. Travelers could quite easily fall among thieves.[2] People who were not Roman citizens did not belong to the privileged minority, and did not have the full protection of the law. If arrested, they could be brutally flogged in advance of the trial.[3]

---

1. The story is found in Acts 16:19-34, and this particular quotation in v. 30. The RSV here has "men" in place of "sirs," but that is an inadequate translation of the Greek *kyrioi*.

2. This is well illustrated by the parable of the Good Samaritan (Luke 10:30-37) and by the large number of soldiers needed to ensure that Paul could be taken safely from Jerusalem to Caesarea (Acts 23:23-33).

3. See the story of Paul's arrest after the uproar in the Temple (Acts 22:22-29).

A very large number of people were, in fact, slaves, entirely without legal rights at all. There were also areas of political unrest, notably Palestine, where Roman rule was bitterly resented, and where ordinary working people were ground between the upper and lower millstone, punished by the Romans if they did not conform, and treated as traitors by their own countrymen if they seemed to conform too willingly.

There are many modern parallels to such an unhappy situation, over which the ordinary people have no control, and from which they cannot escape.[4] Even local governments often find themselves helpless, and hope to find a savior in one of the more powerful nations. But what kind of security, what kind of salvation is possible in such a situation? Can there be a "just and lasting peace"? It was with questions such as these that Jesus seems to have wrestled when he was tempted, i.e., tested, in the loneliness and desolation of the wilderness.[5]

As almost always, the story is told in the light of Old Testament experience, for the desert or wilderness—the *wild* realm in which men and women are *bewildered*—was the place of the Israelite wanderings for forty years (Deut. 8:2), where they had been tried and tested to the uttermost, agonizingly hungry and thirsty (Exod. 16:2–3; 17:1–3; Num. 20:2–13), and where they had also put God to the test (Ps. 95:9). Moreover, it was in the wilderness that they had been saved, and brought to the promised land. In the story of Jesus' temptations it is the *diabolos*, the slanderer and adversary, the source and power of evil, that confronts him, and Jesus' answers are all drawn from Deuteronomy, a book entirely concerned with the Exodus experience.[6] We must, therefore, interpret the testing of Jesus in this context, remembering especially the words of Moses in Deut. 8:2:

> And, you shall remember all the way which the LORD your God has led you these forty years in the wilderness, that he might humble you, testing you to know what was in your heart, whether you would keep his commandments or not.

Jesus could not have lived in Palestine for thirty years without being fully aware of the people's desperate longing for someone who would deliver them from the frustrating and appalling situation in which they found themselves, and he knew also that he himself was destined to be their savior. But by what means could he rightly save them?

Here Arnold Toynbee's discussion of the saviors that arise in disintegrat-

---

4. E.g., Afghanistan, Iran, Poland, El Salvador, Guatemala, Lebanon, the West Bank of Palestine, to name only a few.

5. Matt. 4:1–11; Luke 4:1–13; mentioned briefly in Mark 1:12–13. The three temptations were to turn stones into bread because he was hungry, to worship the devil and so gain all the kingdoms of the world, and to jump down from the highest point of the Temple without being killed.

6. The relevant passage are Deut. 8:3; 6:14–18; esp. v. 16; and 6:12–14.

ing societies is helpful.[7] He distinguishes (1) the "Savior with the Sword," who seeks by military means to bring everything under control and into an orderly pattern, that is, the dictator or the political revolutionary, and (2) the "Savior with the Time Machine," who promises to lead people into an imaginary perfect past by restoring the "good old days," or into an ideal future when all their troubles will be over.[8] To these we should certainly add the "Savior with Largesse," who promises an abundance of material goods, which will enable men and women to be happy in the existing situation.

We meet these saviors every election year, when those who run for office promise that if elected, they will build a strong national defense and maintain law and order, or that they will restore the simple, straightforward morality of earlier times, or ensure that there will be jobs for everyone. Similarly, colonial governments claim that the people under their rule are better fed, better housed, and in better health than they were before. In return, those who resist them promise that once the revolution is over, there will be peace and prosperity.

The diabolical pressure upon Jesus to become the kind of savior people long for cannot be understood if it is not recognized that the needs of the people are brutally actual and intensely serious. The basic needs for survival are food, clothing, and shelter, and subsequently economic security, medical care, employment, and schooling. There is also an urgent need for good government and freedom from tyranny. We need also to have roots, to keep a firm grip upon our heritage, while at the same time reaching forward into the future. To live only in the present is to live a meaningless life.

We are therefore quite justified in seeking to satisfy these needs, but we must recognize that they are also temptations. They encourage an "if only" philosophy: if only we had employment, food, and clothing, if only we could bring everything under our control, if only we were not here, and here were not now, then how easy our life would be! None of these efforts can truly deliver men and women from frustration and bondage, and those would-be leaders who promise *security* to men and women by these methods betray them, because they deny creation. They pretend that what they achieve will not die. But those who say, "If then none of these policies can save us, we have no hope," deny the Creator, for they deny the fact of constant newness in the world.

Jesus, therefore, having wrestled with the temptations which must come

---

7. Arnold J. Toynbee, *A Study of History, Vol. 6* (New York: Oxford University Press, 1939), 175–213.

8. Toynbee adds the "Philosopher Masked by a King," but recognizes that he also must become a "Savior with a Sword."

to everyone who longs to save men and women, made only two fundamental promises to those who heard him: You will die and you will live. You will die, and everything you have will die, because everything in this world is mortal; but you will live because death is never the end, and beyond it is abundant life. You will be safe and secure in this world once you recognize the fallibility and mortality of everything in creation, because nothing ever again can deceive you. "You will know the truth, and the truth will make you free" (John 8:32).[9]

Truly, truly, I say to you, unless a grain of wheat falls into the earth and dies, it remains alone; but if it dies it bears much fruit. He who loves his life loses it, but he who hates his life in this world will keep it for eternal life.

John 12:24–25

Fear not, little flock, for it is your Father's good pleasure to give you the kingdom. Sell your possessions, and give alms; provide yourselves with purses that do not grow old, with a treasure in the heavens that does not fail, where no thief approaches and no moth destroys.

Luke 12:32–33

Sin

We have erred, and strayed from thy ways like lost sheep. We have followed too much the devices and desires of our own hearts. . . . We have left undone those things which we ought to have done; and have done those things which we ought not to have done; and there is no health in us.

Anglican *Book of Common Prayer*

Some readers may reasonably object here that too much emphasis has been laid on the secular aspect of salvation, as meaning safety and security, and not nearly enough on the biblical understanding of delivery from sin and eternal damnation. This is primarily a matter of relationship between an individual and God.

I do not understand my actions [wrote Paul]. For I do not do what I want, but I do the very thing I hate. Now if I do what I do not want, I agree that the law is good. So then it is no longer that I do it, but sin which dwells within me. . . . I can will what is right, but I cannot do it. For I do not do the good I want, but the evil I do not want is what I do. Now if I do not do what I want, it is no longer I that do it, but sin which dwells within me. So I find it to be a law that when I want to do right, evil lies close at hand. . . . Wretched man that I am! Who will deliver me from this body of death? Thanks be to God through Jesus Christ our Lord! So then, I of myself serve the law of God with my mind, but with my flesh I serve the law of sin.

Romans 7:15–25

---

9. John in his Gospel does not tell the story of the temptations of Jesus, but deals with the theme in chapter 6 by showing how the people around Jesus succumb to the same temptations. First, he tells the story, already familiar to his readers, of the feeding of the multitude in the wilderness,

Paul here speaks of himself as a sinful individual, but earlier in the same letter he describes the sin of the Gentiles as being corporate, the product of a thoroughly corrupt community (Rom. 1:18–32). Therefore, he evidently saw sin as something committed by individuals, sometimes deliberately, but often against their will; as also a communal phenomenon; and as a malign power at work in the world, compelling men and women to do what they do not want to do. Men and women are all slaves to their master Sin (the metaphor would have been very familiar to his readers who saw slaves and slave owners every day of their lives) and are consequently compelled to act sinfully. Only one person could set them free from this slavery, Jesus Christ, and he had done so by paying for their freedom with his life, tortured to death so that they might live. Indeed, for Paul the astounding fact was that Jesus paid this enormous price for people who did not in the least deserve it (Rom. 5:6–8, but see all of chapters 5 and 6). The argument is admittedly difficult for people unfamiliar with actual slavery to grasp. However, we may get a good idea of what he meant if we think of confirmed alcoholics or drug addicts. They are often desperately anxious to be free, yet quite incapable of freeing themselves. They can, however, be set free by others who have gone through the same torment, as in Alcoholics Anonymous or among the black Islamic sect.[10]

Sin is therefore a very complex phenomenon, and we must ask whether there is any primary unifying factor, any fundamental "sin," from which all "sins" are derived. We may find it in Rom. 1:25, where Paul asserts that the basic cause of Gentile corruption is that they "turned the truth into a lie, and ascribed to the creation the qualities of a creator."[11] If Christians are right in asserting that the entire universe is necessarily dependent for its meaning upon that which is not itself, upon that which is entirely other than the universe, then it follows that the fundamental and basic error is to speak and act continually as if the assertion were not true at all, as if something within the universe could effectively represent the source of all

---

indicating both the delivery from bondage as in the Exodus and also the prodigality of the coming world, in which the present patterns of society and the marketplace will no longer apply. Instead of having to work for a living, men find food being given away to thousands freely on a mountainside. One group of people think that freedom from the exhausting toil of daily life is all that is necessary (6:25–26). Others decided that if this is what the new world is going to be like, they want to make sure that they will be in control (6:15). The third group demand some kind of miraculous sign (6:30). They want proof in advance that the new world that God is bringing into existence will be satisfactory to them before they will agree to have anything to do with it.

10. See additional notes.

11. This is a paraphrase to bring out the meaning for the modern world. Paul actually says that the Gentiles "exchanged the truth about God for a lie and worshiped and served the creature rather than the Creator."

meaning. This is idolatry, the setting up of some kind of image and worshiping that.

Obviously, if there is really nothing other than the universe, nothing which we might call "God," then the Christian argument is false and the Christian experience a delusion. Paul saw this with the utmost clarity (1 Cor. 15:1–28, esp. vv. 12–19). If Christ has not risen from the dead, if there is indeed no power other than the essentially finite and mortal powers within the universe, then our faith is vain, and "we are of all men the most to be pitied." This dichotomy is basic. Whichever is indeed true, the other must of necessity be altogether a lie, deluding and corrupting humankind, leading them astray and buoying them up with false hopes, causing them to act constantly against the truth.

In defining sin in these terms Paul is by no means alone. The theme runs all the way through the Bible. It is there in the Commandments:

> You shall not make for yourself a graven image, or any likeness of anything that is in heaven above, or that is in the earth beneath, or that is in the water under the earth; you shall not bow down to them or serve them.
>
> Exodus 20:4–5

It is in the closing words of the first letter of John:

> We know that we are of God, and the whole world is in the power of the evil one. And we know that the Son of God has come and has given us understanding. . . . This is the true God and eternal life. Little children, keep yourselves from idols.
>
> 1 John 5:19–21

And in what is probably the most scathing condemnation of idolatry in the Bible (Isa. 44:9–20), we have the portrait of a man who uses the very same thing, the tree he has cut in the forest, for his material welfare, and as being the source of all life and meaning, saying to it, "Deliver me, for thou art my god!" The prophet concludes, "He feeds on ashes; a deluded mind has led him astray, and he cannot deliver himself or say, 'Is there not a lie in my right hand?' "

If we are honest with ourselves, we should probably all admit that in this sense we are in the grip of sin, for our culture so conditions us that we literally cannot ask whether such obviously good and profitable things as physical health, financial security, national defense, democracy, human rights, political liberty, social justice, etc., may not have become lies in our hands. It is their very rightness which deceives us, for we see them as essential for ourselves, a primary necessity for our own existence, before our hands can be free to attend to the needs of the rest of the world. All these easily become for us gods, so that, although we may change a great deal, we cannot truly save ourselves. Only a firm conviction in the *otherness* of God, His otherness from this world and this universe, His love and His power, can persuade us that otherness alone, not we ourselves, can deliver us from disastrous misinterpretation of the world in which we live, that is to say, from sin.

If national defense is indeed an essential good, then the communist nations need to be defended from us—a very disturbing thought! If such things as financial security, physical health, etc. are necessary for human well-being, then, if we understand God at all, we must ensure them first for other communities and other nations. In their security and welfare is our salvation. It may be objected that our salvation is in Christ alone, but "Christ," said Dietrich Bonhoeffer, "was the man for others." It would be even more true to think of him as always the other person, the other social group, the other nation. "And the King will say to them, 'Truly, I say to you, as you did it to one of the least of these my brethren, you did it to me'" (Matt. 25:40).

> Peace cannot be kept by force. It can only be achieved by understanding. You cannot subjugate a nation forcibly unless you wipe out every man, woman, and child. Unless you wish to use so drastic a measure, you must find a way of settling your disputes without resort to arms.[12]

It should now be clear why sin is at the same time corporate, individual, and a power that enslaves men and women. It is corporate, because the very nature of every society is to be a human construction designed for the most effective well-being of its members. Its essential function is the preservation of itself for this purpose. The "others," whether they be deviants within the society or outsiders with different social concepts and constructions, are perceived as antisocial, subversive, even enemies of the state, "godless communists." For any society "otherness" is decidedly something hostile, to be resolutely opposed.

Obviously, all societies in touch with the world beyond them are influenced by many foreign ideas, but they accept these on their own terms. They admit only what they can reshape and incorporate into their own social structure and thinking. What they cannot swallow and digest they wholeheartedly reject. The specifically Christian society, the church, has not been exempt. *Extra ecclesiam nulla salus* (outside the church there is no salvation) has long been the basis of Christian mission.[13] Certainly missionaries are usually dedicated people, seeking very little for themselves, but only to save men and women. But almost universally they have sought to save them from their otherness. It is this otherness which condemns the outsiders to perdition. All societies, therefore, the Christian

---

12. Albert Einstein, *Cosmic Religion* (New York: Covici-Friede, 1931), 67.

13. See additional notes.

society included, despite the enormous good in them, are found to be
fighting against God.[14]

Sin is individual, partly because every individual is inescapably a
member of society, and shares society's sins, and even more because the
very consciousness of being an individual betrays and deludes every one
of us. It starts in the cradle.[15] The immediate necessity is sheer survival,
and this means food and nurture, which is altogether proper. As the child
grows, it becomes increasingly aware of a distinction between itself and
other people, and may spontaneously show great affection for these
others, but its own needs remain urgent and it relies on the others to fulfill
them. There is, therefore, an instinctive, altogether necessary selfishness
in every little human child, which needs to be restrained. Children can,
of course, be taught by word and example to be generous, unselfish, and
forgiving, and they often display these virtues more completely than
adults. But the old Adam is still there, and the built-in tendency to interpret other people and the multitudinous things of the world in terms of
oneself is very strong. It is strong because at the very beginning of our
lives none of us has any other measuring stick. This is original sin—not
that all human beings sin because Adam sinned first, but that Adam sinned
just because he was human.

Finally, sin is a malign power, external to ourselves, compelling us to
do what we do not want, because we are so helpless without society that
we are inevitably shaped by it. We may, and often must, resist its pressures
if we are to stand firm for what is right, but we cannot altogether separate
ourselves from its domination. Those who do so inevitably form another
society, for men and women are by their very nature social animals. Consequently, we are, despite ourselves, conditioned into making the disastrous distinction between ourselves and the "others," and giving primary
attention to ourselves. This is well illustrated by the educational system
of this and indeed every country, for the curriculum is heavily weighted
in favor of our culture and history, with only minimal attention being given
to the culture and history of others.[16]

But the power of sin is felt, and probably more acutely, in another sense.
This, as Paul said in the passage quoted earlier, is the curious and
humiliating fact that again and again we are perfectly able to see what we
ought to do, but somehow we fail to do it. We have been given free will
by God, and quite sincerely want to do what is right. We make all sorts
of good resolutions, but do not carry them out. We find that "the spirit
indeed is willing, but the flesh is weak" (Matt. 26:41). And this is made

---

14. See additional notes.

15. See additional notes.

16. See additional notes.

all the more difficult by the extraordinary fact that the harder we try, the more we are aware of failing. Like Sisyphus in the Greek legend, we valiantly push the great boulder up the mountainside, only to find it every day rolling down to the bottom again. It is a well-attested fact that the greatest and most dedicated saints are those who are most conscious of their sins and of the power of sin. Those of us who are very far from being saints are also little conscious of being sinners, and would be quite offended if we were called sinful. It is not a word we like to use.

Redemption

Clearly, left to ourselves, we are helpless against sin. The early Christian writers were not being unreasonable when they spoke of all men and women as being slaves, bought and sold like merchandise, compelled by their master to do things they hated doing, and unable to claim any rights or protection from the law. For a slave to be redeemed, i.e. to gain his freedom, was a difficult and costly business. Sometimes a generous owner would grant his slaves freedom in his will. Occasionally a slave could accumulate the money to buy his own freedom, or more often a wealthy person would pay for ransoming one or more slaves, perhaps in fulfillment of a vow made to the gods. It is against this background that we have to understand the term "redemption" and the paying for "ransom." In our modern world it might be easier to think in terms of "hostages," with which Americans became uncomfortably familiar in 1979–1980, or of people who have been kidnapped. Their release is also obtained only at a price.

To early Christians, intensely conscious of a freedom they had never known before, the metaphor of ransom was natural and easy to understand. The person who had set them free was Jesus, and the price he had paid was his own life. The difficulty arose when men started asking to whom the ransom had been paid, and developed theories that it had been paid to the devil, or perhaps to God. The discussion went on for centuries and made sense to people who moved in a different milieu from our own, but it makes little sense today. Very few people in the modern world can visualize the devil demanding a price and accepting payment. We need therefore to find our own metaphors.

"Price" does not necessarily mean payment from one person to another. We often say at the completion of a piece of work, That cost me a great deal of time and energy, or, if complimented on some hard-earned skill, a person might reply, I paid a big price for it, meaning that he or she had had to sacrifice other pleasures in order to attain it. When a desperately sick child is saved from death by the devoted care of his or her parents, the cost is the parents' time and the pleasure and luxuries they might

otherwise have enjoyed. But these have not been given to anyone else, nor
has the child received them. What the child has received is new health.
The price that is paid and the benefit received are not necessarily the same
thing. The metaphor of a price paid for sin is still a valuable one, but only
if it is not pressed too far.

Another biblical metaphor, very applicable to our modern world, is that
of a door or gate. "I am the door;" said Jesus, "if anyone enters by me,
he will be safe, and will go in and go out and find pasture" (John 10:9),[17]
and elsewhere he spoke of the narrow gate through which one can enter
eternal life, though only a few find this gate (Matt. 7:13-14; Luke 13:24).
The door was also described as a prison door, behind which the dead and
those who had not heard the Good News were confined (1 Pet. 3:19).
Today it might be helpful to think of the Iron Curtain or the Berlin Wall
or, perhaps, if our minds reach out so far, of the Great Wall of China, built
two thousand years ago to keep out barbarian nomads and "foreign
devils." On one side of these walls men and women perceive freedom and
harmony, on the other tyranny and oppression. To find an unguarded gate
and to escape through it to freedom on the other side is to be both saved
and safe.

This is a useful metaphor, but it has this danger: we may too easily think
that we are already on the safe side of the wall. It might be better, therefore, to think of the great barriers which separate human beings from each
other: barriers of language, culture, religion, sex, race, color, and of
course national frontiers. These last pose a special problem, because the
self-determination that human freedom and human rights have demanded
has created many more separate nations than have ever existed before, and
therefore no less vast an increase in national frontiers, which are
defended, if it seems necessary, by force.

Thus understood, the barriers behind which all human beings live con-
stitute barricades in which we must desperately seek for gates, if the
human race is to survive. Only if we find these gates shall we all "go in
and out and find pasture." But we deceive ourselves if we think that it is
ever simple to go through the gate, once found, or that life on the other
side will be immediately easy. Being saved and redeemed is very much
like coming to terms with a foreign culture, and learning a foreign language, which means, of course, thinking in entirely new terms. It is
seldom smooth sailing. The Roman slaves who were freed always had the
problem of how to earn their living, and those who have been long in
modern prisons have great difficulty in adjusting to the world outside.
Going through the gate and beginning a new life on the other side is fas-

---

17. Almost all translations have here, quite reasonably, "be saved," but Jesus was speaking of
helpless sheep in danger from robbers and wild beasts, and in urgent need of food.

cinating and exciting, but it is far from easy. It means "putting off the old nature and putting on the new nature" (Eph. 4:22–23), asking about everything, What is this? What does that mean? and thus learning to speak and understand a new language. It is for this reason that only a little child can enter the kingdom of heaven, for children are of all people the most eager to learn new words and phrases and to discover the meaning of everything (Matt. 18:3).[18]

Nor should we expect that those who have found these gates are going to be popular. Anyone who has been abroad for any length of time soon discovers that only a handful of people at home are genuinely interested in what he or she has to say. Indeed, there will be quite a number of people on both sides of the barrier who are suspicious and hostile. People with foreign ideas are never altogether welcome and are often seen as dangerous.

There is no safety, no salvation, no redemption from a paralyzing slavery, where barriers of any kind exist, where there is no reconciliation. We cannot be free from sin if we know only our own world and disregard all that lies outside, if there is no "breaking down the dividing wall of hostility" (Eph. 2:14), but where this is done sin is conquered and men and women are redeemed.

Of course, we must not exaggerate. At best this is a parable. We are never redeemed and we never conquer sin by anything that *we* do. We are utterly incapable of setting ourselves free, and if we had been left to ourselves, we should still be at the mercy of sin. The New Testament message is "gospel," that is, "good news," because it proclaims that Jesus Christ paid the price of our freedom in the torment of the crucifixion, and overcame sin by allowing the sinful purposes of men to do their utmost, and emerging triumphant from the criminal's grave to which they had condemned him.

> There was no other good enough
> To pay the price of sin.
> He only could unlock the gate
> Of heav'n, and let us in.
>   Cecil Frances Alexander (1848)

Nevertheless, in one sense we are still responsible for our salvation, since we have to accept it and act accordingly. The prison doors are wide open, but we have to dare to come out and live in this new world of freedom, with its new modes of thought, its new language, and its new manner of life. Christ delivered the world from bondage, and destroyed the barriers between male and female, black and white, Jew and Greek. Yet this

---

18. Some contributors objected to this interpretation, saying that the passage really refers to the innocence of little children.

work still remains to be done again and again in this present world if the work of Christ is to be brought to fruition. Now that he has ascended to heaven, we are on earth his hands, his feet, his ears, and his tongue. His work is now done through us.

But how little it is done! If the argument and belief of Christians are right, the whole power of Christ and the Spirit is there to strengthen them, but they pay so little attention. One of the clearest and most absolute commands of Christ is "Love your enemies and pray for those who persecute you" (Matt. 5:44). Individually there have been many Christians who have done so, but it seldom forms part of the regular Sunday worship in the churches, and in some liturgies such prayers are even marked as optional. As an example of what should surely be done in all churches at all times, it is worth concluding this chapter by quoting a sixteenth-century prayer, which, in a time of great political danger and tension, was required to be said in all the churches:

> Most Merciful and Loving Father, We beseech Thee most humbly, even with all our hearts, to pour out upon our enemies with bountiful hands whatsoever Thou knowest may do them good, but chiefly a sound and uncorrupt mind, where through they may know Thee and love Thee in true charity and with their whole heart, and love us, Thy children, for Thy sake. Let not their hating of us turn to their harm, but, seeing that we cannot do them good for want of ability, Lord, we desire their amendment and our own. Separate them not from us by punishing them, but join and knit them to us by thy favorable dealing with them. And seeing that we be all ordained to be citizens of the one everlasting city, let us begin to enter into that way here already by mutual love, which may bring us right forth thither,
>
> through Jesus Christ, Our Lord
> Amen
>
> (A prayer of the time of Queen Elizabeth I of England, appointed by the government for use in times of national emergency. What government today, even in a "Christian country," would urge the use of such a prayer in time of war?)

ADDITIONAL NOTES

10. This is well described in *The Autobiography of Malcolm X* (New York: Grove Press, 1965), 259–62. One contributor pointed out that the parallel is inexact, since the Christian understanding is that Jesus did not sin. Nevertheless, he certainly experienced the torment inflicted by the power of sin when he was crucified, and the agony of struggling to resist the terrible pressure of sin, for he was tempted in every respect, just as we are (Heb. 4:15).

13. One contributor commented: "This section is unfounded and *wrong*. The basis of missionary activity is that there is no salvation outside of Jesus (whether this is represented by the church or otherwise), because Jesus himself said, 'I am the way, the truth, and the life: no man cometh unto the Father, but by me' (John 14:6). He made it very clear that he was the bread of life, and the only true way, and he commissioned his disciples to spread the good news of his death, resurrection, and forgiveness."

14. One contributor disagreed: "Though saving people from their cultural otherness

may be a fault which crept into some missionary activity, it is wrong to condemn the majority of the missionaries who attempt to bring God's truth and salvation to those in ignorance. It was not 'otherness' but sin that condemned the unbelievers. I believe that most missionaries consciously realized this. Are we to say that Paul was fighting against God through his missionary efforts?"

There is admittedly much truth in this comment, and, of course, Paul cannot be said to have been fighting against God. But he was firmly opposed to imposing a foreign culture upon the converted Gentiles, as is clear from his letter to the Galatians. It is not missionary *efforts* that are being criticized here, but many missionary concepts and methods.

15. One contributor asked for this quotation to be included: "For man, as a result of his fall from Divine Grace, is cursed by an infinite craving, which nothing can satisfy for long. In this sense, indeed, man is searching for God in his sin—but only in this sense." D. R. Davies, *Down Peacock's Feathers* (London: Centenary Press, 1943), 70.

16. There was considerable questioning of this paragraph by some of the contributors. One wrote: "This is not necessarily bad. We need an identity. You are ignoring the importance of belonging. There are many advantages in being a member of a group with a history and a culture."

There is, of course, nothing wrong about being a member of such a group. Sin comes in when this group is exalted above other groups.

Another contributor commented: "But is this sin? What is sinful about being educated more in one culture than another? Maybe it is not the best approach, but it is not sinful. It does not contradict any of God's laws. To distinguish ourselves from others is not sin."

11

GOD AND HISTORY

There is no *scientific* presupposition of historical method which requires historians to rule out the possibility of divine action in history.

Alan Richardson,
History, Sacred and Profane

The Importance of History
for Christians

All the three great monotheistic religions, Judaism, Christianity, and Islam, are "historical religions."[1] In each of them the entire system of belief is based, not upon philosophical reflection, but on the conviction that at a specific time and place in the history of the world something happened. The "something" was so luminous that it not only cast a brilliant light on all that had gone before, but pierced the future like a searchlight, illuminating the part ahead. For the Jewish people the critical event was the Exodus from Egypt, and especially the experience at Mt. Sinai: the revelation to them of Torah, the "Teaching." For Muslims it was the revelation to Muhammad on Mt. Hira, and, in the years that followed, the making known of the Qur'an, and the Hijrah, the "going out" of the first Muslims from Mecca to Medina in A.D. 622.

For Christians the climactic event was, of course, the life, death, and resurrection of Jesus of Nazareth. In this it is similar to Judaism and Islam. However, it may be said to be more profoundly and completely "historical" for two reasons:

First, Christians believe that in Jesus of Nazareth God revealed Himself, not *to* a man, but *in and through* a man. God, therefore, participated in human history in every respect, just as human beings do. Since, as we

---

1. The greatest contrast to these is Hinduism, which is largely uninterested in history, viewing it as part of the *maya* or "deception" of the world. Admittedly, the great epic of the *Mahabharata* is based on history, but research into the history of India, and the writing of Indian history books, did not begin until British occupation in the eighteenth century.

have seen, what we perceive as events in time and space are for God always now, His participation in history is no less a constant than are creation and resurrection. Consequently, all human history must be in some sense the activity and self-revelation of God.

Second, from the very beginning Christians have always seen the death and resurrection of Jesus, and the coming of the Holy Spirit, as the fulfillment of all previous history, which was leading up to this event. Subsequent history is seen as having a new quality. It is as if all the earlier history of humankind had narrowed down to this point, concentrated in Jesus, Son of man and Son of God, and after him has been continually broadening out from generation to generation. This is the age of the Spirit.[2] This thinking is markedly different from that of Muslims, for whom the years before Muhammad are *iyyām al-jahalīyah* (days of ignorance) and therefore not worth recording.[3] The Christian understanding does not, however, differ so greatly from the Jewish, since it was from the Jewish scriptures that the early Christians had learned their history. What had happened and been said before the time of Jesus was for them of enormous importance, and they scoured the Scriptures to discover what relation the activity of God in the past had to His manifestation through Jesus in their own time.

Therefore, before we tackle the question of God's activity in the history of our own day we need to examine carefully (1) what exactly we mean when we use the word "history"; (2) what is the nature of Old Testament history; and (3) why the early Christians saw Jesus as the fulfillment of that history.

What Is History?

In general, history means either the events of the past or the record of such events. But generalizations are misleading. Certainly all past events belong to history, but we can know only a minute fraction of them. Even if we say that history means only all remembered and recorded events, there are still problems. We have to ask, What actually happened; how can we know it? and What is the meaning of these events? The second question cannot be avoided, for every historian must select what seem to be significant events and relate them to each other. No history book, however comprehensive, is ever just a list. It is always an interpretation of events, and

---

2. This theme is developed at length in Oscar Cullmann, *Christ and Time: The Primitive Christian Concept of Time and History*, trans. Floyd F. Filson (Philadelphia: Westminster Press, 1964). Not all scholars, however, accept his whole argument.

3. This must not be exaggerated. Muslims by no means reject all pre-Islamic history. They believe Abraham to have been the first true Muslim, and many historical persons, e.g., Moses, David, and especially Jesus, have a very important place in the Qur'an. However, none of this is told as continuous history, such as we find in so much of the Old Testament.

behind this is a mental picture, a point of view, an understanding of the world, which cannot be set aside by even the most objective scholar. Every historian is conditioned by the culture of his nation and his century, and this affects also the question of what actually happened. Even if it was only yesterday, the complete evidence is never available. The event is over, sliding rapidly into the past, even before the question is asked, and those who perceived it at the time wore tinted glasses.

We can never answer these questions finally, because new evidence may come to light. New experience may compel us to revise our interpretation. Yet this does not mean that we can give no answers at all. We must attempt answers, using scholarly study and research, for if we have no grasp of the past, we shall never properly understand the present, which has grown out of it.

Essential to any understanding of history is the concept of interaction, both among human beings and between them and their environment. Any serious student of history must begin with the premise that all human activity is marked by continuity, one thing leading to another, and by change, sometimes gradual and sometimes sudden. The changes, especially when catastrophic, may deflect the continuity, but they cannot destroy it. As excellent example is the Communist continuation of czarist foreign policy after the Russian revolution.

Is there any universal pattern to history? Can we say, for instance, that despite many setbacks it is marked by progress upon which we may rely, or that it records developing human skill, constantly increasing knowledge, and ever-greater human control over nature, all bound to continue? There have been many attempts to write a philosophy of history, but none have won general acceptance. Every author writes from within his or her own culture and, however vast the learning, none is capable of knowing *all* history, even of what we call the major civilizations. We cannot speak of historical laws with such incomplete evidence. We can speak only of tendencies. We can, of course, perceive patterns because among large groups of people we can recognize tendencies so evident and powerful that we can predict the outcome with some assurance. But the behavior of individuals is only partially predictable. The ever-present element of free will, ability to choose, freedom to change one's mind, even a "conversion experience," a complete change of heart involving a totally new way of life—all this forbids us to lay down the law about history.

Historians, therefore, cannot predict. They can say, "Other things being equal, this is what will happen," but they know full well from their studies that other things seldom remain equal. They have seen how the sudden death of a powerful ruler and the accession of someone much weaker has altered the pattern of events. They have studied the options which at one time were open, but became closed because some statesman or politician refused to listen, and established a policy that turned out to be disastrous.

The Munich meeting in September 1938, a year before World War II began, provides a vivid example. Britain and France could then still have remained faithful to their treaty with Czechoslovakia, and have withstood Nazi expansion, or at least prevented it taking the form it did. The choice was there, but once it was made the options were closed. As Winston Churchill said in the subsequent House of Commons debate, "You had the choice between dishonor and war. You chose dishonor; you will get war."

Political decisions are, of course, by no means the only events in history. There are a great many others, "wars and rumors of wars," dynastic marriages, elections, strikes and lockouts, bills passed or defeated in Congress, earthquakes, and exceptionally rich harvests. "What is essential to the understanding of change is no single type of event. *It is the event as such:* the intrusion, the impact, the impingement upon a given mode of social behavior of some force that cannot, by its nature, be deduced from that mode of behavior."[4]

History in the Old Testament

Out of all the thirty-nine books of the Old Testament only four do not directly discuss history,[5] and the history they recount covers at least nine hundred years—a truly remarkable record.[6] To the great body of information in the strictly historical books we must add the prophetic writings, for their teaching directly concerns the historical situation of their day.

The close relationship of the Old Testament to history is far more profound than the mere fact that there is a great deal of history in it. The essential feature is that some of the leading thinkers in ancient Israel were the first people in the world to write what we today would term "history," antedating Herodotus, the so-called father of history, by about five hundred years, and Confucius, the first true historian of China, by at least four hundred years. Of course, official records had been kept in Mesopotamia and Egypt for well over a thousand years earlier, and these are of great importance for our modern understanding of the ancient world. But they are essentially detailed lists, full of information, but lacking any answers to the question, What is the significance of these events? Similar records

---

4. Robert A. Nisbet, *Social Change and History: Aspects of the Western Theory of Development* (New York: Oxford University Press, 1970), 281. Emphasis added.

5. These are Leviticus, Proverbs, Ecclesiastes, the Song of Solomon. It may be objected that Ruth, Esther, and Jonah are not authentic history. Nevertheless, they are written in historical terms, and so, to a more limited extent, is Ecclesiastes. Leviticus also is set within the framework of the Exodus. Job, though regarded by many as concerned with primarily the individual, is more probably a response to the tragedy of the exile in Babylon.

6. This is assuming that the Exodus took place in 1250 B.C. The earlier period of the Patriarchs cannot be dated with any certainty. The terminal date is the Maccabean revolt, which began in 168 B.C.

were kept in Israel also from the time of King David onward, after about 1000 B.C., and these are mentioned as source material in the two books of Kings (e.g., 1 Kings 11:41; 14:19, 29; 15:7, 23). But these two books are clearly distinct from the records. They use the records as primary sources, but they select and interpret the information. The accounts of history before the monarchy are not based on exact records, for there were none, but they also are interpretations.

All the historical books are rooted in the actual history of the Israelite people, notably in the extraordinary reversals of their situation, which forced upon them the urgent question, Why? Once we were slaves in Egypt, but now we are free; once we wandered in a bleak and barren wilderness, but now we live in our own country; once we were a loose confederation of tribes, but now we are an imperial kingdom. Why did these things happen to us, and what is their purpose?

The questions became still more demanding as history continued, for Israelite imperial power was of short duration. They were caught in the endless power struggle between East and West, between the great kingdoms of Egypt and Mesopotamia. No ruler since King David, and perhaps not even he, was free to pursue an independent foreign policy. In 722 B.C. the kingdom of Israel was crushed by the Assyrians, and in 587 Judah was destroyed and all the leading people thrust into exile in distant Babylon. In 539 Cyrus, a "barbarian" from the inner recesses of the Persian plateau, conquered Babylon and enabled the exiles to return and rebuild Jerusalem, but they had been stripped of all political power. The Persian empire was as vast as the United States before the addition of Alaska and Hawaii, but the province of Judah was only twenty-five miles long by twenty miles wide, and Jerusalem within its walls no larger than what we would call a village.

The Prophetic Interpretation

The magnificent teaching of the prophets was a response to these hammer blows of history, and an answer to the ancient question of Gideon, "Pray sir, if the Lord is with us, why then has all this befallen us?" (Judg. 6:13). "The year that King Uzziah died," when Isaiah was sent to speak to an unresponsive people (Isa. 6:1ff.), was also the time when a new policy of military expansion began in distant Assyria, and the fate of both Israel and Judah was then determined. The events could be very close at hand, as in the case of Gideon, busy hiding his family's food from the marauding Midianites, or they could be a thousand miles away, but the question was the same: What does it all mean? In the words already quoted, there is "no single type of event. It is the event as such" that is essential.

Events are things that happen to us, and in each, however great or small, we are confronted by the absolute and final Reality, that is, by God Himself. Before it happens it is not a fact, only a possibility. But immediately it happens, at that very instant, it is absolute and irrevocable.

> The Moving Finger writes; and having writ
> Moves on: nor all thy Piety nor Wit
>   Shall lure it back to cancel half a line,
> Nor all thy Tears wash out a word of it.
>   Edward Fitzgerald,
>   *Rubaiyat of Omar Khayyam*, 51

Every event has the power to say, What are you going to do now?

We give our answers within the iron framework of time. We answer *now*, but our decision on how to answer, how to interpret the imperious event, is based on our knowledge of the unalterable *past,* and our hopes and fears about the *future,* still unknown. There are for us no facts in the future, only possibilities, which may or may not happen. Much of the past has escaped from human knowledge, but the future lies altogether beyond it. The future is the property of God.

> The purpose manifest in history is the purpose of a transcendent God. . . . The meaning of history, therefore, is determined by that which lies beyond history.[7]

For God, as we have seen, there is no past or future. He is not imprisoned in time, which He Himself created. He dwells in eternity, and everything for Him is now.

> The secret things belong to the LORD our God, but the things that are revealed belong to us and to our children for ever, that we may do all the words of this law.
>   Deuteronomy 29:39

The word of God, therefore, proclaimed by the prophets, and preserved in the Scriptures, was spoken in what for them was the present, but it depended upon a proper understanding of the past, notably the Exodus experience and the Torah given on Sinai. Yet these warnings and promises concerned the future, for by the mercy of God it is not entirely hidden from our eyes. Although future events are among the "secret things," we may learn the kinds of things that could happen from our knowledge of the past. If we make mistakes similar to those of our forefathers, we shall almost certainly suffer similar disasters, but we cannot make the *same* mistakes, or experience the *same* results, for our situation is never the same as theirs. The future remains open for us, although, as we have seen, there may come a point when disaster can no longer be avoided.

But the judgment is final in only one sense. It marks quite definitely the end of a chapter, so to speak, but it does not close the book. God is forever

---

7. C. H. Dodd, *The Kingdom of God and History* (Chicago: Willet Clark and Co., 1938), 22.

the Creator, and the "valley of trouble" is always a "door of hope."[8] Even in the depths of despair amid the ruins of Jerusalem the poet could still write,

> Remember my affliction and my bitterness,
>   the wormwood and the gall!
> My soul continually thinks of it
>   and is bowed down within me.
> But this I call to mind,
>   and therefore I have hope:
> The steadfast love of the Lord never ceases,
>   his mercies never come to an end;
> they are new every morning.
>   Lamentations 3:19–23

This strong sense of hope was a remarkable feature of Israelite, and later Jewish, understanding. In much of the ancient world hope was thought of as deceptive and treacherous. Great would be the rejoicing if it were fulfilled, but only too often the longed-for relief never came, only desolation, loneliness, and despair. There were, of course, many who despaired in Israel, and in their distress cursed God and their king, because wherever they looked they saw nothing but "the gloom of anguish" (Isa. 8:21–2). There were also many false hopes, such as the expectation of rapid delivery from exile, which Jeremiah wholeheartedly condemned (Jer. 27:14). Yet with increasing assurance those prophets whose words are preserved in the Bible insisted that disaster, however savage and overwhelming, must always presage a new beginning and yet more glorious future. Disaster they saw as inevitable, because men and women by folly and disbelief bring it upon themselves, but no less inevitable is the new life beyond the disaster.

Covenant and Promise

Fundamental to the Old Testament understanding of historical events were two firmly held beliefs: (1) that at Mt. Sinai, God and the people of Israel had entered into a covenant, or mutual agreement, binding upon both sides. The terms of this agreement are what we call today the Ten Commandments.[9] (2) That God had made certain promises to the people of Israel, and that since the word of God cannot be broken, these promises must assuredly be fulfilled.

Both covenant and promise are first recorded after the universal flood

---

8. Hos. 2:15. The Valley of Achor (i.e., trouble) was where Achan, by his dishonesty and theft, brought disaster upon the Israelites as they entered the promised land (Joshua 7, esp. vv. 20–26; see also Isa. 65:10).

9. The Ten Commandments are to be found in Exod. 20:1–17 and Deut. 5:6–21. The account in Deut. 5:1–27 makes clear the covenant character of the commandments. The development of the covenant concept in ancient Israel is well discussed in Delbert R. Hillers, *Covenant: The History of an Idea* (Baltimore: Johns Hopkins University Press, 1969).

had subsided. "Then God said to Noah and to his sons with him, "Behold I establish my covenant with you and your descendants after you," promising also that "the waters shall never again become a flood to destroy all flesh" (Gen. 9:8–17). But more important for subsequent history in Israel were the repeated promises made to Abraham and the covenant established between him and God.

> Now the LORD said to Abram,[10] "Go from your country and your kindred and your father's house to the land that I will show you. And I will make of you a great nation, and I will bless you.
>
> > Genesis 12:1–2; see also 12:7;
> > 13:14–17; 15:1; 18:13–15; 22:15–18

> I will establish my covenant between me and you and your descendants after you throughout their generations for an everlasting covenant.
>
> > Genesis 17:7; see the whole passage,
> > 17:1–21, and also 15:1–20

No less significant was the covenant made by God with King David, and through him with all those of his descendants who became kings of Judah. This is why Matthew's Gospel begins with the statement that Jesus was "the son of David, the son of Abraham" (Matt. 1:1), for the good news is that in Jesus of Nazareth God has been faithful to His promises.

Covenants, of course, involve responsibilities, and the descendants of David could not escape retribution if they failed to keep their side of the agreement (2 Sam. 7:14). Similarly, the people of Israel and Judah were required to adhere to the terms of the covenant made at Sinai. A significant feature of this covenant is that it says nothing at all about payment from one party to the other. There is no clause requiring the people to bring sacrifices to God (see Psalm 50). The prophets insisted that sacrifice, and even prayers, had nothing to do with the agreement made at Sinai. This could not be fulfilled in the Temple, but only in the marketplace, the open space at the gate of the town where all the buying and selling took place, and where also the judges administered justice. It was there that the greedy merchants said:

> When will the new moon be over,
> > that we may sell grain?
> And the sabbath,
> > that we may offer wheat for sale,
> that we may charge a high price for a small measure,[11]
> > and deal deceitfully with false balances?
>
> > Amos 8:5

---

10. Abram was the earlier name of Abraham (Gen. 17:5).

11. The RSV has the more literal translation, "that we may make the ephah small and the shekel great."

There also the corrupt judges "acquit the guilty for a bribe, and deprive the innocent of his right" (Isa. 5:23). In the prophetic thinking God was not prepared so much as to listen to those who maltreat or neglect their fellow men and women (Isa. 1:14–17).

The constantly repeated accusation of the prophets was that both the people and their rulers totally misunderstood their own history and the shattering events of the times in which they lived. They insisted that it was useless for people to crowd into the Temple and beg for deliverance, or bolster their hopes with the conviction that God would not allow Jerusalem to be destroyed because it was His holy city:

> Behold, you trust in lying words to no avail. Will you steal, murder, commit adultery, swear falsely, burn incense to Baal, and go after other gods that you have not known, and *then* come and stand before me in this house, which is called by my name, and say, "We have been saved"—only to go on doing these horrible things?
>
> Jeremiah 7:8–10 (trans. D. B.)[12]

God's passion for justice and integrity are such that He will stop at nothing in order to thwart bad government, dishonesty, injustice, neglect of the starving and destitute, and all "man's inhumanity to man." And so Jerusalem, that used to be called "the joy of all the earth" (Ps. 48:2; Lam. 2:15), was laid level with the ground.

But this could not be the end. Though the people might break their side of the agreement a thousand times, God could not break His.

> My heart recoils within me,
>   my compassion grows warm and tender.
> I will not execute my fierce anger,
>   I will not again destroy Ephraim;
> for I am God and not man,
>   the Holy One in your midst,
> and I will not come to destroy.
>   Hosea 11:8–9

There would have to be a new covenant (Jer. 31:31–34), and a new kind of humanity to understand and maintain it (Ezek. 36:22–27).

The New Agreement

The new covenant and the new kind of humanity are exactly what all the New Testament books were written to describe. Every writer is convinced that the slate has been wiped clean, that the old covenant, so constantly broken, has been set aside, and all past failure to keep it has

---

12. This is part of Jeremiah's sermon at the Temple gate in 609 B.C. (see also Jer. 26:1–6). All the sins of which he accuses the people are breaches of the covenant (Exod. 20:3, 13–16).

therefore been annulled. The Epistle to the Hebrews develops this theme at length: just as the earlier covenant had been ratified with the blood of oxen offered in sacrifice (Exod. 24:2–8), so now the self-sacrifice of Jesus, and the blood which he had shed when he was flogged and crucified, ratified the new agreement (Heb. 9:15–28, but see the extended discussion in chapters 8—10). There is also a new creation, a new world in which the old sex and race barriers no longer apply (Gal. 3:28; Eph. 2:14-16). There is a new kind of person, "begotten, not of different kinds of blood, nor of the will of the flesh, nor of the will of man, but of God" (John 1:13, trans. D.B.).[13]

Nevertheless, the earlier covenant, although now set aside, was not for that reason to be downgraded, since apart from it the new covenant could never have been understood. Only those trained from childhood to think of this world and of God's relationship to human beings in terms of covenant could have perceived that there was in fact a new agreement. The new covenant could not abrogate the old without undermining its own validity. The covenant at Sinai was understood to have its foundation in the covenant with Abraham, and the still earlier covenant with Noah, and the new covenant in Jesus Christ had the sure foundation of Sinai, renewed and confirmed with the house of David. It was the assurance to men and women in an unstable and menacing political situation that covenant, agreement, fellowship, is always the basis of true society, and that even when the old agreement lies shattered in pieces,[14] God is forever ready to begin again on the same friendly family basis.[15]

Christian Convictions and the History of Our Own Day

In the light of all this, how should we respond to the complex events of our own day, confronted, as we are, by the Absolute, by God Himself? We do not, of course, respond to history in general, nor to the infinite reality of God, which we can neither know nor comprehend. We respond to things that happen to us, to events, to God made known in history, as "incarnate," as expressed in human terms.

The criterion for our response must always be the Christ event, the birth, life, death, and resurrection of Jesus. By this all other events are measured and acquire meaning, and by this every response is judged. Yet in its day it was a commonplace and insignificant event. It took place in a small corner of the Roman empire, and the rest of the world—Asia, the

---

13. See additional notes.

14. This is the meaning of the word used in Jer. 31:32.

15. See Hos. 2:14–15; 11:1–4, 8–9.

Americas, and the Antipodes—proceeded in complete ignorance of it. The Christ event is not self-explanatory. It must be seen against the background of the time, and in terms of God's ongoing revelation of His will and purpose in all that had led up to the time of Jesus—in covenant, judgment, and promise.

Covenant, when one pauses to consider it carefully, is a surprising religious concept, since covenant is always established by discussion and debate. Any treaty or agreement imposed by the powerful upon the weak is self-defeating and will be overthrown at the earliest opportunity. Since nowhere in the Bible is it ever suggested that a divine covenant was imposed upon the people, but rather that it was freely entered into and continually renewed, we have to conceive of God as maintaining constant conversation and discussion with men and women. The relation is eternally I-Thou, in which each speaks directly to the other, and neither treats the other as an object to be spoken about, as a mere It.[16] It is an awe-inspiring thought that at every moment, in everything that happens, God is talking to us and we to Him, but the Bible requires us to think in this manner.

The biblical understanding is also that covenant is the only sound foundation of society, and that this is universally true. Other methods of establishing society, other responses to the events that crowd in upon us, involve the worship of other gods, the exaltation of other principles, and therefore saying, "No!" to God Himself, and demoting Him to the level of an It. Only by friendly conversation is contact with God maintained and a stable society sustained. History, whether past or present, must, in the biblical understanding, be interpreted in these terms. Only in full communion can there be community.

Covenant inevitably issues in judgment and promise. There is promise, because all covenants and agreements are made with an eye to the future. They offer assurance of benefits to come if the agreement is kept, and they promise always some measure of safety, for example, financial security in old age, protection from thieves, from foreign invasion. The divine covenant promises ultimate security, that is, salvation. However, no treaty or agreement, not even the biblical covenant, can guarantee immediate and total security here on earth, because no covenant can annul the innate human freedom to act in a completely contrary manner. "In the world you have tribulation," said Jesus, "but be of good cheer, I have overcome the world" (John 16:33).

Judgment is there in a triple sense. First, since no true agreement is ever imposed, all concerned must judge for themselves whether they will enter into the agreement. Second, agreements do not keep themselves. The

---

16. Martin Buber, *I and Thou* (New York: Charles Scribner's Sons, 1970).

societies involved must be frequently assessed and judged to ensure that the agreement is being maintained. Third, those believed to have broken the agreement must be brought to judgment, and if they are found guilty, some form of restraint must be imposed. "Justice must not only be done; it must be seen to be done." In the Christian understanding all humanity was brought to the judgment seat, and justice was both done and seen to be done, when Jesus took upon himself to pay the penalty so that the accused might be allowed to go free.

As we turn the searchlight of covenant, judgment, and promise upon modern societies and present history, it is easy to demonstrate that communist countries and other dictatorial systems are not characterized by agreement based upon free discussion and debate, that they make promises far beyond what they are able to fulfill, and that they grant to some people power such as no human beings have a right to possess. But when the searchlight swings around to illuminate our own society we are usually less discerning. Certainly, discussion and debate form the basis of every democracy, and this is good, but in practice democracy generally achieves its purpose by balancing the selfishness of one group against that of another. The principle of all elections, that the will of the majority should prevail, is a useful rule of thumb for maintaining internal order, since a discontented majority could overthrow the system, but there is no evidence at all that the majority are the wisest and best informed of the population, and plenty of evidence that where majority opinion prevails, minorities find themselves discriminated against and even oppressed.

There are therefore dangers involved in transferring the biblical oracles and promises to our time, and especially for Christians in the United States. Biblical history, in both the Old and New Testaments, is the history of a small country, without great material resources, and at the mercy of the great world powers. The United States, however, is one of the superpowers, similar to Assyria, Babylon, or Rome, not a downtrodden and oppressed little nation. When the prophet cried out, "Comfort, comfort my people!" (Isa. 40:1), it was not to the mighty Babylonians that he was speaking.

Moreover, not only event, but also continuity and change, are the essence of history. Because of continuity, biblical history and oracles, the judgments and promises, are still valid for our own day. But because of incessant change, sometimes gradual, sometimes abrupt, we stand in peril if we apply them literally. To do so is to forget that God is Creator, and that the world is new every day.

The New Testament has very little exact advice about how we should respond to political events. The Christian, therefore, must do so as he or she thinks fit, remembering that the only right decisions are those made according to Truth, the fundamental nature and conditions of human existence, and the will and purposes of the Creator. We must interpret the impact of events in terms of our own finiteness, weakness, and mortality, and respond to them in terms of the one, infinite God, altogether Other, and working everlastingly for the ultimate well-being of His creation. To respond sinfully is to do the opposite, to take something within this finite universe and use it as the ultimate authority for our action.

There is a host of false gods ready to be used. We can start with ourselves, and make our own personal needs and livelihood the criterion. But the sincere Christian, rightly rejecting this, may easily fall into the trap of using another finite god, just because it is not myself, but something other. Lives of great devotion and self-sacrifice have been lived out in service to the community, the church, the nation, and surely such self-sacrifice will not be forgotten by God. But how often, how very often, what is being served so selflessly is *my* community, *my* church, and *my* nation. The more evidently good the object of devotion, the greater is the danger of a sinful response. The profound tragedy of Christian history is that the community of believers, the church, has so little perceived what she above all ought to have known, that there is indeed only One God, and that this One God is not herself.

Honest individuals may become so convinced of the justice of their cause that they cannot see beyond it. We speak of "a just and durable peace,"[17] so admirable an aim that we fail to see that it is an empty promise. We should work toward it, but we cannot achieve it. All our efforts are bound to be finite and less than absolutely just. International problems are so complex, with suffering and anxious people on both sides of the dispute, that we can never be truly just to all. To take only one prominent example, it is utterly impossible, whatever enthusiasts of both sides may say, to reach a fully just solution in the Palestine dispute. If we are just to the Palestinians on the West Bank, we shall be unjust to those Israeli families who were encouraged to settle there, and did so in good faith. But if we strive to be just to them, we shall be unjust to the dispossessed Palestinians, whose land they took. There is no way round this problem, and it applies no less severely in all major conflicts.

The Christian must recognize this, and see every political settlement, not as a solution to a nagging problem, but as a temporary respite, a breathing space giving opportunity to start afresh, and to undo at least something of the injustice we committed in our efforts to be just. One might well, without irreverence, venture to say in the language of the Sermon on the Mount, "You have heard how it hath been said by them of old time, 'Repent of the evil you have done.' But if you repent of your

---

17. This oft-quoted phrase originated with John Foster Dulles, the Secretary of State in the Eisenhower administration, and himself a devout and eminent Christian, but Christians must realize that as a political goal it is thoroughly misleading.

evil actions, what do you more than others? Do not even Gentiles the same? But I say unto you, 'Repent of the good things you have done.' "

One further question remains. If events in history are to be seen as God confronting us directly with the question, What are you going to do now? must we then say that everything that happens in history is the work of God? What are we to make of such appalling atrocities as the atomic destruction of Hiroshima and Nagasaki, or the saturation bombing of Hamburg and Dresden by the Allies, when even more people died? What are we to say about the Holocaust, or earlier in history the Inquisition, with all its brutalities done in the name of Christ? Have we the right to say, in any sense at all, that they are "of God"? But if they are not of God, then where was God in the terrifying firestorm that swept the city of Hamburg? Where was He at Auschwitz and Belsen? And where is He now in Lebanon, in Afghanistan, in Iran, and in Central America? Is the God whom we worship and adore only a *deus otiosus,* an absentee landlord, or is He a savage and jealous deity, commanding destruction?

"Does evil befall a city, unless the Lord has done it?" asked Amos (3:6). By this he seems to have meant that violence and destruction, which he has no hesitation in calling evil, do not happen unless behind them somewhere there is solid reality, some challenge from God, which we ought to have perceived, and to which we should have responded, but failed to do so. God does not command men and women to be violent, to torture, kill, and destroy. There is nothing good at all about these actions. The good resides only in this: they reveal with blinding clarity the enormous evil of which human beings are capable and which, if we judge only in terms of this immediate world, they will undoubtedly commit, thinking that they are doing the best they can in the circumstances, that they have no alternative. If we do not honestly realize this truth about ourselves, the "day of the Lord" will indeed be darkness and not light (Amos 5:18).

ADDITIONAL NOTES

13. All English translations have "born" rather than "begotten." However, the Greek word *egennēthēsan* can mean either. Since the emphasis in this passage is on "will," it seems better, in light of the ancient understanding that the will of a child came from the father rather than the mother, to say "begotten" in place of "born." Also, the normal translation of the next clause is "not of blood," although the Greek is clearly plural. The phrase almost certainly reflects the belief that different kinds of people had different kinds of blood, one bloodline being better than another. Though certainly false, this was a very natural idea among people who were thoroughly familiar with rearing animals. It persisted well into our own century in the belief in some quarters that black and white blood should not be mixed by intermarriage.

12

CHRISTIANS AND THE END-TIME

What we call the beginning is often the end
And to make an end is to make a beginning.
T. S. Eliot,
"Little Gidding," *Four Quartets*

The End of the World

The world in which we live is passing away. This simple statement can
be the source of either immense apprehension or profound relief. It has
a very different meaning for the wealthy in Beverly Hills and the helpless
victims of a police state. On one level it merely reflects the fact that we
live in a world of constant adjustment, of transition, change, and endings.
In each of these we sense, at times with fear and anxiety, our finitude and
our powerlessness to achieve all that we desire or hope to be. We cannot
control the course of distant events. We hope only that with each unrepeat-
able moment, each tick of the clock, we may have the courage to face the
unknown.

But on another level the statement elicits a more profound response than
the realization that all things are transitory. For many the end appears to
be a cosmic and imminent event, whether this is understood in religious
or nonreligious terms. People have been fascinated, and at times panic-
stricken, by projections of the possible effects of the Comet Kohoutek, or
the rain of deadly ash from Mt. St. Helens. Both in this country and in
Japan some scientists have in recent months predicted for the near future
major, and possibly catastrophic, volcanic and earthquake activity. In
popular literature and film we have a veritable doomsday industry, predict-

ing "Apocalypse Now!"[1] Some preachers have quoted the Bible to show that global politics, especially in the Middle East, denote the cataclysm preceding the triumphal return of Jesus Christ, and a popular bumper sticker darkly announces: "Ready or not, Jesus is coming!"[2]

Dire predictions of the end of the world are not new. They have been often heard in times of great crisis, or at significant points in history. The year A.D. 1000, the end of the first millennium after the estimated date of Jesus' birth, stimulated both faith and frenzy. As we draw near to the end of the second millennium we may expect similar manifestations. But this time there is a great difference. We have now the capacity readily at hand to end the world as we know it. Nuclear war would not bring the universe to an end, but it could destroy life on this earth, and make the survivors— if, indeed, there are any—envious of the dead. We must postpone discussion of this until the end of the chapter, for first we need to look at the traditional Christian understanding of the end-time.

Eschatology and Incarnation

Christianity is rooted in history, and believes that history has a purpose and direction. Only partially does it look back to a golden age;[3] far more insistently it looks forward to the future. It understands the course of human affairs to be under the direction of God, who creates and sustains the world. It perceives history, therefore, to be the arena in which human beings decide whether or not they will cooperate with the divine purpose. What is done by them in time has consequences for eternity. This is true not only for the critical events of the life of Jesus, but also for the unique choices made by each individual person. But the ultimate significance of all these historical events will be discerned only in the future. It will be made clear only at the end of time, which the early Christians believed to be very close at hand. It would establish the kingdom of heaven, and usher in the "day of the Lord," heralded by the prophets (e.g., Isa. 2:12; 13:6), and long awaited by people in exile and under oppression.

The end of time is the eschaton, and eschatology therefore the study of the "last things" (eschata). As usually understood by Christians these include a person's destiny: death, judgment, heaven or hell, and for the totality of humankind, general resurrection, the final judgment, and a "new heaven and a new earth" (Rev. 21:1). These are the marks of the

---

1. E.g., Doris Lessing's *Four-Gated City*, or Nicholas Roeg's film, *The Last Wave*.

2. William Martin, "Waiting for the End," *The Atlantic Monthly* 249 (June 1982): 31.

3. The United Monarchy under David and Solomon was regarded by many Jews as an ideal period, and Christians have often thought of the early church in the same way. Both agree, however, that earlier history presages an even more glorious future.

kingdom, understood by New Testament writers both to fulfill ancient prophecy and to initiate the final age:

> "The people who sat in darkness
> have seen a great light,
> and for those who sat in the region and
>   shadow of death,
> light has dawned."
> From that time Jesus began to preach saying, "Repent, for the kingdom of heaven
> is at hand."
>
> Matthew 4:16–17;
see Isaiah 9:1–2

For the writers of the Gospels the good news of Jesus is not only that he proclaimed the end of the age, but that what he proclaimed is here and now realized. An irreversible process has begun. It will be completed in the future, but it casts its light already on the present. The prophets had seen the future hidden in the present, and Christians must now similarly discern "the signs of the times" (Matt. 16:3). They cannot, however, draw up a timetable, since it is not for them to "know times or seasons which the Father has fixed by his own authority" (Acts 1:7). Yet even now Christ is seated at God's right hand (Eph. 1:20), the position of power, from whence "he shall come again with glory to judge both the quick and the dead."[4]

The end is not yet, but Christians believe the incarnation of Christ to be the guarantee of the end. Christian faith and action, therefore, do not lie outside history, apart from the present world. Just as Jesus lived in and for the world, so must his followers. To proclaim the kingdom, raise the dead, heal the sick, cast out demons—this, and not eschatology, is their primary concern (Matt. 10:7–8). These are authentic signs of the end, but they are done now in the present. Thus, eschatology and incarnation are twin facets of the completion of God's promises, and both provide the context for the church's ministry and mission.

Apocalypse[5]

Very much of the biblical writing about the end-time is in the form of what we know as "apocalyptic," from the Greek word *apocálupsis*. This literally means "taking the lid off" something, and therefore *disclosure* of hidden knowledge, *manifestation, revelation*. The main aim, therefore, of all apocalyptic writing is *clarification*, the revealing of hidden meaning

---

4. The Nicene Creed.

5. For a list of apocalyptic writings see additional notes.

in an otherwise baffling, contradictory, and incomprehensible situation. However, the normal reader's immediate response to apocalyptic writing is exactly the opposite. He finds it grotesque and obscure, full of absurd images and exaggerated fantasy.

Why should this be so? At the surface level an important reason is that all apocalyptic belongs to times of great tension, "distress of nations in perplexity . . . men fainting with fear and with foreboding of what is coming on the world" (Luke 21:25–26). Both biblical apocalyptic and nonbiblical apocalyptic of the same period reflect the thinking of a community struggling to be faithful to God while suffering under the domination of a pagan, and often brutal, foreign power. In such circumstances to be too explicit is not safe.

Another surface reason is the persistent human desire that things should be simple and straightforward. We prefer a literal description to one that compels us to search for deeper meaning. This very human tendency has led many readers of apocalyptic material in the Bible either to reject it out of hand as impossible and even repulsive, or to expect literal fulfillment of the prophecies.

The third, and more profound, reason for the confusion is the total impossibility of expressing divine activity within the limits of human speech. Imagery, hyperbole, and symbolism are the only means available to those who struggle to convince men and women of the otherness of God, and His infinite power, love, and justice. Apocalyptic literature, therefore, must be viewed as great art is always to be viewed—not as a literal, photographic image, but as a picture full of profound, but often hidden, meaning.

Apocalyptic and eschatology have this in common: neither treats historical events as mere shadow play. For each, history is deadly serious. Apocalyptic seeks to reveal the fundamental meaning of brutal foreign domination, cruel persecution, and complete helplessness to take any effective action against overwhelming military and political power. No writer of the period could suggest to his readers that their miseries were anything but real. The apocalyptic authors argued that beyond them is even more profound reality, which in due course would prevail. The arrogant pomp and power of the earthly rulers would then be shown to be but empty sham, and the faithful to have had true value, for

> the kingdom and the dominion
> and the greatness of the kingdom under the whole heaven
> shall be given to the people of the saints of the Most High.
> Daniel 7:27

For Christians in the United States to understand apocalyptic writing is very far from easy, since only a few have lived in a police state and known deliberate oppression at first hand. Black people, with their memories of slavery and experience of cruel discrimination, are far better equipped than whites to interpret the images, and best equipped of all are those Christians, whatever their color, who dwell under tyranny and must read their Bibles only in secret.

Nevertheless, though it is not easy, it is essential for Christians to come to grips with apocalyptic, since there is so much of it in the Bible. It has its roots in the sufferings of the exile, for example, the Isaiah Apocalypse (Isaiah 24—27) and Ezekiel 38—39, but the chief flowering came in the midsecond century B.C. with the deliberate attempts of Antiochus IV to suppress Judaism. The Book of Daniel belongs to this period, though it is told in terms of the Persian empire much earlier. Apocalyptic became a fully developed literary movement between 100 B.C. and A.D. 100, when Roman control became more and more absolute. Christian apocalyptic is to be found in the Gospels (Matt. 24:4-36; Mark 13:3-37; Luke 21:8-36), in the epistles (2 Thess. 2:1-12; 2 Pet. 3:1-12), and supremely in the Book of Revelation, often called the Apocalypse of St. John the Divine. Irenaeus, writing in the second century, says that this was written about A.D. 95-96, near the end of the reign of Domitian, the sixth Roman emperor to be proclaimed a god.

The book opens with seven compelling letters to churches in western Asia Minor, and then develops a series of vivid, but often violent, visions in which there is war in heaven, and Satan, the anti-Christ, the vicious beast, is overthrown and Christ, the spotless lamb, is triumphant. The New Jerusalem comes down from heaven "prepared as a bride adorned for her husband." Though the cowardly and faithless will be cast into a fiery lake, God Himself will be with those who have stood firm. "He will wipe away every tear from their eyes, and death shall be no more, neither shall there be mourning nor crying nor pain any more, for the former things have passed away (Rev. 21:4; but see the whole chapter).

Early Christians, as well as later ones, have been disturbed by such imagery. Cyprian, Eusebius, and Luther are among the many who have not found such revelations revealing. Modern commentators often discover more value in the seven letters with which the book begins, warning Christians of all ages about false prophets in the churches, faithlessness within every Christian, and the violence from heaven that comes more to test the church than to punish the persecutors.[6] Nevertheless, there it is in the Bible, and to understand apocalyptic today we need to enter with great humility into the sufferings of the oppressed and tortured, to sit where they sit, and share their sense of helplessness, their desperate fear that

---

6. Miles Bourke, foreword to Paul Minear's *I Saw a New Earth* (Washington: Corpus, 1968), viii.

God has deserted them. What we must *not* do is to take the visions literally, to seek to identify particular tyrants with the beast, or to use the violent images as justification for our own violence and brutality against those we perceive to be evil. The whole purpose of apocalyptic is summed up in the valiant statement to Nebuchadnezzar in Dan. 3:16–17, "We have no need to answer you in this matter. If it be so, our God whom we serve is able to deliver us from the burning fiery furnace, and he will deliver us out of your hand, O king." Violent resistance is discouraged, for it would be only "a little help" (Dan. 11:34).

The Millennium

The term "millennium" is very loosely used in modern speech to mean a situation at the end of the world when all problems will be solved and everyone will be happy. This is very far from its original meaning, and from the discussions about the millennium which have so often exercised Christian thinkers. The concept occurs in only one place in the Bible, the twentieth chapter of Revelation. There the writer speaks of a thousand years during which "that ancient serpent, who is the Devil and Satan" (v. 2), will be imprisoned, and those Christians who have been put to death for their faith will come to life and reign with Christ. At the end of the thousand years Satan would be let loose again to ravage the earth, and there would be a great battle, in which he would be defeated and cast forever into the lake of fire. Then, and only then, would all the dead be raised to life and be judged "by what was written in the books, by what they had done" (v. 12). Those whose names could not be found in the Book of Life would be thrown into the lake of fire. Then at last will come "a new heaven and a new earth" and "death shall be no more" (21:1–4).

The question of how these thousand years should be interpreted has greatly troubled the minds of many in the Christian community, though it has been more persistent in the Western church than in the Eastern, which discourages speculation on the matter. Already in the Jewish community there was the idea of "the Sabbath of the Messiah," still to come in the future, which would last a thousand years.[7] Some of the early Christian Fathers, for example, Papias, Irenaeus, Tertullian, and Lactantius, accepted the principle of the Jewish interpretation and saw the seven days of creation as prefiguring the six millennia of world history, with the seventh day being the final millennium, during which Christ's reign will be

---

7. The concept of a thousand years started during the Persian empire, when Jewish scholars were trying to reconcile the six days of creation with Zoroastrian belief that the age of the earth is six thousand years. They did so by equating one day in God's sight with a thousand earthly years, on the basis of Ps. 90:4, the only psalm they believed to have been written by Moses.

established on earth. There were premillennialists, who argued that Christ would return to the earth before this last millennium, and postmillennialists, who believed that he would come at the end.

The millennialist fever was dampened already in the early church by the long delay of Christ's return in glory, and in the fourth century Augustine sought to settle the matter by saying that the dominion of Christ, the last epoch in human history, had already begun. Christ comes in glory every time the Lord's Supper is celebrated, and the kingdom is proclaimed by the reading of Scripture. The eternal Sabbath would come indeed, but would not be of this earth. God's rule and judgment operate, not only at that final day, but in every present moment.[8] In Augustine's day it was becoming more and more easy to identify the kingdom of God with the new Christian empire.

During the Reformation, and right up to the present time, the millennial hope has played a vigorous part in the thinking of many Protestant groups, especially in this country, and mainly among the more fundamentalist communities. It cannot, therefore, be neglected by those concerned with the faith of Christians. Yet the so-called mainline churches tend to discourage such inquiries as being divisive, and as leading to extravagant speculation, the "cunningly devised fables" against which Scripture warns us (2 Pet. 1:16; see also 1 Tim. 1:4; 4:7; 2 Tim. 4:4). We would probably be wise to be very cautious. All discussion about the future, even on the purely earthly level, is speculation. We can have no certainty at all about what the world will be like so soon as the year 2000, whether there will be war or peace, famine or plenty. If, then, we cannot predict earthly things, how can we dare to predict "the times and seasons which the Father has fixed by his own authority" (Acts 1:7)?

The Last Things

A popular cartoon shows a person saying, "Eternal Judgment, Hell, Death, Separation! That kind of religious talk scares me. Let's talk about Santa Claus, the Easter Bunny . . ." Difficult and frightening things do indeed come to mind when we begin to think about the fate of humanity, the end of our world, and the coming of the kingdom. They have all the terror, not only of the unknown, but of the unknowable. Yet the biblical images do not represent Christ only as the stern Judge, but also as Savior, and in this we should take comfort. "Fear not, little flock, for it is your Father's good pleasure to give you the kingdom" (Luke 12:32).

Traditionally, Christians have believed the last things to include the fol-

---

8. See additional notes.

lowing elements. First is death in this world, but, as we have seen in the chapter on resurrection (chapter 7), this is understood to be not the end but the entrance to a new condition, for the person is in no way destroyed by death. Together with death comes judgment. Traditional interpretations saw the particular judgment of the individual being repeated at the general judgment, the great assize on doomsday, when humanity will be judged as a whole. Then the sheep will be divided from the goats, the sheep to sit on the right hand of God, and the goats to be assigned to the left (Matt. 25:31–46). More horrific images developed in the Middle Ages, as in the *Dies Irae* of Thomas of Celano,

> Death and Nature shall stand stricken
> When the hollow bones shall quicken
> And the air with weeping thicken.

This was based upon the grim prophecy of Zephaniah:

> The great day of the LORD is near,
>   near and hastening fast.
>
> A day of wrath is that day,
>   a day of distress and anguish,
> a day of ruin and devastation,
>   a day of darkness and gloom.
>   Zephaniah 1:14–15

At the same judgment the powers that have resisted or opposed God will be finally overcome, ending the continued existence of rival and combating forces.

This final judgment will be preceded by the Parousia, the so-called Second Coming or Advent of Christ in glory (Matt. 10:23; 16:27ff.; 19:28; Acts 1:11; 2 Pet. 1:16; Rev. 1:4, 7). The term "second coming," however, suggests an absence of Christ from the world and his followers between the time of his ascension and his final enthronement, which Paul in Ephesians claims is not true, for he is even now reigning (Eph. 1:20).

Between the particular and the general judgment the person was believed to be in an intermediate state. Some have spoken of a soul sleep, others of the soul disappearing with the body and being created anew at the general resurrection, Jesus himself being the "first fruits" from among the dead.

> In a flash, at a trumpet crash,
> I am all at once what Christ is, since he is what I am, and
> This Jack, joke, poor potsherd, patch, matchwood, immortal
>   diamond,
> Is immortal diamond.
>   Gerard Manley Hopkins,
>   *That Nature Is a Heraclitean Fire*

After resurrection and judgment every human being will be either admitted to eternal life, to heaven, the celestial city and our true homeland, or condemned to damnation in hell, "where their worm does not die, and the fire is not quenched" (Mark 9:48).[9]

However, there are two problems about this traditional interpretation, even though it has solid biblical foundation. First, how could the loving and compassionate God permit such eternal punishment? Some have suggested that at the final judgment the evildoers will be simply annihilated, rather than suffer eternally, but this would suggest that there was no good in them at all, which is a very savage judgment. Others believe that salvation will be universal, even Satan being reconciled with God, since it is God's will that all be saved. But if even Satan is to be reconciled, then what advantage is it to refrain from evil now? Others still have argued that hell can be experienced already in life. Father Zosima said of it, "I maintain that it is the suffering of being unable to love."[10] But since it is clear that heaven can be experienced only partially on earth, why should hell be any different?

The other problem arises from what has been said earlier about time and eternity. Beyond death, beyond the realm of time and space, there is no before and after. The ancient and the medieval world could reasonably speak of individual judgment being followed by general judgment at a later date. We can no longer do so. Nor can we think of heaven and hell as places. We need, therefore, to be very cautious in our discussion of what, for the want of a better word, we still call "the hereafter." We clearly cannot achieve any kind of accuracy in our discussions of the end-time.

Justice, as far as we can understand it, requires punishment and reward; mercy requires forgiveness. We believe God to be eternally just and eternally merciful, and eternity to be other than time. Therefore, "eternal punishment" does not mean "everlasting punishment," nor does the time dimension have any existence in eternity. God does not have to wait until after the punishment is over to be merciful, nor does the person who is judged at death have to wait for a thousand years until the decision is repeated at the general judgment. In the consummate nowness of eternity there is no conflict. Punishment and complete forgiveness can occur at the self-same instant, and judgment, properly the assessment of our quality, never has to be done all over again. This is a mystery, and we shall not understand it until we ourselves are transferred from time to eternity.

---

9. Our English word "hell" comes from the North German *hel*, meaning "the realm of the dead."

10. Feodor Dostoyevski, *The Brothers Karamazov* (Chicago, 1932), 169.

The End-Time and Our Own Time

What if this present were the world's last night?
John Donne, *Holy Sonnets*.
Annunciation, 13.

At the beginning of this chapter it was pointed out that we are the first of all generations on the earth to have ready to hand the power to destroy all life, to condemn the earth to death. In the past it was only in visions that people could speak of fire "which fell on the earth; and a third of the earth was burnt up; and a third of the trees were burnt up; and all green grass was burnt up" (Rev. 8:7). Now we know that we ourselves could in fact bring it about, that the nuclear arsenals of the Soviet Union and the United States are already sufficient to surpass the apocalypse, and leave no shred of living tissue on the surface of the globe. And we are only at the beginning. At the time at which this book is being written less than forty years have elapsed since the first two atom bombs were dropped on Hiroshima and Nagasaki. Only two nations at present have this awesome power, and the other members of the nuclear club are still few. But who is to say how widespread nuclear weapons will be in the year 2000, less than twenty years from now, and whether nuclear power will still be restricted to governments, or whether it will have become available to resistance movements and terrorist groups?

Perhaps the most extraordinary feature of our present situation is the attitude of the churches, which is to say the attitude of Christian people. There have certainly been powerful voices urging the end of all nuclear weapons, and condemning their use in no uncertain terms. There have been determined efforts to prevent all use of nuclear power. What is extraordinary is not the lack of response, although in many areas this has been very small, but that the response has been so unbiblical. The use of this particular power is condemned, but without any recognition that *all* power belongs to God, and that men and women are answerable to God for any use that they make of power. Some Christians have even gone so far as to suggest that a nuclear holocaust would be a good thing, because it would hasten the end-time. Arrogance could scarcely go further. Of one thing we may be sure: those who take upon themselves to urge destruction of God's creation for the purpose of hastening salvation will not find themselves set at His right hand in the judgment.

What is so very unbiblical in the Western Christian attitude of today is the quite startling lack of humility and penitence. This is true of the whole range of Christian churches, from the Fundamentalist churches, which pride themselves on their increasing numbers, to the mainline churches which pride themselves on their status and superior scholarship. Personal penitence is certainly there, but corporate penitence hardly at all. As

Christian men and women look back on the last two hundred years, and the constantly increasing use and misuse of technical power, how very faintly indeed is heard the authentic biblical response:

> O Lord, the great and terrible God, who keepest covenant and steadfast love with those who love him and keep his commandments, we have sinned and done wrong and acted wickedly and rebelled, turning aside from thy commandments and ordinances; we have not listened to thy servants and prophets. . . . To thee, O Lord, belongs righteousness, but to us confusion of face, as at this day.
>
> Daniel 9:4-7[11]

A nuclear war on even a moderate scale would not merely kill immediately a fantastic number of people; it would condemn no less vast a number to a more prolonged and agonizing death; it would altogether disrupt the world's economy; and would attack in the womb the still unborn. And yet the United States has already declared publicly that in the event of Soviet penetration into the Persian Gulf it would be prepared to use nuclear weapons.

Yet, though the most immediately terrifying, nuclear warfare is only one of our present dangers. No less alarming is the possibility that we may be irreversibly disrupting and destroying our environment, that we may already have set in motion processes which are beyond our control. The climate of the entire globe takes its start from the equator, and the equatorial forests are essential to this process. Yet we have been destroying them wantonly, with no thought of the consequences. We do not as yet know what effect our modern industrial society is having on the ozone layer in the atmosphere, but we do know that serious disruption of it could render human life on this planet impossible. We do not know what to do with nuclear and other toxic waste, though it is constantly increasing and we know it to be deadly. We know that all forms of life on this planet are interrelated, and yet because of human misuse species are progressively disappearing.[12] We experiment with cloning, but we cannot foretell what it will lead to. We have no right to argue that in view of the nuclear danger our stewardship of the environment may now be abandoned for quick gains, since the end of the world is near. We have no right to use the biblical message as an excuse for playing God. On the contrary, it would be thoroughly biblical if our ultimate destruction were brought about, not by God's intervention, but by our own flagrant disobedience of His commandments and ordinances.

Constantly in the past, and again in the present, Christians have succumbed to identifying the kingdom beyond time and space with a particu-

---

11. See additional notes.

12. One contributor pointed out that species disappear constantly by the process of natural selection. However, modern human misuse of the environment has caused the rate of disappearance to go far beyond what is natural.

lar earthly dominion—the Holy Roman Empire, Holy Mother Russia, the Pax Britannica, or the Pilgrim Nation of America, "God's Own Country." The temptation to equate worldly majesty and might with divine approval is very strong, and from time to time nations have asserted a messianic role in the world. But this tends quickly to disintegrate into self-deception and arrogant destructiveness, as when the concept of the Millennial Kingdom of the Saints was used to justify the thousand-year *reich* of the Nazis. Nations and powerful political groups which use apocalyptic images are likely to find that "antichrist" or "Babylon" are more truly applied to themselves.

The signs and symbols provided in the Scriptures are ambiguous at best, and provide no blueprint for events in the days ahead. These writings of consolation addressed to the afflicted in the past may prove consoling to ourselves as well, because of their deep sense of humanity, and because we hear in our own day echoes of those ancient crises. The words of apocalyptic preachers were not spoken uncaringly over the heads of the audience. They summoned Christians then, as Christians now are summoned, to be ready at every moment to meet their Lord, to stand steadfast, hoping for him with the oldest of all Christian prayers: *Maranatha!* "Come, Lord Jesus!" (1 Cor. 16:22).

ADDITIONAL NOTES

5. The term "apocalyptic" has been used so widely by scholars that it is difficult, if not impossible, to define exactly to which books it rightly applies. However, there is general agreement that at least the following should be included: (1) in the Old Testament: Isaiah 24—27; Ezekiel 38—39; Daniel; Joel; Zechariah 9—14; (2) in the Apocrypha: 2 Esdras (in Roman Catholic Bibles 4 Ezra); (3) outside the Bible, such books as 1 Enoch, Jubilees, 2 Baruch, the Apocalypse of Paul, the War of the Sons of Light against the Sons of Darkness, etc. The New Testament apocalyptic writings are listed in the text.

The subject of apocalyptic and the apocalyptic books is excellently presented by D. S. Russell in two short books, *Between the Testaments* (Philadelphia: Fortress Press, 1960) and *The Jews from Alexander to Herod* (New York: Oxford University Press, 1967).

8. A more secular development of millennial ideas occurred during the Renaissance and the Reformation periods in Western Europe. This was the concept of "Utopia," i.e., "nowhere," a term invented by Thomas More. The idea developed in response to the discoveries, explorations, and settlements in the New World that were interpreted in terms of both the Garden of Eden and the World to Come. The great Utopia-makers, Thomas More himself, Thomas Müntzer, Thomaso Campanella (*City of the Sun*), Francis Bacon (*The New Atlantis*), Samuel Butler (*Erewhon*), and countless others during the last four centuries, blended elements of millenarian fervor with images of the terrestrial and celestial paradise to describe their ideal societies which challenged the corruption of the world around them.

Some were detailed and explicit in describing the perfect state, but others, such as Karl Marx with his concept of the future proletariat society, were silent about the exact dimensions of the world to come. Yet all these writings, as well as experiments in Utopian living, have deeply affected American society. Thoreau's Walden, Emerson's Brook Farm, the Shaker villages, and others as well, have their roots in Rev. 29:4–6, and the reign of saints in new-found harmony with God.

11. As far as we have been able to discover, none of the so-called mainline churches provide for the reading of this magnificent statement of national penitence (Dan. 9:3–19) at any time in the lectionary for the Sunday services of worship. The Roman Catholic lectionary for daily readings prescribes vv. 4–10 for Monday in the second week in Lent, and the Episcopal Church has vv. 4–10 in the second week in Lent every other year. The Presbyterian Church recommends the reading of the whole passage for certain "special occasions," such as times of national mourning. The neglect of so important a part of the Book of Daniel is a sad commentary on the apparent triumphalism and self-satisfaction in the churches of today.

13

CHRISTIAN WORSHIP

Religious worship is a universal phenomenon. As far back in human history as we can trace, men and women have brought offerings, as well as prayers and praises, to the divine. Even in the modern secularized world, with all its techniques of brainwashing and thought control, there is no country in which worship does not continue.

This is a fact, but not necessarily a good fact. Worship has often sanctified brutality and corruption, arrogance and complacency. There is an ancient and prolonged record of human sacrifice, drunken orgies, and wholly unrestrained sexual license, all done in the sanctuary and offered in adoration to the god or gods. There is, of course, a quite different aspect of human worship. It has been the greatest of all stimulants for human art and skill, to which Stonehenge, the Parthenon, the Dome of the Rock in Jerusalem, the Temple of Heavenly Peace in Peking, among a multitude of other shrines, all bear witness. At the other end of the scale it has the utmost simplicity—a lotus leaf offered to Krishna, the sign of the cross made by an unlettered peasant, the mezuzah on a Jewish threshold, the *kalima* whispered into the ear of a dying Muslim. Everything of which humanity is capable is gathered together in worship.

In this chapter our subject must be the worship done by Christians, which has its own special character, but we shall not understand it if we do not see it as part of the totality of human religious practice.

The word means literally "worth-ship," according full value to something or someone. For example, in the traditional Anglican wedding service the husband says to his bride, "With this ring I thee wed, with my body I thee worship, and with all my worldly goods I thee endow." In the modern world people worship all manner of things, national flags, wealth, obsessive loves, and even themselves. But primarily the word is kept for describing the human response to the presence and power of God. It is the glorification of God and the sanctification of man, whereby God is praised and human beings are endowed with holiness.

Throughout human history religion has provided the images, symbols, and rituals needed to express our experience of the sacred. And they are also the active process whereby we seek to express the meaning of meaning, the fundamental basis of all meaningfulness. They are central to the daily round of mundane activities, not marginal. To experience the sacred, the holy, the Absolutely Other, is to find the true heart of reality in an otherwise pathless and chaotic world. We live normally in what Mircea Eliade has called "profane time and space," in contrast to "sacred time" and "sacred space."[1] When we worship, when we approach the Absolutely Other, we enter the sacred and participate in eternity. Past and future become "now," so that at Christmas Christians proclaim, "Christ is born *today*," and at the Passover supper the Jewish father tells his children, "On *this night* the Holy One brought us out of Egypt." Not only time is annulled, but also space, and we are in the midst of all our fellow worshipers throughout the world. Even when alone in the desert the devout Muslim closes his devotions by turning his head to the right and the left, saying each time, *salaam 'aleikum*, "peace be upon you," to all Muslims everywhere, who join with him in worship.

The symbols and rites of worship mark both the daily round of ordinary life and also the moments of change and crisis, especially birth and death, easing us through these moments of drastic change. Therefore, worship is a vital activity, enabling each person to perceive how the world truly works, how society functions, and to plumb the deepest levels of his own consciousness.

Christian worship performs the same functions. The religious services for Christmas, Epiphany, Good Friday, Easter, and Pentecost each give shape and structure to critical moments of revelation in Christian experience. And every Sunday, most notably in the Eastern orthodox liturgy, the doors to the world are closed and the gate of heaven opened. Men and women then join in the eternal worship of the angels before the face of Almighty God.

The distinctive feature of Christian worship is the relationship to God as Father, Son, and Holy Spirit. It is the response to God's revelation of Himself in Jesus Christ, and the power of the Spirit to bestow new life. Obedient to Jesus, and empowered by the Spirit, Christians, alone among the monotheists, venture to address the transcendent God as "Father." This has profound implications. Christians do not worship an unknown God, but "God in man made manifest," to whom they can both listen and speak. Their worship, therefore, centers in the active power of the divine

---

1. Marcea Eliade, *The Sacred and Profane: The Nature of Religion*, trans. Willard R. Trask (New York: Harcourt Brace Jovanovich, 1959).

"word," both in the reading of the Bible and in the reenactment of the Last Supper. The "word" is both the medium and the message. What is said in the Scriptures and done in the Son, is in worship returned to the Father, through Jesus Christ and the power of the Holy Spirit. So God is active, giving power to both the message and the response. His word does not return to Him empty, but accomplishes His purpose, and prospers in the work for which He sends it (Isa. 55:11).

> We can never have too big a conception of God, and the more scientific knowledge (in whatever field) advances, the greater becomes our idea of His vast and complicated wisdom. Yet, unless we are to remain befogged and bewildered, and give up all hope of ever knowing God as a Person, we have to accept his own planned focusing of Himself in a Human Being, Jesus Christ. If we accept this as fact, as *the* Fact of history, it becomes possible to find a satisfactory and comprehensive answer to a great many problems, and, what is equally important, a reasonable "shelf" on which the unsolved perplexities may be left with every confidence.[2]

Worship is a history lesson. It is a faithful remembering, meditating on, and reenacting the past. "This do in remembrance of me," said Jesus at the Last Supper, when he broke the bread and gave the wine (Luke 22:19–20; see 1 Cor. 11:24–25). The biblical word is *anamnesis* (the opposite of amnesia), the never forgetting of the whole process of salvation from sin, death, and ignorance. Remembering Jesus and all that he did is not the same as remembering Caesar or Napoleon in our studies. The worshiper does not merely repeat the events of Jesus' life; he or she is genuinely present, and participates in his ministry, suffering, death, and resurrection. "Were you there when they crucified my Lord?"

By so doing Christians gain a new understanding of their identity. They are taught to welcome the revealed Word of God, to make it known, and indeed to *be* that Word, proclaiming it not only with their lips, but in their lives.

> For central as is the relationship between the separate individual and God, each man needs an experience of life in the great family of God if he is to grow to understand the real nature of that love and the real character of his response to that love, to say nothing of growing to understand and to live creatively with his fellows.[3]

Therefore, Christian worship is not only a matter of prayer, praise, and remembering this history of our salvation. It involves also repentance, change, judgment, and putting on a new life. Confronted not only by God, but by ourselves in relation to God, we seek completeness, holiness, and salvation.

---

2. J. B. Phillips, *Your God Is Too Small* (New York: Macmillan Co., 1960), 135–6.

3. Douglas Steere, *Prayer and Worship* (New York: Association Press, 1952), 36–37.

Christian worship, no less than Christian life, is primarily communal. "Where two or three are gathered in my name, there am I in the midst of them" (Matt. 18:20). In worship we are together with Christ, who gave his life "for many," who preached to the multitudes, and taught his disciples to be self-sacrificing pastors of his flock. Certainly, we need also to pray in private. "Go into your room and shut the door and pray to your Father who is in secret" (Matt. 6:6). But prayer is never solitary. Even alone, a Christian begins with the words "Our Father," and often ends a prayer by saying, "We ask this through Jesus Christ our Lord, Amen." The words of prayer are powerless if they are not joined to the Word of God, and it is in the church, the congregation, the community of the faithful, that the unity of the Word is most visibly present in Scripture, preaching, sacraments, and people. In worship one encounters God, but also other people, one's neighbors and companions, those friends with whom one breaks bread.[4]

The Worship of Israel

Christian worship developed out of the worship of Israel. Its foundation was the Last Supper of the disciples with Jesus, and this had taken place "on the first day of Unleavened Bread, when they sacrificed the Passover lamb" (Mark 14:12, 22–25; 1 Cor. 11:23–6). At the Passover feast the blood of the slain lamb anointed the doorposts of Jewish houses, saving their firstborn from the angel of death (Exod. 12:1–28). These words and symbols opened new levels of understanding for Christians, as they struggled to comprehend to the full Jesus, the Lamb of God slain to take away the sin of the world. In sharing together this Christian Passover they participated in Jesus' sacrifice, and partook of its saving effect. So too, the crossing of the Red Sea was for them a foreshadowing of baptism. By passing through the water the pilgrim Christian moved from the bondage of sin to the land of safety. Now, with his fellow Christians, he could eat the manna, the "bread from heaven" (John 6:30–35; 1 Cor. 10:1–5, 16).

Israel had sought by various means, in sacred word and ritual acts, to sanctify life, time, and space in response to God. Ordinary, everyday activities became profound symbols of the divine. The three feasts of Passover, Weeks (Pentecost), and Booths (Tabernacles) sanctified seedtime and harvest, and all the laborer's toil. They looked back to Creation and the Exodus, and forward to the great "Day of the Lord," when Elijah would come again. The Sabbath rest and the Temple, the visible shrine of God's presence, sanctified time and space. The ritual acts of circumcision and bar mitzvah made the young boy a true son of the covenant, and

---

4. "Companion" comes from *panis*, the Latin word for "bread."

a full member of the worshiping community. By pilgrimage also men and women were bound together in fellowship.

> I rejoiced when they said to me,
> "Let us go to the house of the Lord."
> Now we stand within your gates.
> O Jerusalem:
> Jerusalem that is built to be a city
>   where people come together in unity;
> to which the tribes resort, the tribes of the Lord,
>   to give thanks to the Lord himself,
>   the bounden duty of Israel.
>   Psalm 122:1–4 NEB

But there were also those spokesmen for the Lord who questioned the sincerity of such worship, and even described it as sinful (Amos 4:4–5). They demanded interior conversion, saying, "Get yourselves a new heart and a new spirit" (Ezek. 18:31). Yet it was not a question of either/or, but one of both/and.

> For thou hast no delight in sacrifice;
>   were I to give a burnt offering.
>   thou wouldst not be pleased.
> The sacrifice acceptable to God is a broken spirit,
>   a broken and contrite heart, O God,
>   thou wilt not despise.
> Do good to Zion in thy good pleasure;
>   rebuild the walls of Jerusalem,
> then wilt thou delight in right sacrifices.
>   Psalm 51:16–19

In ancient Israel the experience of God, whether by one or by many, meant the delivery of a special saving word to the whole people, a revelation linked to the life and fate of the community, remembered and repeated by them in their worship, even when they were words of judgment and doom.

When the Israelite prophets spoke of the proper responses to divine revelation, they struck themes that reappeared in the teaching of Jesus. How can people say that they worship God, the source of life, if they do not love and care for those who lack life's bare necessities, the helpless widows and orphans? There is no true worship where the poor are oppressed and the covenant is not kept. So it is also in the New Testament. "If you are offering your gift at the altar, and there remember that your brother has something against you, leave your gift there before the altar and go; first be reconciled to your brother, and then come and offer your gift" (Matt. 5:23–4). Worship, therefore, does not end when people leave the sanctuary, nor does it even begin there. God is everywhere, and especially does he watch over the starving and the victims of injustice. Worship and ministry are therefore not separate. Both are rightly described as "service," and only together are they the faithful response to God.

Jesus, Prayer, and
Christian Worship

Jesus regularly took part in the worship of his day, and he understood his own ministry in terms of that worship.

> Jesus came to Nazareth, where he had been brought up; and he went to the synagogue, as his custom was, on the sabbath day. And he stood up to read; and there was given to him the book of the prophet Isaiah. He opened the book and found the place where it is written,
> "The Spirit of the Lord is upon me,
> because he has anointed me to preach
>   good news to the poor,
> He has sent me to proclaim release
>   to the captives,
> and to set at liberty those who are oppressed.
>   Luke 4:16–18

"Today," he said, "this scripture has been fulfilled in your hearing" (4:21).

Constant prayer was the essence of Jesus' life, the means whereby he maintained his close relation with the Father. It was in solitary prayer that his day began (Mark 1:35), and when the crowds pressed upon him he would go alone into the wilderness or on the hills to pray (Matt. 14:23; Mark 6:46; Luke 5:16). By this quiet communication with God he was refreshed and strengthened in the great crises of his life: at his baptism (Luke 3:21), his choice of the twelve apostles (Luke 6:12–13), the recognition by Peter that he was the Messiah (Luke 9:18–22), the transfiguration (Luke 9:28ff.), and supremely during his agony in Gethsemane (Matt. 26:39–44; Mark 14:35; Luke 22:39–46). He urged his disciples to pray continually lest they should succumb to temptation (Mark 14:38) and become fainthearted (Luke 18:1ff.).

An important part of his ministry was teaching people how to pray, how to speak in response to God's action in their lives. In his parables he urged them to persevere in their prayers, like the unexpected and unwelcome guest knocking on the neighbor's door in the middle of the night (Luke 11:5–8), and to be always humble and penitent, like the despised publican, rather than the arrogant and self-assured Pharisee (Luke 18:9–14). When St. Benedict in the sixth century composed his rule for religious communities, he adopted this view of prayer, saying that it should be frequent, humble, devout, and brief.[5]

---

5. *Rule of Benedict*, chap. 20.

From the teachings of Jesus, and notably the Lord's Prayer, used by all Christians, we learn that prayer is speaking to God, not a speech about God or a compendium of proper beliefs. It includes asking for our primary day-to-day needs, for food and freedom, whether from sin or from debts of any kind, no less than the obviously religious need of fulfilling the will of God. Famine and the tax collector are just as much the concern of the Christian as is the devil.

Christian worship goes beyond prayer. It includes sacred ceremony or *sacrament*, the "outward and visible sign of an inward and spiritual grace given unto us, ordained by Christ himself, as a means whereby we receive the same, and a pledge to assure us thereof."[6] The direct command of Jesus to baptize all nations (Matt. 28:19) gave new meaning to the ritual washings that were common in both Jewish and pagan communities. Baptism became the means of a completely new start, the making of new men and women in Christ. So too the celebration of the Lord's Supper, the Eucharist (thanksgiving) or Holy Communion, was enjoined on Christians everywhere by Jesus' simple imperative, "Do this in remembrance of me."[7]

Ideally, the fullness of prayer life and worship encompasses the whole of Christian action and ministry. Paul expressed this when he contrasted the Jewish and the Christian understanding of God's Temple as a place of prayer and worship, God Himself dwelling in the Holy of Holies. But through the work of Christ the new Temple, the new place of His indwelling, became the individual Christian and the corporate body of Christ (Eph. 2:20–22). The Christian life, therefore, ministry and all its activities, became also prayer and worship. Christians are to offer their bodies as a living sacrifice, holy and acceptable to God (Rom. 12:1). Their whole life is to be a prayer. Most simply is it said in St. Benedict's humble words, *Laborare est orare* (To work is to pray).

Christian Worship in the
Modern World

Nearly two millennia have gone by since the first baptisms and the first celebration of the Lord's Supper. The Christian church has spread throughout the world, and its worship is continuous.

> As o'er each continent and island
> The dawn leads on another day,
> The voice of prayer is never silent,
> Nor dies the strain of praise away.
> John Ellerton, 1870

---

6. Anglican *Book of Common Prayer*, The Catechism.

7. See additional notes.

There are now many churches and sects, and changes are taking place before our very eyes. The center of gravity is shifting away from us, and it is probable that in less than twenty years' time the majority of all Christians in the world will be black. There is consequently an immense variety of worship. The Ethiopian Church celebrates the Eucharist with dances and drums, and the Society of Friends sit in silence, dispensing with sacrament altogether and awaiting the guidance of the Spirit before they speak. In the heart of Africa Christians seek to relate their worship to their own cultural heritage.[8]

All Christian communities use rites and signs, because it is by doing things in common that we maintain community. Some Christian traditions maintain a strongly formal worship, but even those who decry ritualism and formality develop their own patterns of regular worship. This is inevitable. The worshipers need to feel at home. Sacramental actions, including, of course, the two major sacraments of Baptism and Eucharist, are the focal point of Christian worship, actions that touch the lives of the members at crucial moments, strengthening them by the rites of passage. Those Christians in Germany who sang Martin Luther's hymn, *Ein Feste Burg Ist Unser Gott,*[9] in defiance of Hitler's tyranny were no less performing a sacramental act than was the Archbishop of Canterbury when in the same period he crowned King George VI of England, or the Pope celebrating Mass in St. Peter's in Rome. The army padre secretly administering rice and water in place of bread and wine to prisoners in a Japanese military camp in World War II was doing the same. Theologians may write or debate, but it is by observing Christians as they pray and minister that one can judge if the word that is preached is truly the Living Word. "You shall know them by their fruits" (Matt. 7:16).

Inevitably Christian worship and ministry develop and change to meet new demands and address new questions. From within itself the Christian community makes the necessary arrangements to provide a fit and proper ministry, called from its own ranks by God. But the tendency has too often been to look at worship and ministry from within one's own particular church or communal tradition, and to see this alone as the realm of the sacred amid a profane world. But Christians do their community a disservice if they totally exclude the "psalms and hymns of praise" that have fortified countless other Christians. Every Christian is heir to the whole of Christian tradition—the Orthodox liturgy, Wesley's Methodist hymns, Bach's Lutheran Masses, Cranmer's prayers, and the sermons of Martin Luther King, to name only a small fraction.

Worship too easily becomes compartmentalized, merely what an

---

8. A good example of this is the Church of Christ on Earth by the Prophet Simon Kimbangu, which has about five million adherents and maintains itself from its own resources, without foreign help.

9. "A Mighty Fortress Is Our God."

approved Christian does on Sunday in a mainline church. Therefore, we urgently need the rebuke of the charismatic storefront churches. It can also degenerate into preaching from the Bible and administering the sacraments within a church building, altogether separate from the cries and hunger of the world. Mere attendance at church does not make Christians. Yet clothing the naked and feeding the starving, urgent and primary though this is, does not satisfy all their needs. There must also be a saving word for their troubled spirits.

The world of the late twentieth century is so very different from the world of the first century, when Christian worship began, or the medieval period when the great cathedrals were built, that we have difficulty in knowing just how we should worship today. Some say that we should maintain unbroken the great heritage of the past, others that modern worship requires modern language and modern images. Both are almost certainly right, but how are they to be reconciled? To cling to an unchanging past is to deny the Creator, but to reject the past is to deny God's mighty acts in history. The adherents of both positions are apt to make absolute statements, and to be scornful of those who do not accept them. What then are we to do?

The problem is so complex that we obviously cannot propose solutions, but we can suggest some principles. Certainly, however we shape modern worship and liturgy, all must be done in love and charity. This has often been lacking, and the unity and fellowship of Christ's church have suffered in consequence. New liturgies and revised prayer books have caused splinter groups to break away from both the Roman Catholic and the Episcopal churches, but expressions of grief have been few. We should be prepared to be a great deal more patient, allowing, and even encouraging, experiment, but also cherishing what we have inherited from those who have gone before us.

We must beware of familiarity, and yet not despise it. Familiar words and actions, and familiar tunes to sing, enable worshipers to feel at home in the house of God, and are therefore very necessary. Yet they can easily lull us into comfort and complacency, so that we ask no questions about what we are doing. We should probably beware of "experts." Of course, we should respect, and listen carefully to, the scholars in any field of study, but they are apt to dictate to the churches. That certain actions were performed in worship by early Christians does not make them automatically right, nor are certain kinds of music more right and holy than others. It has been caustically said, and with some measure of truth, that "some organists would rather go to the penitentiary than play hymn tunes written in the nineteenth century," for they reject them as both sentimental and musically inferior. Admittedly, we should always try to offer the best to God, but excellence is not the only criterion. Honesty and sincerity are no less necessary. Sentiment is an essential feature of human relationship, although not the most profound or noble. Inferior, apparently tawdry, offerings to God, made in all sincerity, are acceptable in His eyes, and should not be despised by those who claim to know better.

Finally on this subject, we should be very cautious about ordering our patterns of worship by majority opinion. We too easily imagine that we can resolve our disputes by putting the question to a vote. But all voting involves division, and leaves many unhappy and dissatisfied—a very shaky foundation for the worship of Almighty God. Moreover, the history of the church provides us with no evidence at all that the majority is necessarily right. Indeed, if the majority had been right in the mid-first century A.D., there would be today no church at all.

But what of private, individual worship, when a Christian goes into his or her room and shuts the door? It is enjoined in the Sermon on the Mount, and, as we have seen, was the common practice of Jesus himself. It is no less necessary to Christian life than corporate worship. Yet it also has become a great deal more difficult in the modern world. It is not that Christians are persecuted in the West, or in a great many other countries, though they certainly are in some. The problem might be indeed easier to resolve under persecution, for then we should be driven to pray in secret, and our sufferings would compel us to seek strength from God.

No, the problem is that modern life provides no place for private prayer and gives it no encouragement. In the past, in all the so-called Christian countries society acknowledged the necessity of prayer and respected the prayerful. Today the personal Christian life has been rendered more difficult, not because it is forbidden, but because it is increasingly a misfit. There is no common assumption, as there was in the past, that people *need* to pray.

Curiously, also, many churches today accept this situation and give little encouragement and little instruction in private prayer. There are, of course, notable and important exceptions to this generalization, but it remains true that the individual Christian is today strangely lonely from Monday to Saturday. He or she knows quite well that a Christian ought to pray every day, to read the Bible, and to meditate on its teaching, but has very often only the vaguest idea of how to set about doing it. We shall have to consider this question more carefully in the final chapter. For the moment we can do no more than bring it into the open.

ADDITIONAL NOTES

7. Gregory Dix, in his book *The Shape of the Liturgy* (London: Dacre Press, 1970), 744, has a magnificent passage about the celebration of the Lord's Supper:

Was ever another command so obeyed? For century after century, spreading slowly to every continent and country and among every race on earth, this action has been done, in every conceivable human circumstance, for every conceivable human need from infancy and before it to extreme old age and after it, from the pinnacles of earthly greatness to the refuge of fugitives in the caves and dens of the earth. Men have found no better thing than this to do for kings at their crowning and for criminals going to the scaffold; for armies in triumph or for a bride and bridegroom in a little country church; for the proclamation of a dogma or for a good crop of wheat; for the wisdom of the Parliament of a mighty nation or for a sick old woman afraid to die; for a school boy sitting an examination or for Columbus setting out to discover America; for the famine of whole provinces or for the soul of a dead lover; in thankfulness because my father did not die of pneumonia; for a village headman much tempted to return to fetich because the yams had failed; because the Turk was at the gates of Vienna; for the repentance of Margaret; for the settlement of a strike; for a son for a barren woman; for Captain so-and-so, wounded and prisoner of war; while the lions roared in the nearby amphitheatre; on the beach at Dunkirk; while the hiss of scythes in the thick June grass came faintly through the windows of the church; tremulously, by an old monk on the fiftieth anniversary of his vows; furtively, by an exiled bishop who had hewn timber all day in a prison camp near Murmansk; gorgeously, for the canonisation of S. Joan of Arc—one could fill many pages with the reasons why men have done this, and not tell a hundredth part of them. And best of all, week by week and month by month, on a hundred thousand successive Sundays, faithfully, unfailingly, across all the parishes of christendom, the pastors have done this just to make the *plebs sancta Dei*—the holy common people of God.

14

THE MISSIONARY IMPERATIVE

Go therefore and make disciples of all nations, baptizing them in the name of the Father and of the Son and of the Holy Ghost, teaching them to observe all that I have commanded you; and lo, I am with you always, to the close of the age.

Matthew 28:19–20

Then he opened their minds to understand the scriptures, and said to them, "Thus it is written, that the Christ should suffer and on the third day rise from the dead, and that repentance and forgiveness of sins should be preached in his name to all nations, beginning from Jerusalem.

Luke 24:45–47

Necessity is laid upon me. Woe to me if I do not preach the Gospel!

1 Corinthians 9:16

The Necessity of Mission[1]

It is evident from these, and many other, passages in the New Testament that the command to proclaim the good news of salvation through Jesus Christ, and to turn men and women from "vain things to a living God who made the heaven and earth and the sea and all that is in them" (Acts 14:15), is in the Bible an absolute command. There is no hint of a suggestion that the message could be modified, or toned down to suit the culture and outlook of the hearers.

Although the great missionary enthusiasm became evident only after the death and resurrection of Jesus, the absolute command was already there, firmly established in Torah and the prophetic teaching. The Jewish people had been summoned to be "a light to the nations," that the salvation of God might "reach to the end of the earth" (Isa. 49:6). They had long maintained, as did Paul, that "although there may be so-called gods in

---

1. See additional notes.

181

heaven and earth—as indeed there are many 'gods' and many 'lords'—yet for us there is one God, the Father, from whom are all things, and for whom we exist" (1 Cor. 8:5–6). Paul, it is true, added the words, "and one Lord, Jesus Christ, through whom are all things and through whom we exist," but though this deepened the message, it did not change its significance, or make it any less universal.

Upon this basic and primary conviction the Christian church, though sadly rent asunder, has been solidly established, and has spread to every country in the world. This missionary outreach began only a few weeks after the resurrection of Jesus, and is still at work today. Yet its great development in the modern world, from the late eighteenth to the early twentieth centuries, has been little noticed by historians. The first edition of the multivolume *Cambridge Modern History* has in its index only one entry under "missionary," and that is the battle of Missionary Ridge in the Civil War.[2] Church historians have, of course, had more to say, but they tend to overplay the good aspects, soft-pedaling the bad, and to neglect, sometimes completely, the tremendous missionary outreach of the Eastern Orthodox churches in Asia.

The effects of this missionary drive have been stupendous, and have largely determined the character of the modern world. In every developing country what we would term modern education, modern health care, and modern social work were initiated by Christian missionaries. The state took over later. We must, however, not exaggerate or be misled. All the world's great civilizations, in India, the Far East, and the Muslim world, have a history of education, care for the sick, and food and shelter for the destitute. The oldest university in the world is al-Azhar in Cairo. China has a long tradition of medical care, whose significance the West is only now beginning to recognize. In Buddhist India under the Emperor Asoka there were hospitals, not only for people, but also for animals.

Christians must always beware of saying, in defense of the faith, that Christian charity surpasses that of others, a claim too often made, but nothing less than arrogant. They have no monopoly on lovingkindness, nor can it be shown that they have excelled in it. Nevertheless, in one area Christians have indeed taken the lead: dedicated service to the suffering and desolate in lands far distant from their own. Only Christians have gone to live among lepers.[3] In obedience to Christ, they went in the first place to proclaim the gospel, the good news about Jesus. But wherever they found suffering, ignorance, or need, the Holy Spirit used them for healing, comfort, and the spread of knowledge. Out of this service devel-

---

2. The second edition, however, pays more attention to the subject although the treatment is still somewhat inadequate.

3. As late as 1950 the only center in France for the treatment of leprosy (properly today called Hansen's disease) was run by the French Protestant Church.

oped the schools and universities, the hospitals and village clinics, the social services, which in most countries have now been taken over and developed by the state.

It is an impressive record, but no cause for boasting, since it has also a very ugly side. The undeniable self-sacrifice and readiness to share in Christ's sufferings are balanced by no less evident arrogance, blindness, and selfishness. Probably the worst feature was the inability of even the most dedicated to escape from the confines of their own culture, and the failure to recognize that they, who had come to save others, were themselves imprisoned. It was British, French, German, American, and Russian education that was carried to foreign lands, because the missionaries themselves knew no other. Children in British missionary schools studied British history; in French schools they spoke of France as *notre mère*, "our mother," and even obediently repeated the absurd statement, "Our ancestors, the Gauls"; in American schools they no less obediently revered American democracy. In World War I little children in China were urged to take sides in a conflict whose center was halfway across the globe.[4]

Together with this wholesale transfer of foreign cultures came also the unhappy divisions of the Christian church. During all the nineteenth century and much of the twentieth, division, suspicion, and jealousy between different mission stations were common, though fortunately by no means universal. Converts were baptized into different churches, learned different rituals, and acquired different identities, so that in the same small town one person might say, "I am a Southern Baptist," while another replied, "I am a Swedish Lutheran." There were certainly efforts to overcome this, and under the principle of comity churches agreed not to poach on each other's territory. But this did not remove the division. Those in northern Iran who were converted became Presbyterians, while those in the south became Anglicans.

Another great weakness, indeed a sin, of missionaries was their paternalism. They were willing everywhere to serve the local people as doctors, nurses, and teachers, but they had no intention of serving under them. They taught them to be teachers, doctors, and nurses themselves, but they did not grant them full control or appoint them to top positions. They did not trust them as far as that, and this has caused much resentment.[5]

Finally, much missionary work was marred by pride and self-

---

4. There is a moving portrayal of this in A. J. Cronin's novel, *The Keys of the Kingdom* (Boston: Little, Brown, and Co., 1941).

5. The great and dedicated missionary Albert Schweitzer, so much venerated in the West, who devoted his whole life, without thought of self, to the hospital at Lambarené in what is now the country of Gabon, has been much criticized by Africans for his constant paternalism.

satisfaction, the constant penalty of great achievements. The great temptation of those who have set high standards for themselves is to be betrayed by the very excellence of their intentions, and to "trust in themselves that they are righteous and despise others" (Luke 18:9). The good is always the enemy of the best, and many missionaries were quite incapable of perceiving their mistakes and weaknesses, and so saw no necessity for improvement.

The Winds of Change

The first half of this century has seen great changes in the missionary outreach and the attitude to other religious cultures. The traditional evangelism is by no means ended, as is clearly shown by the work of Billy Graham and others. Also, missionary self-satisfaction may have reached its height in the first third of the century, a religious parallel to the widespread belief in human progress. Yet new and serious questions were beginning to be asked, questions of great importance for Christians today.

The first concerned the scandal of church disunity. How could a church divided against itself bear true witness to the *one* God and Father, and the *one* Lord and Savior, Jesus Christ? A second question was that of divine revelation. Were Christians justified in believing, as they had always done, that the truth about God had been revealed to Christians only, while those outside were pagans dwelling in darkness? A third question concerned the function of missionaries in relation to the now vast numbers of people who had renounced past beliefs and been baptized into the Christian faith. Did these people still need spiritual guidance and material help from those who had converted them?[6]

Christian disunity and its consequences were first discussed on an international scale at an important missionary conference held at Edinburgh, Scotland in 1910. As a result of this the International Missionary Council was formed a few years later, and then, very shortly after World War I, two other international and interchurch groups: the Faith and Order movement, and the Life and Work movement. In 1948 these united to form the World Council of Churches. The World Student Christian Federation also played an important part, not least in helping to maintain communication throughout World War II between churches in Germany and occupied countries with churches in the Allied Nations at war with Germany.

The second question, that of divine revelation, dominated the World Missionary Conference held at Tambaram, Ceylon (now Sri Lanka) in

---

6. In early 1945, at a conference in Jerusalem attended by missionaries from a number of Middle Eastern countries, one of the delegates ventured to say, "Conditions will be very different after the war; we must prepare our own departure." The other missionaries united in rejecting this. "What a pessimistic outlook!" they said, "Of course we shall always be needed."

1938, when for the first time delegates from the "younger churches"[7] out-numbered Western missionaries. The purpose of the conference was to "state the fundamental position of the Christian church as a witness-bearing body in the modern world, relating this to different conflicting views of the attitude to be taken by Christians towards other faiths, and dealing in detail with the evangelistic approach to the great non-Christian faiths."[8] A profound and scholarly book was written in advance by Hendrik Kraemer of the Netherlands, a very experienced missionary with considerable knowledge of the other great religions.[9] In it he adopted the position of Karl Barth: that Christianity is the one true faith, and that other religions, whatever their merits, are therefore false. He wrote, "The missionary is a revolutionary and he has to be so, for to preach and plant Christianity means to make a frontal attack on the beliefs, the customs, the apprehensions of life and the world, and by implication (because tribal religions are primarily social realities) on the social structures and bases of primitive society. . . . Missions . . . imply the well considered appeal to all peoples to transplant and transfer their life-foundations into a totally different spiritual soil, and so they must be revolutionary."[10]

The book was much debated at the conference, and the majority took Dr. Kraemer to task for his absolutism, which, they said, their own experience did not support. They urged a more tolerant view of other religions, primitive or advanced, arguing that Christianity could claim no monopoly on spiritual truth.

The third question came to a head at the next World Missionary Conference, held at Whitby, Ontario, in 1947. Many delegates were profoundly conscious of imperialism, both Western and Japanese,[11] and feelings ran high. The issue seemed so delicate that the missionaries and delegates from the younger churches agreed to meet separately, so that all might express their views freely without fear or favor. When the two reports were presented to the whole conference, they were found to be in close agreement, recommending strongly that the time had come for full independence from Western tutelage. The delegates were amazed and interrupted their discussion to sing the doxology, in thanksgiving for this manifestation of the Holy Spirit powerfully at work in their midst.

These conferences were all markedly Protestant, though not completely

---

7. I.e., the churches in Asia, Africa, and the Pacific, which had come into existence as a result of Western missionary efforts.

8. Minutes of the *Ad Interim* Committee of the I.M.C., Old Jordans, 1936.

9. Hendrik Kraemer, *The Christian Message in the Non-Christian World* (1938; reprint, Grand Rapids: Kreger Publications, 1963).

10. Ibid., 342. See also additional notes.

11. Many churches represented had suffered severely from Japanese expansionism before and during World War II.

so. Missionary activity by the Russian Orthodox Church had, of course, been abruptly halted by the communist revolution in 1917, but other Orthodox churches were deeply concerned, since many of them existed within the Muslim world, which does not permit proselytizing. The ancient Mar Thoma Church in western India, which claims descent from the apostle Thomas, contributed much to the discussions. Roman Catholics were also deeply interested and kept in close touch, though they could be present only as observers. Vatican II has opened all three questions to an even wider debate in Roman Catholic circles.

Christians and Other Religions in the Late Twentieth Century

Then slowly answered Arthur from the barge,
  "The old order changeth, yielding place to new,
And God fulfills himself in many ways,
Lest one good custom should corrupt the world."
                                              Tennyson,
                                The Idylls of the King:
                          The Passing of Arthur, 407–10

That the old order is changing with incontinent speed is beyond all question. The urgent problem facing Christians, remembering their long history of missionary endeavor, and also confronting their task in the present world, is this: How is the unalterable truth to be proclaimed in a rapidly altering world? What indeed is the gospel, and what merely our interpretation, colored by our own cultural thinking? Within the limits of this chapter we can make no more than suggestions for discussion and debate. Not all will agree with them, and some will be strongly opposed. Many may consider the questions themselves unnecessary, for the answers are there already in the Bible, and, however changing the world, the biblical message is not subject to change.[12]

Our situation today is, in one important sense, strikingly different from that of the early missionaries, about whom we read in the Book of Acts. They nowhere encountered what we call "world religions." But we must take them with utmost seriousness, for the continents are today so closely interlocked, politically, economically, and technologically, that we cannot escape the question of their cultural and religious relationship. Here the New Testament gives us no *direct* answers. We must read between the lines and frame our answers according to the profound spirit, rather than the letter, of Scripture.

---

12. One contributor commented, "This is absurd! Any work, particularly the Bible, is not straightforward, and is always open to interpretation for the thinking mind." Nevertheless, there are people who think along these lines.

As we survey the great religions of the world, clearly so satisfying to their adherents, we cannot help but ask, Do the Scriptures and the Christian faith contain everything necessary for salvation? Are these alone adequate for humankind? The answer seems to be both yes and no. It is firmly yes because centuries of Christian experience have demonstrated the absolute validity of Christ's death and resurrection and the infinite power of the Spirit. The men and women who accept these wholeheartedly have no need to search for other gods. But it is also no because the many millions of people who know nothing of Christ are nonetheless created by God, and are His children. It is sheer impossibility that He should have neglected them throughout these same long centuries, and have granted them no light in the darkness. It is also no because our present encounter with beliefs so different from our own is a major event in history and, as we have seen, in every historical event we are confronted directly by God. To Him we must answer.[13]

To take but one example, Islam has been for fourteen centuries of all religions the most resistant to the Christian message. Christians would be wrong to close their eyes and call this invincible ignorance. They should rather ask God, What are You teaching us? What new revelation is enshrined in this intransigence? What repentance are You demanding?

The answer could well be: You have treated me lightly. I made Myself known to you, but you have quarreled bitterly among yourselves about My nature. You have sought to define Me exactly, and have portrayed Me in pictures and images. You have burnt at the stake men and women who defined Me differently. You have acted in My name as if you were the masters. Therefore, I have raised up, and maintained, a people who bear witness five times a day that I am One, and that I am Eternal, dwelling in light unapproachable, and altogether beyond any human definition. Perhaps this is not the answer, for we are only at the threshold of knowing how to respond, but it is not impossible that this is what we should confess.

As we have seen in earlier chapters, there are for Christians certain constants which cannot be surrendered or denied. They include at the very least the following: creation, incarnation, resurrection, salvation, the gift of the Spirit, and the last judgment. Upon such solid foundation stones the entire Christian experience and teaching are built. But Christians should remind themselves that they experience all these things in time, and therefore in finite terms, whereas for God they are timeless and eternal. He is constantly, unwaveringly, and eternally the Creator, the Savior, the life-giving Spirit, and the Judge. Christians, with excellent reason, have seen in Jesus of Nazareth the climactic example of incarnation,

---

13. See additional notes.

crucifixion, and resurrection, but they commit a grievous mistake if they claim these as a Christian prerogative.

There cannot be another Jesus of Nazareth, and so there can never be another crucifixion of Jesus nor a resurrection of Jesus. "We know that Christ being raised from the dead will never die again" (Rom. 6:9). But this has not terminated either crucifixion or resurrection, and therefore incarnation is not terminated, though it cannot happen again in that particular form.

If we ask ourselves, Has God been, or can He be, incarnate in other religious traditions? the answer is, He must be! "No one has ever seen God" (John 1:18), nor can He be perceived directly by any human being. All that He does or says must have human form, must take definite shape inside the cultural framework that human beings inhabit. God, if He is to be known at all, must become visible or audible in human behavior, human words, books written by human beings, and so on. All divine activity must have human shape or it would not be perceived at all. Therefore, difficult though it may be for Christians to grasp, God must be indeed in some sense "incarnate" in the Qur'an, in Krishna as we meet him in the Bhagavad Gita, in the Enlightenment of the Buddha, in the Tao of the Chinese.[14]

This suggestion will doubtless shock many readers, but it needs serious thought. Students of comparative religion have often pointed out how much the great religions have in common. They all insist upon compassion, mercy, forgiveness, generosity, humility rather than arrogance, the down playing of the self; they all maintain that faith without works is dead and that worship, however passionate and devoted, is valueless without love and charity. Christians certainly agree, for it is clearly written in Scripture, but they should ask themselves, Where did the others get all this from, if it was not from God?[15]

Of course, there is corruption in other religions, just as there is in Christianity. "There is no distinction; since all have sinned and fallen short of the glory of God" (Rom. 3:22–3). Especially vulnerable to the corrupting power of sin are religious institutions, and those who hold power in them, whatever their creed may be. Other religions are not necessarily superior to Christianity.

Perhaps they may be superior in some areas, and have grasped more fully the divine revelation. We dare not rule out in advance the possibility that they may have something to teach us. Therefore all Christians should approach other religions in humility and lowliness of heart. The proud and self-assured will never learn anything. This is no whit less true for those

---

14. This is not to deny in the least the uniqueness of Christ, but Muslims make the same claim of uniqueness for the Qur'an.

15. See additional notes.

committed to traditional evangelism and conversion. No one, in any walk of life, has the right to teach, who is not from the beginning and continually thereafter ready to learn.

Together with humility must go repentance, and perhaps most of all repentance for our scandalous divisions. There is little hope that Christians may proclaim effectively "one body and one spirit . . . one hope . . . one Lord, one faith, one baptism, one God and Father of us all" (Eph. 4:4–6) from the basis of a church split into 20,800 separate parts.[16] The younger churches, which of necessity live in close proximity to adherents of other faiths, have seen this clearly, and have set a shining example of striving for union. The formation of the Church of South India in 1947, and the Church of North India in 1970, are landmarks in the slow progress toward Christian unity. Also in 1970, fifty-three Protestant communities in central Africa came together to form the Church of Christ in Zaire. These have not been the only reunions, and in this matter Christians in Africa and Asia are apostles to their brethren in the West.

The urgent question is whether conversion is still today the best witness to Christ. Is it not possible that, as in the politically divided world, the true Christian function is reconciliation? Did Christ die upon the cross so that men and women might be converted to Christianity? Or did he die so that all the scattered children of God should be reconciled to their Father in heaven and to each other?[17]

Conversion does indeed bring men and women to salvation, though we should remember those Pharisees of whom Christ said, "You traverse sea and land to make a single proselyte, and when he becomes a proselyte, you make him twice as much a child of hell as yourselves" (Matt. 23:15). But it also increases enmity and dissension, for those from whom the converts are taken often feel angry, insulted, and betrayed. Moreover, in societies where the family or the tribe play an essential role, and all things are done in common, conversion of individuals can be destructive.[18] Missionaries have sometimes argued that the destruction is necessary, and have rejoiced over those who have forsaken all to follow Christ. Certainly, one may wholeheartedly admire the sacrifice, but is the motive of those who caused the separation equally admirable? Jesus indeed foresaw that his coming would bring not peace, but a sword (Matt. 10:34), for new truth in any form is not immediately accepted, but provokes much argu-

---

16. David B. Barrett, ed., *World Christian Encyclopedia* (New York: Oxford University Press, 1982).

17. Two contributors argued that reconciliation can come only by means of conversion, since they are essentially the same.

18. This is very well presented by Vincent J. Donovan, a Roman Catholic priest and missionary, in his book *Christianity Rediscovered: An Epistle from the Masai* (Maryknoll, N.Y.: Orbis Books, 1982).

ment, even angry and bitter quarrels. But is not such quarreling a matter for tears rather than rejoicing? These questions are not easy to answer, but they must be asked in all seriousness.

Reconciliation is never easy. When people in both camps are convinced that all right and truth are on their side, those in the middle are likely to find themselves doubly condemned as "traitors," for both groups demand one hundred percent support of their cause. Moreover, it is not enough for the reconcilers merely to stand in the middle. They must seek to *belong* to both sides, and understand the passionate convictions from within. In the great conflicts by which the world is rent today we urgently need people who know from the depths of their being what it feels like to be black in South Africa, and also what it feels like to be white; what it feels like to be Russian and what it feels like to be American; to be Israeli and to be Arab; to be rich and to be poor; to govern and to be governed. In missionary terms this means knowing, to the fullest possible extent, what it means to be a Christian, to think as a Christian, act as a Christian, believe as a Christian, perceive the world as a Christian, and also what it is to think as a Buddhist, believe as a Buddhist, perceive the world as a Buddhist (or in other contexts, as a Hindu, a Taoist, a Muslim, an animist, an atheist).

Reconciliation comes only at great cost. "All this is from God, who through Christ reconciled us to himself and gave us the ministry of reconciliation" (2 Cor. 5:18). This reconciliation took place when there was someone who knew from within his own being what it meant to think, and act, and perceive the world, both as God and as a human being, and could therefore bind the two together into one. But this was done only at the cost of much suffering, and upon the cross by the agonizing sensation that he had been cast off, not only by men and women, but also by God (Mark 15:34). We have no evidence or promise that the ministry of reconciliation entrusted to us will be easier. Yet it would be worth it.

But Paul speaks also of a new creation. "The old," he says, "has passed away, behold, the new has come" (2 Cor. 5:17). As with all the other constants, creation is eternally now with God, and those who have been reconciled to God, and committed their lives to Him, need to make his nowness part of their own perception. In this age, as in every age, the old has passed and the new has come. We must examine seriously the old structures, whether they belong in the new or not, and among these are all the methods, perceptions, and goals of those who seek to make Christ known to the world.

Salvation and the gift of the Spirit are no less constants, always now with God, but experienced by human beings in time, not only the past and present, of which we have some knowledge, but also the future, which we do not know at all. It is therefore exceedingly dangerous for finite mortals to assert that they already know to the full what salvation and the gifts of the Spirit are. The future is still to come, and with it, almost certainly, new disclosures of what salvation and the Spirit mean for God.

No one can state in advance what God may, or may not, do. During the Babylonian empire most people in Judah were convinced that God could not allow His Temple to be destroyed, and when Jeremiah and Ezekiel insisted that He could and would, they refused to listen. Nevertheless, so it happened. Much earlier Isaiah had said that God was using the Assyrian army to punish Judah and Jerusalem, but then also the people failed to understand. "Whatever was written in former days was written for our instruction" (Rom. 15:4), and the warnings of the prophets remain valid for us today. God used the Assyrians and Babylonians to punish His people, and it may well be that He is using Muslims, Hindus, Confucians, agnostics, and communists, all "men of strange lips and with an alien tongue," to save His people, saying to them, "This is rest . . . and this is repose" (Isa. 28:11-12).

The Last Judgment is no less a constant, thought this may sound like a contradiction in terms, for what is last belongs to the end of time. This is true, just as creation belongs to the beginning of time. But God is eternally judge, and His judgments are always final, for they allow of no appeal to a higher court. Judgment, final and irrevocable, comes upon the human race in every hour, indeed in every minute. Medieval Christians were more conscious of this than we are, for they were more conscious of death, and more aware, therefore, that God may say at any time to those who feel secure, "Fool! This night your soul is required of you" (Luke 12:20). Therefore, when Christians consider the adherents of other religions, they need to consider as now the Last Judgment so vividly portrayed in Matt. 25:31-46. There it is the *nations*, the pagans, the worshipers of other gods, the rank outsiders, who are summoned before the Son of man, and many will instantly be admitted to the kingdom of heaven. They had been wholly ignorant of the gospel, even perhaps antagonistic, but had manifested to the full the fruits of the Spirit. For them there is a kingdom prepared from the foundation of the world.

ADDITIONAL NOTES

1. A number of general comments on this chapter were made by contributors, some of which are quoted here:

"I have started to think of things that I never thought of before, and some serious questions have come to my mind. (1) If the God of Christians is the God of all other religions, why did He send such different messages? (2) If all the religions are true, what was the purpose of Christ coming to earth? (3) How can all the different religions be true at the same time, since they all demand one hundred percent participation? (4) If Jesus was God, then what he said was true. How then can the other religions also be true? (5) If the other religions are true, what are we to make of such passages as 'I am the way, and the truth, and the life; no one comes to the Father, but by me' (John 14:6)?"

"This chapter helped me wrestle with some personal problems I had concerning Christianity's relevance to other religions. Open-mindedness of religious people (although this could be detrimental in excess) is, I feel, one of their most important attributes; a greater awareness and appreciation for God is facilitated by acknowledging that He works in ways we cannot know."

"I find the subject of Christianity and other religions exceedingly difficult, because so often the main imperative of missionary work, which is, as I see it, to spread the knowledge and love of God, seems to get lost in a whirlwind of arrogance, narrow-mindedness, and religious labeling. To many, including myself, the word missionary has negative connotations—pompous people going into foreign countries, destroying viable customs, ways of life, and beliefs, all in the name of God, although, as you later state, there are other ways of being a missionary."

"Although you have pointed out the good, and especially the bad, points, we must remember that what missionaries do is beyond the call of duty. God has given them very special talents, and sometimes the resourceful use of these talents can be very hard. We need to give the missionaries more credit."

"I think that his chapter *totally* misrepresents the topic of Christians and other religions. All sorts of statements are put forward without explanation, and without pointing out that there are very good reasons why a large part, if not the majority, of Christians would vehemently disagree with you. . . . There seems to be little recognition of the fact that everybody cannot be right, and that there is a very real possibility that millions of people could be deceived by false prophets and false teachers. . . . Christianity does not claim to be another religion; it claims to be the truth about God and reality. There is no middle ground. It is either the truth, or it is a lie."

10. It is only fair to report that Kraemer himself greatly modified his views in later years, as shown in his book *World Cultures and World Religions: The Coming Dialogue* (Philadelphia: Westminster Press, 1960). Nevertheless, he did say, in another book published at the same time, "When we probe more deeply into the religions in one way or another they are shown to be religions of self-redemption, self-justification, and self-sanctification and so to be, in their ultimate and essential meaning and significance, *erroneous*." *Why Christianity of All Religions?* trans. Hubert Hoskins (Philadelphia: Westminster Press, 1962). This is a very dubious statement.

13. The majority of contributors strongly approved of this paragraph, but not all did so. Some disagreed with the yes, and some with the no. One wrote, "When you describe the views of Karl Barth and Hendrik Kraemer, I was appalled that anyone could be so narrow-minded and yet consider themselves true Christians. I was relieved to know that other delegates at the World Missionary Conference disagreed with these men."

Another commented, "The whole emphasis in the New Testament is that only through Christ's death and resurrection are we saved. To say or imply that it is okay to be of any religion is then contrary to what the Scriptures say, and I do not think that you bring this point out. I feel that it is the key difference between Christianity and the other religions. If it did not matter what religion people believed in, or who they worshiped, then there would not be any point in Christianity."

15. One contributor answered the question in these terms: "From Satan, the counterfeiter, very possibly. What better way to deceive someone than by throwing in some of God's truth with the lies?"

15

CHRISTIANS AND SOCIETY

I'm just a poor, wayfaring stranger
Traveling through this world of woe.
Traditional ballad

Christians understand themselves to be the people of God, who live *in* the world but are not *of* the world. The world in this view represents humankind as it is estranged from God, cast out of the Garden of Eden, and wandering in the wilderness. In this world human beings are also alienated from each other, at odds with nature and society. There is a yearning to find a home, reconciliation through a covenant, and that kingdom where the barren desert is transformed to paradise (Isa. 41:17–20). Until the whole world understands the redemption won in Christ, and until the kingdom is finally and completely established, the Christian remains "an alien in an alien land," a stranger, and a sojourner. "Foxes have holes, and the birds of the air have nests, but the Son of man has nowhere to lay his head" (Matt. 8:20). "Here we have no continuing city, but we seek one to come" (Heb. 13:14 KJV).

At the same time Christians affirm a no less forceful vision of the world, as created, sustained, and redeemed by God, the lover of "all that exists, with loathing for none of the things that He has made" (Wisd. of Sol. 11:24). He so loved the world that He sent His only begotten Son, Jesus Christ, to reconcile the world to Himself. This, then, provides the model for Christians to imitate as they live in the historical and material world. They are asked quite simply, How can you say that you love God, if you do not love your neighbor? Love is not abstract; it must be put into practice.

When we move from this panoramic view to a consideration of *how* a Christian lives, or ought to live, in this complex world we encounter some of the most pressing questions of our day. What does a religion and

193

community committed to a kingdom not of this world have to do with everyday justice, politics, or questions of economics and culture? What has the Christian faith in general, or specific Christian churches, have to do with the Pentagon, the Kremlin, or Wall Street? Most people would agree that religion can make a valuable contribution to questions of ethics in our national and cultural life. There is clearly a public role to be played by Christians in the order of the world. But how and when should this intervention be made, and what are its limits?

Modern experience offers conflicting examples of what can happen in a state when religious authorities either take control of political affairs or are systematically excluded. Does society prosper or suffer when religion is alienated from political life? What happens if religion is made the central force in society, fashioning the laws and customs according to its own beliefs, although the body politic may contain many nonbelievers? Are there risks for religion when it becomes politically involved, or is a significant element lost from national culture and political life when religion is excluded? These are some of the questions to which we must turn, noting certain models suggested during Christian history, and how they might apply today.

Christ and Culture

This heading comes from the title of a book by H. Richard Niebuhr,[1] which dealt with the social responsibility of Christian churches in an increasingly secular world. Some of the questions had been openly discussed since at least the time when Edward Gibbon, in his book *The Decline and Fall of the Roman Empire* (1776), had cast a cold and wary eye on Christianity as other-worldly, making no contribution to material civilization or progress. It could even be thought of, as some Christians did, as removing any need for involvement in a world that was passing away. It was accused of crippling moral initiative in this world by its promise of a better world to come, of perpetuating reactionary systems, and of encouraging a slave mentality.

Niebuhr's study can provide a valuable basis for our own questions. He was careful to define his terms. "Christ" is for the Christian both Jesus of Nazareth confined within time and space, and also the risen Christ, one with the absolute God. "Culture" (from the Latin *colere,* to cultivate, the opposite of "wild" or "unrestrained") denotes orderly well-mannered society, including learning, knowledge, arts, and sciences—all that makes society meaningful, safe, and enjoyable. These elements of the collective life are never addressed in the Gospels. Niebuhr identified five different

---

1. H. Richard Niebuhr, *Christ and Culture* (New York: Harper & Brothers, 1951).

relationships of Christ to culture: (1) Christ Against Culture, (2) The Christ of Culture, (3) Christ Above Culture, (4) Christ and Culture in Paradox, and (5) Christ the Transformer of Culture.

The first two are absolutist, either opposing Christ to culture or identifying him with it. The last three, however, recognize the conflicting claims of both Christ and culture. They perceive the absolute purity of God made known in Jesus Christ and the world, and also the necessity of culture in this world, an essential part of the purposes of God. They do not reject the world as utterly corrupt, but neither can they say it is altogether good. All recognize that Christ came to save the world, but why, from what, and to what end? Here they disagree. The First Epistle of John represents "Christ Against Culture":

> Do not set your hearts on the godless world or anything in it. Anyone who loves the world is a stranger to the Father's love. Everything the world affords, all that panders to the appetites or entices the eyes, all the glamour of its life, springs not from the Father, but from the godless world. And that world is passing away with all its allurements, but he who does God's will stands for evermore.
>
> 1 John 2:15-17 NEB

For such Christians the sole authority and source of life and knowledge is the explicit word of Christ, although obedience to Torah may be included. They urge men and women to confront the sensuality, superficiality, and materialism of society by adhering to the Sermon on the Mount, not as an outline of ideals, but as a practical political and social program. Tolstoy, the nineteenth-century Russian author, provides an excellent example. Confronted by the meaninglessness of existence, he accepted the Gospels as his absolute authority. To be faithful to the life and teachings of Christ meant living at peace with all men. He was an absolute pacifist. Since weapons and violence are evil, one must love one's enemy unconditionally, and never resist the evildoer by force. He also believed that private property and all institutions, the church included, are evil inventions of the devil.

Such absolutists have been few in number, but they are of great importance, for they set an example of complete Christian dedication. "So shines a good deed in a naughty world."[2] Yet the dangers of fanaticism, hypocrisy, and spiritual pride are not far distant from such believers. Tertullian, for instance, was only too ready to unchurch those believers who did not share his rigorous vision of Christians in flight from the godless world. There is also the danger of seeing the world in crudely Platonic terms, as a prisonhouse from which the pure soul must escape.

The "Christ of Culture" group is very apparent in our own day. They seek to reconcile gospel with contemporary science and knowledge, but

---

2. Shakespeare, *The Merchant of Venice*, 5.1.88.

the danger here is that many identify the two. For them knowledge is salvation. Peter Abelard in the twelfth century spoke of Jesus as the great moral teacher, who "in all that he did in the flesh . . . had the intention of our instruction," and who completed the teaching that had been begun by Socrates and Plato. From this perspective Jesus is a messiah of the mind, whose actual physical and historical life tends to be downplayed. His teaching is seen as totally reasonable and rational, and the non-reasonable element in the gospel, for example, miracle and resurrection, is disregarded. This group rightly emphasizes the need to recognize and obey truth in whatever guise it comes, whether in religious belief or in scientific discovery, but it tends to deify humankind and temporal institutions, and so fails to take the Creator seriously. Culture is always a human construction, and to deify it is idolatry. Nevertheless, it is built from divinely created material.

The last three groups all perceive the relationship between Christ and culture as a dialectic, in which two opposing realities must in some way be reconciled. The "Christ Above Culture" thinkers begin from the truth that Jesus Christ is both God and man. They see culture, therefore, as both divine and human, holy and sinful. Their aim is to give proper obedience to both, and strive to "render to Caesar the things that are Caesar's and to God the things that are God's" (Mark 12:17). Clement of Alexandria in the second century and Thomas Aquinas in the thirteenth are notable representatives of those who see nature and grace cooperating, the latter perfecting and completing the former, which even in its fallen, sinful, diminished state may serve as a vehicle of divine power.

Dualists, such as Paul, Luther, and Kierkegaard, see "Christ and Culture in Paradox," drawing sharp distinctions between them. They believe that Christ and the world must be kept clearly distinct, and never be confused or synthesized. Yet the rulers of the world have a definite place in the divine purpose, and should therefore be obeyed, even when they are pagan. "Let every person be subject to the governing authorities, for there is no authority except from God, and those that exist have been instituted by God" (Rom. 13:1). Augustine agreed that the Christian, having dual citizenship in the City of God and the City of Man, should obey the earthly rulers, for their function is to provide order, peace, and happiness, all of them gifts of the Spirit. Similarly, Luther argued that Christians should cooperate even with corrupt, tyrannical, and oppressive rulers, since the power they exercise fulfills some hidden divine purpose. This view maintains the needed social order and security, but at a great cost in human misery. This, it is insisted, can be relieved only by the direct intervention of God.

The final group are the conversionists, who believe in "Christ the Transformer of Culture," for they see the Creator and Redeemer as continually at work. For John Calvin in France and Geneva, and F. D. Maurice in Britain,[3] a new world is always in process of being made. They see redemption and resurrection, not merely as past actions, but as present events. The Word becoming flesh initiated a process that will culminate in the gradual transformation of the world, and allow the faithful to participate in eternal life within time. Having entered history, the Word of God is expressed and transformed in the words of men, but the same Word in turn judges and transforms human ideas and structures.

Eschatology and Incarnation

In the light of Niebuhr's categories, let us now look at two divergent perspectives in the modern world. We may call them "eschatological" and "incarnational," corresponding to Niebuhr's dualist and conversionist models. Both share the biblical understanding that the faithful are required to speak in the name of God concerning the moral character and political life of the nation, just as the prophet Nathan rebuked King David and John the Baptist confronted Herod (2 Sam. 12:1-10; Mark 6:14-29). Both groups perceive religion to be not primarily a private individual matter, but public and communal, affecting and guiding the nation. They see, therefore, religion as essentially political. God is the God of history, forever involved in human affairs.

The two groups, however, diverge on the question of how general or specific the role of the church should be. Since it deals with social concerns, the church has to be political, but should it engage directly in politics? Or should it stay out of politics so as to preserve the validity of eternal truths? Might such a disengagement be itself used for political ends, by muzzling the prophetic critique of society? Could the revival of politically active religion lead also to the revival of old-time fanaticism and intolerance? The tremendous contributions of Christianity to culture need to be seen against such dark images as the Inquisition, the Holocaust, and apartheid.

Should the churches confine themselves to discussing only abstract principles underlying specific policies and government programs, which in themselves are controversial? Should they take a stand, not only on major social problems, like militarism, racism, materialism, and economic injustice, but also on more specific questions, such as military involvement in Central America, capital punishment, gun control laws, the Panama Canal treaty, the Equal Rights Amendment, and abortion? One cannot always make neat distinctions between principles and policies.

---

3. Frederick Dennison Maurice (1805–1872), an Anglican theologian deeply interested in social questions, and one of the founders of the Christian Socialist Movement. Niebuhr included the author of John's Gospel among the conversionists, but not all would agree.

Even those conservative Christians who in general oppose political involvement, being more concerned with personal salvation, are nonetheless vocal about such political issues as divorce, alcohol and drug addiction, abortion, school prayer, teen-age suicides, organized crime, and sexual exploitation.

Christians who understand this world to be primarily a preparation for the next adopt a dualist position: Christianity has no right to play a social, political, and economic role. Its mission is entirely spiritual, and the function of the church is to bring men and women into the presence of God. It should help the believer to know, love, and serve God in this life, and to be happy with Him forever in the life to come. Poverty, injustice, inhumanity, and oppression may hinder the free proclamation of the gospel, but they are understood to be the result of original sin, and therefore inevitable. The Christian should strive to overcome these obstacles, but this is not the primary object of the church's mission. Christ, they say, came as a savior, not as a social worker. The only biblical commission is to gather the believers together, so that they may prepare themselves by prayer, faith, and hope for the kingdom that God will establish at the end of the world. Christians are not required to build the kingdom of God, but to make themselves ready for it.

The strength of this position is its insistence that we cannot be saved by sheer socialization, personality development, liberation from oppressive structures, or an end to poverty. Salvation comes only through Christ, and is mediated to us by the reading of Scripture, prayer, sacrament, and charity. Christianity's primary task, therefore, is to refashion men and women in Christ's image, for if all the physical and social ills of humanity were suddenly to vanish, we should still need him who takes away the sin of the world. This stress upon heavenly citizenship is a sobering corrective to those Christians who have allowed themselves to become too comfortable with the world as it is. It also sets us free from submission to all totalitarian claims:

This citizenship transcends in prophetic judgment all political systems. All human freedom depends finally on the value of human life and the freedom from paralyzing fear that a transcendent allegiance bestows.[4]

This eschatological view reminds Christians that discipleship is costly, and that the words of consolation and power found in Scripture cannot be fully understood by those who have never suffered want, oppression, or persecution. The eschatological preacher might well ask his congregation, Were Christian leaders crucified in our nation last year, or were they

---

4. Pastoral Letter of the House of Bishops, General Convention of the Episcopal Church, 1982.

instead given high positions? If we are not victims, we are likely to become victimizers, who need to hear Christ's first spoken command: "Repent!" (Mark 1:15).

Incarnationalists view things differently. They see the primary function of Christians to be the imitation of Jesus, who became directly involved in the world. Love of one's neighbor demands this full involvement; it is not merely helping individuals. It requires vigorous social and political action, aimed at making structural changes in the principalities and powers of this world. God certainly initiates the kingdom, but He does so by sharing our humanity, our flesh, and the struggle of our life in the person of Jesus Christ. This biblical understanding of God actively engaged in the process of creation, through Christ and all those who belong to the body of Christ, must be taken seriously. If Jesus Christ is indeed the final truth about humanity, as Christians claim, then Christians must assist in the full development of humanity, and struggle ceaselessly to transform the human realm into the kingdom of God, a kingdom of peace and justice in place of "dark Satanic mills." John Chrysostom in the fourth century, seeing this in terms of the destitute and oppressed, ventured to put these words in the mouth of Christ:

> It is such a slight thing I beg. . . . Nothing very expensive. . . . Bread, a roof, words of comfort. If the rewards I promised hold no appeal for you, then show at least a natural compassion when you see me naked, and remember the nakedness I endured for you on the cross. . . . I fasted for you then, and I suffer hunger for you now; I was thirsty when I hung on the cross, and I thirst still in the poor, in both ways to draw you to myself and to make you humane for your own salvation.[5]

Just as Chrysostom summoned Christians to see the poor in a way they had not done before, so the incarnationalist looks afresh at faith and the language of faith. In his book, *Theology and Political Society,*[6] Charles Davis seeks to bind Christian faith and political action together, on grounds of the biblical condemnation of wealth and social oppression. For him theology is not a set of dogmas, principles, or metaphysical beliefs, but a political activity, the wholehearted engagement by Christians for the purpose of human liberation. Those who deny this and stress inward sanctification are too often reactionary defenders of the status quo. They do not regard the status quo as itself political, but only any opposition to it.

---

5. John Chrysostom, quoted by William J. Walsh and John P. Langan, "Patristic Social Consciousness—The Church and the Poor," in *The Faith That Does Justice: Examining the Christian Sources for Social Change* (New York: Paulist Press, 1977), 132.

6. The 1978 Hulsean Lectures at the University of Cambridge. Published by the University Press.

In Davis's view true faith is collective, the remembrance of history, of the covenant, and the promises made by the whole community. It therefore requires practical political action directed against all forms of ideology and idolatry.

> This is the so-called "performative approach." Faith can never be a matter of disembodied words. It must be incarnate in *praxis* (faith-in-action). Faith is a transforming acceptance of the Word, which challenges us through the cries of the poor and oppressed. Only in liberating *praxis* can we give to the world that "warm welcome" that constitutes faith. Faith is not a passive waiting upon God's decision to act; rather, it seizes the initiative and reshapes the world by its God-given power. Faith, therefore, is not a passive virtue. It does not protect us from the world; it remakes the world. It is active engagement in the service of the Kingdom of God.[7]

This kind of faith involves creating new language and reshaping patterns of thought, which are affected and changed by action, and which themselves change and affect the action. For example, if the Christian idea of God as personal is to be powerful and persuasive, there must be a society in which "person" has meaning. If the idea of a just God is to make any sense, there must be a just and humane society to give it credence. If Christian beliefs are to be meaningful, Christian language must be rooted in social reality.

This is not a new insight. When early Christians described Christ as Lord and spoke about the kingdom, they were using the language and images of their own political society. We have grown so accustomed to the traditional imagery that we are hardly conscious of how greatly Christianity is affected by its cultural environment, for example, in diverse forms of worship, or how it has molded culture, as in the influence upon society of such holiday as Christmas and Easter, which themselves have been shaped by customs borrowed from many cultures.

In Latin America fabulous wealth and absolute poverty often exist within sight of each other. There Christians influenced by liberation theology have sought to discover in the Bible and Christian tradition resources for enabling the poor to find greater freedom and better economic conditions. As in other similar situations, the call to revolution and the desire for nonviolence exist together in uneasy tension. Many view the church's growing commitment to the poor as revolutionary and foreign, too dependent upon European political ideas or Marxist economics. The liberation theologians insist that they are making a response that is both indigenous and biblical in order to find just ways of distributing wealth and power. For was not the advent of Christ heralded in these terms?

---

7. Richard P. McBrien, *Catholicism*, vol. 2 (Minneapolis: Winston Press, 1980), 968.

He hath put down the mighty from their seat;
   and hath exalted the humble and meek.
He hath filled the hungry with good things;
   and the rich he hath sent empty away.
Luke 1:52-3 Coverdale

It is possible to read the story of Jesus' birth and see only angels and eternal light. Or one can see a direct message to indigent shepherds on the fringes of society, to poor people shifted about by a distant emperor for census and tax purposes, a pregnant young woman with no shelter, a king desperate for power, the senseless slaughter of innocent civilians to protect his dynastic dreams, political refugees, and displaced persons. To read the Gospels in this manner is to perceive the possibility of altering unjust society. To those who say that Christians are required only to worship God, liberation theologians reply that worship and prayer are themselves political, for they seek the transformation of the world into the kingdom of God, and they ask for daily bread amid economic systems which do not provide it. For the multitude of dispossessed in today's world the Christian faith is the guardian of moral courage, freedom, justice, and liberation. It protests against idolatrous and demonic distortions of power, whether by the omnipotent state or the religious community itself, which still today so often "slays the prophets." Viewed from this perspective, the Bible provides a constant record of liberation—from Egypt, from Babylon, from the might of Rome, and on Calvary from the bondage of sin.

Some Concluding Questions

The world in which we live today is in many important respects altogether different from what it was in the past. These differences may be summed up in the one phrase: the knowledge explosion. This is evident in a variety of spheres. In earlier days societies could exist separately, but now we have discovered each other, and what is done by one people has repercussions all over the globe. Scientific and technological research have so vastly increased our knowledge that we live in a world of specialists, with universalists no longer possible. So rapid is modern communication that news from anywhere in the world may demand an immediate response, without time for thought or consultation. Nuclear missiles from the Soviet Union could arrive here in only fifteen minutes. Moreover, we stand only at the doorstep of the transformation of our cultural situation. Nuclear research, genetic engineering, and computer science are still in their infancy, and we cannot begin to foresee their outcome.

This explosion of knowledge means inevitably also an explosive increase in human power and control, but with these disturbing implications: (1) this power will not be available to all. Because of the necessity of specialization, the many will always be the servants of the few, and the greater the power the more complete the servitude; (2) the power will be exercised by fallible, corruptible human beings, prone to think in selfish terms; (3) no knowledge and no power can be forever guarded from being stolen or used for corrupt purposes. No computer code can be devised which will outwit the skill to break the code. Knowledge is in itself neutral, and available to both the just and the unjust; (4) so wayward are the minds of men and women that those who use these new enormous powers for evil and destruction will often be convinced that their goals are altogether good. One American military leader in the Vietnam War said, "We had to destroy the town in order to save it," and now we are solemnly told that our nation will use "peace-keepers" (nuclear warheads) in order to "make the world safe for democracy."

It is against this background that we must reconsider the problem of Christ and culture. We said much earlier in the book that Christians should give thanks for scientific discovery, but what are we to say about nuclear weapons, nerve gas, defoliation, and napalm? Though modern culture certainly includes "learning, knowledge, arts, and sciences," can we truly say today that it "denotes orderly well-mannered society—all that makes it meaningful, safe, and enjoyable"? The "Christ of Culture" requires from us thorough reconsideration. Is it perhaps possible that men and women may so thoroughly misuse the enormous power now entrusted to them that a day will come when "Christ Against Culture" will be the *only* position left for Christians?

What are the abiding values and perspective that can empower the most people, and provide us all with moral courage, energy, and compassion before the mounting problems of the future? Religion can, by its insistence on the power of the word, demonstrate the importance of grounding our common language in reality, and show how this should be done, especially in the language of politics, which so easily drifts into vague rhetoric and meaningless clichés.

"Christ Above Culture" is for modern Americans a very tempting position. With our ideals of freedom of expression, equal opportunities, pluralism, commitment to civil and human rights, a voluntary church, separation of church and state, and religious toleration, many honestly believe that they can indeed "render to Caesar the things that are Caesar's and to God the things that are God's." But can we really do this, and is it self-evident that all these things are good, and deserve our obedience?

For those in the modern world who can adopt none of these three positions, "Christ and Culture in Paradox" seems very persuasive. Even in situations of the greatest degradation, poverty, and suffering, the virtues of love, hope, fellowship, and forgiveness still persist, inextinguishable candles in the grim darkness. American power and American Christianity have no guarantee of survival, and even now missionaries from the Third World are coming to this country. It may well be by God's grace that those who know destitution, oppression, and foreign domination at firsthand will be those who bring into our midst "Christ the Transformer of Culture." Can we in their presence continue to consume the goods of the earth so disproportionately without heeding the stern rebukes of the prophets, many of whom speak from outside the church? To use a biblical phrase, do we consume the portion of widows and orphans? Dare we enter the supermarket without a sense of dread and outrage? Are we sufficiently aware that at the cost of one attack submarine we could erase malaria from the globe, that some four hundred and sixty million people are even now starving to death, that over one billion live in conditions that degrade the very meaning of humanity? The neighbors whom we are commanded to love are no longer merely next door, but all over the world. God made known to us in the Bible is just, and justice demands that the haves do not stand aloof from the have-nots. It demands repentance, and repentance means the transformation of our culture in a measure far beyond what left to ourselves we could achieve. Even so, Come, Lord Jesus!

16

THE CRISIS OF CHRISTIANITY
IN THE MODERN WORLD

Christ is loved as a person; he compels recognition as a world.
Teilhard de Chardin

The world as we once knew it is being shaken to its foundations. Wave after wave of future shock breaks against our political, economic, cultural, and intellectual institutions. Not only our patterns of living have shifted, but also our forms of consciousness. Our authors have described the present time as an "Age of Anxiety" in a shellshocked "Waste Land," a living hell from which there is "No Exit."[1] We seem to be homeless and lost in this desert, and have no words for the stark reality of concentration camps and Gulag, the ceaseless procession of displaced persons and refugees. There is no language suitable for Lebanon and El Salvador.

This is a grim picture, but a true one. Yet it is not the whole truth. Life in very many countries of the world is still well worth living, and even where it is not altogether easy, it still has a great deal to offer, a multitude of little pleasures, sometimes even great contentment. Even so, there are in the strongest societies disturbing cracks and fissures, and over the entire globe looms the menace of nuclear war and destruction of the environment.

Certainly, humankind has faced affliction before. Søren Kierkegaard in the nineteenth century called the bone-deep despair in the eyes of those around him a "sickness unto death," and the Book of Job has spoken to the heart of people in every generation.

Terror upon terror overwhelms me,
it sweeps away my resolution like the wind,
and my hope of victory vanishes like a cloud.
So now my soul is in turmoil within me,
and misery has me daily in its grip.

---

1. The authors quoted are W. H. Auden, T. S. Eliot, and Jean-Paul Sartre.

By night pain pierces my very bones,
and there is ceaseless throbbing in my veins;
my garments are all bespattered with my phlegm
which chokes me like the collar of a shirt.

                                    Job 30:15–18 NEB

But seldom has the sense of abandonment seemed so widespread. There has always been savage cruelty and grim poverty, and the overflowing scourge of the Black Death created a wasteland of anxiety no less terrifying than our own. Then, as now, the senseless suffering and destitution of humanity marked the world as alien, hostile, and absurd. What makes our situation different is on the one hand our awareness of worldwide suffering, and on the other the fact that we are the children of those who believed wholeheartedly in inevitable progress. Not only do we now know that to have been a will-o'-the-wisp, but we live in dread of inevitable destruction. Both Jews and Christians have been heard to affirm that "God is dead."

Numberless contemporary men and women have sought new gods, new sources of life in what some have called postindustrial, postmodern, and post-Christian society. New cults proliferate, promising a new home, a protective and supporting community, or reintegration with nature. Ancient beliefs in occultism, nature worship, witchcraft, and magic flourish once more. Some preach a gospel of material success and self-help; others take refuge in alcohol, or seek to attain ecstasy and heightened awareness by means of drugs. Gurus, or the stars, direct the destinies of men and women seeking oneness with the universe, what Theodore Roszak has called the "counterfeit infinity." All reveal the desperate hunger for identity amidst a massive shift in social and personal ideals, and a political, sexual, and religious revolution. Is there any possibility that the Christian faith can speak to this unhappy world, or is it unintelligible and irrelevant amid the skyscrapers and gigantic cities of today? How valid today is the call of Him who said, "Behold, I make all things new" (Rev. 21:5)?

The World Is All That
Is the Case

Never shall I forget those moments which murdered my God and my soul and turned my dreams to dust. Never shall I forget these things, even if I am condemned to live as long as God Himself. Never.[2]

Part of the crisis in human meaning and values has been the inability of traditional religion and images of God to deal with the horror and devastation of modern experience. Wholesale murder, hunger, poverty,

---

2. Elie Wiesel, *Night* (New York: Avon, 1969), 44.

and despair seem to destroy not only humankind, but also God. As we asked in an earlier chapter, Where was God in Auschwitz, Hamburg, and Hiroshima? Have we become alone in the universe? All too often Christians have so spiritualized the divine presence as to allow no real link between Creator and created world. Or they have claimed that the existence of God is alone sufficient explanation of the apparent meaninglessness of life and the injustice of human suffering. Faith is degraded into resolution of human doubt, fear, and affliction.

> We wish to make religion an escape from the conflict, a haven of refuge from trials of faith, and tend to enjoy the contempt for others which only a sense of religious superiority can give, forgetting that it is he who endures to the end who shall be saved.[3]

Those Christians who preach peace of mind and deny that there is any problem are like Job's three friends. But it was only of Job, the rebel and questioner, that God said, "He has spoken about Me what is right" (Job 42:7).

The modern age is marked, not only by the rise of gigantic cities inhabited by a lonely crowd, but also by the breakdown of more intimate communities and neighborhoods. The new insistence on ethnic identity reveals how effectively contemporary individualism has stolen from us any sense of belonging. Alex Haley in his book *Roots*, written from within the black minority, struck a chord in the hearts of the whole community. Underlying all this is a powerful change in consciousness and the very process of thinking. A great many today would exclude a priori the transcendent and supernatural from any attempt to decipher the universe. Secularism is not only a pattern of life; it is a method of interpreting the world around us. The secular critic, therefore, rigorously separates the educational, economic, legal, and political sections of society from "the domination of religious instruments and symbols."[4] The collective intellectual and political moguls who define our culture no longer give unqualified sanction to religious symbols and practices. Prayers in public schools and Christmas nativity scenes paid for by public funds have become the cause of legal battles, and no longer represent communal unity. Religious believers have become a cognitive minority, a group whose view of the world differs markedly from that of the majority. The dominance of Christianity in this country is over.

There are now strong alternatives to older religious beliefs, and these are held honestly and with dignity. Humanism, with roots deep in classical and medieval religious thought, is today often atheist, agnostic, or existentialist. Following the philosopher Ludwig Wittgenstein, secular humanists

---

3. J. S. Bezzant, "Intellectual Objections," in A. D. Vidler, ed., *Objections to Christian Belief* (New York: J. B. Lippincott, 1964), 111.

4. Peter Berger, *The Sacred Canopy* (Garden City, N.Y.: Doubleday & Co., 1969), 107.

maintain that "the world is all that is the case." There is nothing more to life, they say, than life as it is known in the world, in nature, and in shifting appearances. There is for them no transcendent center of meaning. Humanity is, in Jean-Paul Sartre's words, "condemned to be free," and summoned therefore to build a this-worldly structure of meaning and action.

Others, such as Ernst Bloch, have argued that the Christian meaning of transcendence is today best understood not in terms of otherworldliness, but rather as the consciousness of oppression, and ensuing resistance to the brutal power of this world. Older images of transcendence derived from Hellenistic and medieval forms, and are today useless.

Some types of humanism, however, reject Christian theism altogether, as encouraging dependence, fear, guilt, irrationality, and alienation, characteristic of reactionary systems that merely perpetuate the unjust distribution and ownership of this world's goods. If human potential is to be fully realized, if peace and justice are to be truly established, then, it is argued, there must be an end to the false consciousness created by god-talk. As Frederich Nietzsche said, the death of God is the necessary price for man's coming of age.[5]

Undoubtedly, modern historical and scientific knowledge challenge traditional modes of religious acting and thinking. But we need to be clear how, in fact, these relate to other dimensions of human life. Christianity claims to provide an ideal of the true self, true personhood, and has in the past sanctioned cultural forms, such as class and caste, which it believed to enshrine these ideals. Now science is beginning to alter radically the standard definitions of personhood, with profound implications for the religious perspective. Both must be included in any discussion about the moral and practical implications of such things as genetic engineering, sperm banks, life-support systems, and the right to die. Ought limits to be set to some kinds of research and experiments? Have either science or religion alone the right to determine goals and guidelines?

Christians may be justified in defending traditional views, but what they must never do is to claim *scientific* validity for their opinions, if the scientists themselves are dubious about them, or have been compelled to reject them. "Illusions guide the experimenter," said the great scientist Louis Pasteur, and subjective factors have their part to play in the development of scientific knowledge. But these factors have themselves to be rigorously tested. Religious beliefs, however, cannot be tested in the same manner, and Christians in the past have seldom asserted that the truth of the Christian faith could be objectively proved using the accepted norms of empiri-

---

5. See additional notes.

cal research. If such proof were in fact possible, we would not be talking about Christian beliefs or faith, but about historical or scientific data and knowledge. Christianity would then in effect be conformed to this world, and be limited to what could be rationally demonstrated. It would have no power to witness to transcendent Reality, or to perform those acts of healing and reconciliation which have no parallel in science.

Christianity and the
Modern Crisis

The new world of thought and action faces Christians with a number of far-reaching challenges and opportunities. How does the present position of Christianity in the world differ from that of all the other centuries since the resurrection? What is the outlook for the Christian community in the third millennium? Will it be more difficult to be a Christian then?

Clearly, the temporal power of the state can no longer offer protection or privilege for Christianity in Western society. The state church is disappearing, although there are still countries, even among those claiming to practice the separation of powers, where Christianity receives special treatment, sometimes at the cost of serving as a prop for authoritarian regimes. Governments often support religion, or grant it benign neglect, since religion helps to keep the public peace. But when the government policies themselves are called in question, the church is then said to be interfering in politics, an accusation which had not been made while the church was lending its support. Therefore, some people today urge the churches to relinquish government assistance, for example, tax-exempt status, in order to embrace solidarity with the poor and the life of poverty imposed upon them.

Some observers judge Christianity's achievements in terms of political success, social acceptance, or increasing membership. Full or empty pews become the measuring rod, with the result that the Christian faith is reduced to "a rotarian cult of success and visible results."[6] In recoiling from this we have no need to romanticize the early Christian communities, for the vivid accounts of those in Corinth and Laodicea (1 Corinthians 5—6; Rev. 3:14–17) reveal startling weaknesses.

Nevertheless, the ancient model of the believers' church, rather than that of the state church, seems most helpful for our uncertain future, when privilege may give way to neglect or even oppression. It has been this type of community that has enabled the church to survive under Mao Zedong (Mao Tse-Tung) and in other parts of the Third World. The duty of the

---

6. The phrase comes from Thomas Merton, in his assessment of Christian optimism in contemporary American society.

church anywhere is to be "a light to the Gentiles," not a political institution, and the strength of its witness may depend upon its political weakness. It has always claimed to stand for the powerless in society and even today Christians have spoken with a prophetic voice when they confronted national and technological totalitarianism, whether in Nazi Germany or among the Western exploiters of the Third World.

The churches today are clearly more willing to listen than many of them were prepared to do in the past. They pay more attention to each other, and engage in dialogue, instead of trying to refute unfamiliar opinions. In this country the more conservative churches have recently shown a marked increase in membership, in contrast to the mainline churches, though these still remain vigorous. In Europe, however, church attendance is still uncomfortably small.[7] The European churches, however, were in the years between the wars, more involved in ecumenical discussion and in cooperation with each other. As the Nazi pressure increased, they realized that they had a great deal more in common than had previously appeared. In this country, despite such notable pioneers as Bishop Brent, the founder of the Life and Work Movement, general interest in ecumenical activity did not develop until the 1950s, and widespread conversations between Protestants and Roman Catholics had to wait until Vatican II. All this led to significant advances in biblical, historical, and theological studies, for example, joint translations of the Bible and common texts used in worship. There have also been other signs of renewal: weakening of racial divisions, new liturgies in the more traditional churches, the re-emergence of revivalist spirituality in the Jesus movement, Pentecostal and charismatic groups, and the various storefront churches. More diverse sources of spiritual guidance and practice are being explored, such as using yoga and Zen meditation techniques with Christian forms of prayer.

In the last twenty-five years important changes have taken place. Christians of many denominations have become more ready to include in their fellowship those whom they had previously rejected, such as people from the Third World, blacks, and native Americans. Much of this was certainly inspired by Martin Luther King, Jr., but it is worth remembering the strong initiative taken by students and other groups of young people. The elders often followed in their footsteps. There were, of course, many who held back, fearing a sort of lowest common multiple of all beliefs, a leveling of significant differences which would compromise essential elements of the different traditions. Nevertheless, the goal of church union still remains, and the conversations continue, with from time to time

---

7. The reference here is to Western Europe. Behind the Iron Curtain conditions are different. In Poland church attendance is extremely high, and elsewhere, despite often enormous difficulties, church life, though it is often the life of a small minority, has been strengthened rather than weakened by oppression.

definite steps forward. Christians have begun, though slowly, to recognize how conflicting a message is the gospel, when preached by a divided church to an already fragmented secular society. The ancient explanation of amazement, "See how these Christians love one another!" has become in the recent past an ironic comment on mutual distrust and disunity, which Christians had come to take for granted.

The Christian, therefore, needs to recognize both personal and corporate sinfulness, the pride and self-regard which hinder the gospel message, the failure to perceive Christ except in a manner predetermined by one's own tradition and interpretation of Scripture. Repentance such as this may prepare us to understand the diversity of means used by God to speak the Word to His creation.

> We remember that God has not left himself without a witness in any nation at any time. When we approach the man of another faith than our own it will be in a spirit of expectancy to find how God has been speaking to him and what new understandings of the grace and love of God we may ourselves discover in this encounter. Our first task in approaching another people, another culture, another religion, is to take off our shoes, for the place we are approaching is holy.[8]

On Being a Christian

"Faith" is for the Christian a very rich word. It represents the total human response to all that is experienced as holy and finds expression in both belief and action. The faithful Christian, no less than the nonbeliever, firmly rejects the God that is "too small," the empty, shallow, senseless concerns to which people devote themselves with often fanatical rigor. The Christian refuses to bow before idols, even those of his own fabrication, and for this Christians in the Roman Empire were tried and executed as "atheists." Today, in many countries they would be called disloyal, antisocial, enemies of the state. The Christian is called to abandon what is safe, comfortable, and familiar, and to undertake a risky journey of faith, following the example of Abraham, who was told, "Go from your country and your kindred and your father's house to the land that I will show you" (Gen. 12:1).

God, worshiped and adored by Christians, is the Reality that transcends all earthly phenomena and lies beyond all human skill and knowledge. Mysterious and ineffable, yet known in human experience, in the depths of human existence, God is the fathomless source of being and power. Our first glimpse of this mystery comes from our special capacity to wonder, which Aristotle called the origin of true wisdom and the essence of human nature. To wonder about the meaning of things is to be human. This is how

---

8. M. A. C. Warren, quoted by Ian G. Barbour in *Myths, Models and Paradigms* (New York: Harper & Row, 1974), 178.

we think, act, and have our being. We have, therefore, an inbuilt sense of the Other, expressed in our inner yearning to know the power of our consciences to choose, and the capacity to hunt for the *really* real.

Inherent in this view of humankind is the affirmation that we are not alone, that the universe is not the final source of its own meaning, and that the critical moments of human existence are turning points leading to a transformed life. Those who follow this way are never content with trivial rationalization, hiding the unsatisfactory nature of existence, its limits, frustrations, and pain. This faith offers no superficial remedy for our legitimate doubts, terrors and afflictions. It provides no escape into fantasy or some golden age, whether in the past or future, for truth is both the path and the power to follow it. In this Christians are not alone. All the great religious traditions are systems of faith, although their emphases and images may differ.

What, then, is specifically "Christian" about Christian faith? All religions agree that out of the transcendent mystery something is revealed, but the Christian faith speaks of *who* is revealed.

> He sometimes hides Himself from us; but faith alone, which will not fail us in time of need, ought to be our support, and the foundation of our confidence.[9]

From that cloud of mystery, the symbol of our unknowing, a word is spoken—in Jesus Christ. The mystery has become flesh, the dialogue of heaven and earth is audible, and in Christ Jesus we come to understand both what God is and what men and women are called to become. He is the model of sacrificial service in love and devotion to God and humankind. This is "the way, the truth, and the life." But at the same moment we recognize our failure to respond to that love. Love itself convicts us of our own self-love.

> For a Christian, his Christian existence is ultimately the totality of his existence. This totality opens out into the dark abysses of the wilderness which we call God. When one undertakes something like this, he stands before the great thinkers, the saints, and finally Jesus Christ. The abyss of existence opens in front of him. He knows that he has not thought enough, has not loved enough, and has not suffered enough.[10]

But if the transcendent mystery is present to all humanity simply by virtue of their being human, if God is indeed the universal love that lures the restless human heart, and "moves the sun and other stars," why should we follow the special, and often arduous, path of being a Christian?[11] This question should not be answered lightly. But perhaps we can see that while

---

9. Brother Lawrence, *The Practice of the Presence of God* (Old Tappan, N.J.: Fleming Revell, 1968), 58.

10. Karl Rahner, *Foundations of Christian Faith* (New York: Seabury Press, 1978), 2.

11. See additional notes.

God's embrace of the world is universal, the human response and human questions are partial, limited, conditioned by time and place. I do not love humanity; I love this person or that one. I do not love God in universal form as a transcendent mystery. I love Him, because He loves me, an individual. He calls *me*, and I respond, "Lord, here am I." I do not know why my name is called. I know only that my name is spoken as no other can speak it.

It is the calling, the intimate word of God, that makes men and women Christian. Our minds and hearts have been stirred, perhaps not so dramatically as were those of the apostles, Paul, or Augustine, but stirred nonetheless, and we discover new life, shaped and changed by the faithful response in Christ.

> The finality and uniqueness of Jesus Christ involves a personal response; the judgment about the person of Jesus Christ is a deeply personal matter. As is true of all personal matters, it demands the freedom of faith and it is always open to an eventually deeper revelation. In the realm of symbols, questions of finality and uniqueness do not fit into finished categories, once-for-all realities. Rather, they imply a dynamic process and are basically developments as faith itself.[12]

As members of Christ's body, bearing his likeness, baptized into his death, and making known the reign of God, we are called to proclaim "not only with our lips, but in our lives" the central message of the Christian faith: "God was in Christ, reconciling the world unto himself" (2 Cor. 5:19 KJV).

ADDITIONAL NOTES

5. One contributor commented here: "One problem the modern world has encountered in its attempts to build values and institutions with humanity as the base is the inability to hold to concrete limits and morals. As Dostoyevski said, 'Without God everything is possible.' Without an Absolute transcending the universe, there is no possibility of establishing rational absolutes inside the universe. If man is as free as Sartre suggests, then he is free to rape, pillage, and murder with as much justification as if he chose to love, heal, and serve. In an absurd, meaningless universe there is no reason to do anything other than what you want to do, and no reason for condemning others for doing what they want to do. Thus, modern man is left with the dilemma of knowing full well that what Hitler did was atrocious and wrong, but having no legitimate reason for condemning him.

"Humanism is in many ways an attempt to transcend this ethical nihilism without reference to the transcendent God. Camus, in his book *The Rebel,* seeks to propound the need for moderation and limits in an absurd universe. He says that a man true to his nature, a rebel, must live with the constant tensions of a meaningless death and a will to life, recognizing the value he places in his own life, and the necessity of valuing all life. It is a passionate plea for the need for humanness in our period of inhuman-

---

12. L. Richard, *What Are They Saying about Christ and World Religions?* (New York: Paulist Press, 1982), 68.

ness, but in the end it falls short of rationally transcending the ethical freedom of an absurd universe. This is the chance for theism, and specifically Christianity, to speak truth into the world, and give answers to modern humanity's troubling questions."

11. One contributor answered these questions as follows: "Why should we bother to follow the path of being a Christian? It is the true path (Jesus is 'the way, the truth and the life'). It is the only path (Jesus said that no one comes to God except through him). It is the path of life, a narrow path (Matt. 7:13-14). There is a hell for those who refuse to believe (John 3:18). All of God's blessings and inheritance of eternal life are available to those who accept God's grace in Christ.

"Christianity is not a particular path because Jesus is not a particular Lord. He is universally Lord of all the earth. His truth is universal truth. All religions are not the same, and we, as free people, are not culturally conditioned to the point of complete cultural slavery."

17

DISCIPLESHIP

Until now this book has been written largely in terms of we and us, since Christians are never separate individuals, isolated and alone, but always part of the church, the fellowship, the community of the faithful. Even when cast into solitary confinement and kept from all contact with the outside world, the Christian is not alone. He or she is sustained by the unceasing prayers of those outside, and is forever in communication with Christ and with the blessed company of those who are already in the heavenly realm. Nevertheless, the cruel fact that men, women, and even children are thus imprisoned by totalitarian regimes throughout the world emphasizes that the Christian, though never separate, is nevertheless an individual, a single person with a heavy load of individual responsibility for his or her actions, and capable of feeling desperate and cruel loneliness. It is necessary, therefore, to consider what are the responsibilities of a Christian, what is involved in "discipleship."

To write about this topic is possibly more difficult than writing about any other aspect of the faith of Christians. First, Christians, considered as individuals, are enormously varied, and one can offer no exact prescription for all of them. Second, anyone who ventures to write on this subject must become more and more aware of his or her own inadequacies, and the repeated failures to be a true disciple of Christ. Nevertheless, the effort needs to be made and some suggestions are therefore offered here under the headings of "Believing"—"Doing"—"Praying"—"Repenting"—"Thanking and Hoping."

Believing

"Lord, I believe; help thou mine unbelief." This anguished cry of the father of an epileptic son (Mark 9:24 KJV) is often on the lips of those who think seriously about their own believing. Belief thus examined is never easy. One can, of course, without any difficulty believe without

215

thinking. We do this all the time. We believe in our country, in democracy, in human rights, in our parents, and in our friends, and this means also believing that these things and these people are worthy of our trust. Such instinctive belief and trust is essential. We could never get anything done if we did not take a great many things on trust, without asking continual questions. Nevertheless, unthinking belief, what is often called blind faith, is exceedingly dangerous. Evil is perfectly capable of parading as good. Dishonest advertising can betray many innocent shoppers, and false prophets can deceive even the elect (Matt. 24:24). Only the absolutely true can endure all questioning.

The faithful Christian begins by believing, not only that God is, but also believing in God; believing not only that Jesus died and rose again, but in Jesus as Savior; believing not only in the Holy Spirit, but also that the Spirit is constantly at work in our midst. While all is going well we do not find believing in, and trusting in, God, in a life to come, and in the work of the Spirit very difficult. But when we encounter suffering, deep personal loss, manifest injustice, human brutality, doubts and questions rush in upon our minds, and we do not know whom or what to believe. Life can dissolve into meaninglessness.

It is doubtful whether we are really committing sin when we are in this manner thrust into doubt and even despair, since the questions that are forced upon us are valid questions. It would be more of a sin to try to suppress the doubts, to refuse to face the questions, because that would be manifest dishonesty. It is also not a sin, even in less urgent times, to have grave doubts about whether one can really believe in the virgin birth of Jesus, in the empty tomb, in miracles, in life after death, or any of the other things that Christians proclaim and teach. None of these assertions are exempt from human questioning, and none can be proved empirically. It would be altogether more sinful to believe them for no better reason than that we had learned them in Sunday school, or because as a Christian I ought to believe these things, or because the Bible says so, or out of a sense of duty.

Far more serious is the mental laziness that does not bother about such questions until they are forced on our attention. True faith involves being prepared to do some solid work, to ask the questions boldly, to wrestle with them, to discover what wiser and more experienced minds have said on the subject, to read as widely as possible to reject merely simplistic answers.

But none of this means that there is no room for simple faith. I am doing nothing creditable if I make my own mind the final judge of what is right and true, because that is intellectual arrogance. Nor am I doing God service, or service to anyone else for that matter, if I despise the simple beliefs of the unlettered peasant. Absolute truth has this curious character:

because it contains no falsehood it can be perceived even by "babes and sucklings," and yet its immense profundity exhausts the researches of even the most brilliant scholars. All the great religions of the world are built upon very simple statements, such as "Christ died for us while we were yet sinners," or for Muslims, "There is no god except God Himself, and Muhammad is the one whom God has sent," or for Buddhists, "All life is suffering," and yet no one has ever plumbed these statements to their final depths. True faith is always so simple that even a little child can do it, and so difficult that even the greatest saint grieves because he cannot achieve it.

None of this should surprise us. It is the kind of thing that is bound to happen whenever finite men and women become involved with infinity and eternity. What then should the ordinary Christian do? No exact prescription is possible, since each individual has his or her own problems and difficulties. Yet it is probably true that the best advice for each one of us is Persevere! Don't give up! Being a Christian means betting one's life that in Christ God has truly made Himself known, and that in Christ also we have been already delivered from the power of death and evil. Of course I do not understand it, because I shall never understand it on this side of death, nor will anyone else. But I can understand already what it is about, and the more that I keep at it, and think about it, the greater understanding I am likely to have, and the more solid, I hope, will be the foundation on which I build.

Doing

Faith is not true faith unless it issues in action. To proclaim the faith without doing anything about it is to indulge in those "idle words," for every one of which we are told that we "shall have to give account thereof in the day of judgment" (Matt. 12:36 KJV). "Faith by itself, if it has no works, is dead" (James 2:17). Yet it is no less true the other way round. "What must we do," the people asked Jesus, "to be doing the works of God?" and Jesus answered them, "This is the work of God, that you believe in him whom he has sent" (John 6:28-9). Faith and deeds are therefore intimately related and we cannot separate them.

Once again, the question of how to show forth our faith by our works is not altogether easy to answer. The first duty is probably obedience, something very difficult for the independent modern mind to accept. We must begin by obeying God as made known to us in Christ Jesus and in the Scriptures. There is no lack of moral instruction in both the Old and the New Testaments, but difficulties undoubtedly arise when we begin to ask what exactly we are supposed to do. A valuable principle to begin with is that if there should seem to be a conflict between the Old Testament and the New, as, for instance, in how we should treat our enemies, precedence should be given to the New Testament. For Christians Christ must remain the ultimate arbiter of their actions.

However, both the Old and New Testaments tend to establish principles of moral action rather than go into details, though admittedly the Old Testament is in some matters more precise. It is all very well to be told that we must love our neighbors and also our enemies, but what does this mean in practice? Clearly there is a special problem when love and authority have to be combined. How does one exercise love and control at the same time? This is a constant difficulty for all parents, teachers at every level from kindergarten to graduate school, judges, government officials, and many others as well. In what proportions must justice and mercy be mixed so as to provide the most healing medicine?

There is no clear-cut answer, nor is it correct to say, as some have done, that love always finds the answer. The love of God certainly knows the answer, but none of us possess that love in the needful abundance. We are left with the uncomfortable conclusion that we must do the best we can, fully knowing that we are bound to make mistakes. Certain guidelines are all that we have. First, it is seldom love to conceal the truth. It is never love for parents to gloss over the faults of their children, or for teachers out of the kindness of their hearts to award grades that have not been earned. Situations where the truth would do more harm than good are a great deal more rare than most of us would like to believe. Nevertheless, they do exist. There may certainly be occasions when it is kinder to hide the truth from someone who is desperately sick in the hope that he or she would be more able to face the shock at a later date. One cannot legislate for every occasion.

One thing is certain. No faithful disciple of Christ will ever withhold forgiveness, or carry resentment, envy, or contempt in the heart. If I am to be obedient to Christ, I must take active measures to annul all antagonism. If I have any reason to think that I have hurt someone inadvertently, or that someone I know is displeased with me, perhaps for no reason at all that I can perceive, I must seek that person out and try to put the matter right at the earliest opportunity. It is no less certain that love is generous, and that giving is not true giving until it hurts. With all the constant inflation in the modern world the need to take thought for the future, to provide for the education of one's children, to take precautions against phenomenal hospital expenses, and for many the possibility of prolonged unemployment, is unquestionably urgent. It would be idle to pretend otherwise. Yet the command still remains that we should trust God wholeheartedly and "not be anxious about tomorrow, for tomorrow will be anxious for itself" (Matt. 6:34). Every individual Christian must resolve this dilemma for himself or herself. No one person can instruct another on this matter. But for all the guiding principle must be: Do not assess your giving in terms only of what you can afford after providing for your own family's needs and pleasures. Run at least some risks, and even at times some alarming ones. Otherwise there is no confidence in God at all.

Finally, every Christian must be prepared to be honest and open about the faith. For some this responsibility comes more easily than for others, who are private persons, unwilling to wear their heart upon their sleeve. They do not enjoy speaking out in public, or even to an acquaintance, about matters that are dear to them, or they are afraid of ridicule or hurting the feelings of those who do not agree. Again there can be no cut-and-dried instructions, but every Christian needs to examine himself or herself on this matter, and seek both the guidance and the strength of the Spirit, lest silence be an escape of selfishness.

Praying

It should be clear from what has been said already that the Christian life cannot be lived on purely human terms. It has no reality or meaning at all apart from God, in the fullest sense of that word. There is no Christianity without recognition of, and obedience to, the Creator and Sustainer of all that is, the authority and saving power of the Son, and the guidance, strength, and comfort of the Spirit. The life of discipleship is therefore lived in constant conversation with God, walking hand in hand with Him along the tortuous path of life, straying neither to the right hand nor the left. This intimate conversation we call worship. It can be done—indeed must be done—both communally in open fellowship with others as a community and in privacy as individuals. The basic elements of this worship have been beautifully set before us by Archbishop Cranmer in the traditional exhortation at the beginning of Anglican Morning and Evening Prayer, described as the time

> when we assemble and meet together to render thanks for the great benefits we have received at his hands, to set forth his most worthy praise, to hear his most holy Word, and to ask those things which are requisite and necessary, as well for the body as the soul.

Although this description is of corporate worship, the same principles apply to private prayer, and the order is worth consideration. It does not begin as one might expect, with adoration and praise of the infinite God, but with something very much more simple—the saying of "thank you." Some, it is true, find speaking to God in private prayer so easy that the words flow from their lips, but for many others it proves very difficult. They feel that they ought to be doing something, but they don't know where to begin. The very simplicity of "thank you" opens the door for us. It is a phrase everyone learns as a child, and continues to use until speech is no longer possible. There is no difficulty at all about saying thank you, and no harm in beginning all prayer in this way. We need, of course, to pause from time to time and think for what things we ought to give thanks. They cover an enormous range, from the heartfelt relief at escape from imminent death to the simple pleasure given by a letter from a friend or the glimpse of a tree in the fall. Quite possibly most of us ought to give thanks far more often than we do. Saint Teresa of Avila said that we should thank God for everything that happens to us, but that is a goal to aim at, not something we can do at the very beginning.

Some find it easier to pray kneeling at their bedside or before a crucifix, some sitting quietly in a chair, sometimes putting another chair in front of them so as to increase the sense of talking to somebody. Some pray standing, some walking back and forth so as to concentrate their thoughts. There are no rules about such a matter. Everyone must do what seems most natural and helpful. But to whom are we talking? The obvious answer is God, but for many this is of little help. God seems so vague, so unlike a real person. As one puzzled worshiper put it, "I find that when I pray I can only think of God as a vague grey blur up in the top right-hand corner of the room." Again there are no rules. We may speak to the Father, or if that term offends us to the Mother (though we must be careful not to attribute sex to God), and visualize, if we will, the perfect human father or mother. We may talk to Jesus, or we may address the Spirit. We must do whatever brings us nearer to the presence of God, and as through the years we continue both to pray and to think about prayer, the stumbling words and inadequate images with which we began will give place to what is more profound.

The "most worthy praise" is something different. It is the daily recognition of the glory and majesty of God, the Creator of all that is, and at the same time the infinitely small entering into every nook and cranny of our lives. It is the recognition of our salvation, and of Jesus of Nazareth who saved us. It is the grateful acceptance of the endless comfort and power of the Spirit. We must, of course, try to make this part of our own thoughts and language, but for the fullest recognition it is probably helpful to draw upon the words of those who have gone before us, upon the language of the Bible, especially in the Psalms and the epistles, but also in the language of the historic liturgies, or worship services, of the church. In using these words we join that great company of Christians, in heaven and on earth, united in the praise of God: Father, Son, and Holy Spirit.

"To hear his most holy Word." This is an essential feature of all worship, public or private, if it is to be the true "worth-ship" that we discussed in an earlier chapter. In our modern busy and secularized world there are many Christians who do not fully grasp what an amazing and infinitely rich treasure we possess in the Bible. It is a whole library of books, and by reading and meditating upon it our understanding of God and His purposes is steadily enriched. We never come to the end of it. Some parts speak immediately to us, but some passages, even some whole books, we may find puzzling, perhaps desperately difficult to understand. But we should not condemn it for that reason. It would be sad indeed if we were ever able to put it on one side, saying, I now understand it all. Part of the rich delight of the Bible is that never, however long we live, can we come to the end of exploring it. The more we read it, the more we meditate upon it, the more it speaks to us directly, and the more it has to say. It is a great part of the miracle of the Bible that, far more than any other great religious book, it lends itself to translation, and the work of translation into all the languages of the world never ceases. Every Christian throughout the world knows the Bible in translated form; even those who speak Greek or Hebrew as their native tongue encounter one of the two Testaments in translation.

We should, of course, seek help. There are a large number of manuals to assist us with our daily reading and meditation, and an almost infinite number of books, great and small, about the Bible. There are available to us many commentaries on single books of the Bible. Little by little, as year succeeds to year, each one of us should try to become familiar with the whole Bible and, as far as possible, persist in reading all of it. One of the most powerful and insidious temptations, both for the single person and for the community as a whole, is to slip, almost unconsciously, into reading only those passages and books with which we are comfortable, and leaving on one side those which threaten and disturb us.

Only toward the end of our prayers should we turn to asking for what we think to be "requisite and necessary." Thanksgiving, praise, and instruction all come first. In asking, which we are fully encouraged by God to do, the most immediate necessity is to be honest. Trusting God wholeheartedly involves telling Him what we really think, not merely what we have been told we ought to think. If much of what we ask for at first is superficial and unworthy, we shall learn this little by little, and be able to put such thoughts completely out of our minds. Their place will be taken by more profound understanding. But nothing is to be gained by dishonest thinking, whether spiritual or intellectual. If we are truly honest with God, we will find ourselves saying again and again something like this: This is how it seems to me, O Lord, and this is what I would like, what I hope for. Such hopes may be altogether unworthy, or even perhaps wrong, but no harm is done if we remember to say also, and at the very least *try* to mean, Nevertheless, not what I want, but what you want, be done.

The exhortation quoted at the beginning of this section says nothing about praying for other people. Since it is a preparation for confession of sin, it quite properly concentrates our attention upon ourselves and our own community. Nevertheless, every sound act of worship must stretch out to include other people, since Christ died, not for us only, but for all men and women. To pray without giving serious thought to these very many others is not true prayer at all. When we are aware of sickness or distress it is possible to be quite specific in our prayers for other people, but probably most often we can pray only in general terms, trusting in God to do for them what is best.

Since the human mind is often forgetful, and since it is also a creature of habit, there is great value in having some kind of prayer calendar, a list of people for whom we should pray, so that none are forgotten. This list could stretch over a week or even a month—everyone must decide for himself or herself what is best, considering only that it is very easy to be forgetful. Certainly to be regularly included are those whom we are tempted to omit: the desperately unhappy, the starving, the persecuted and oppressed, and also the enemies. These include all who in some way or another appear to set themselves against our way of life and what we believe to be true, all who seem to threaten our well-being. The more godless we believe communism to be, the more fervently we should pray for the well-being of communists.

Repenting

Our word "penitence" comes from the Latin *poena*, meaning "punishment." Penitence, therefore, means feeling and expressing sorrow for our sins, in the earnest hope that we may escape the well-merited punishment. This is a perfectly valid way of looking at the matter, but it might be more valuable to think of it in Old Testament terms. The words used there are *nacham* (comfort or ease) and *shuv* (to turn), and the sense is that human sin inevitably causes intense suffering and unhappiness, and that it is only by turning away from sinful behavior that we can be at ease and comforted. For *teshuvah* (turning), it has been said, the world was created.

Blessed is the man
  who walks not in the counsel of the wicked,
nor stands in the way of sinners,
  nor sits in the seat of scoffers.
                                                        Psalm 1:1

With these words the Book of Psalms opens, setting before us a vivid picture of someone strolling along a path that leads in the wrong direction, then pausing to stand and talk with people who are full of bad advice, and finally sitting down and becoming one of their company. It would certainly be better, as the psalmist says, not to have got involved with such people in the first place, however witty and knowledgeable they may seem, and we would be right to be sorry about it, but the essential feature of repentance is to get up, bid them farewell, and try to get back to the right road. Sometimes the track that leads back to it is not too difficult, though it is seldom really easy. Always some help is needed, and we must ask for that help in our prayers. But there are times when the problem of extricating oneself from the sheer power of the wrong way of life seems altogether insoluble. For this reason the true worshiper is never alone in prayer. Not only does he or she have Christ close at hand, but help is available from other men and women: close friends, sage counselors, and people who have gone through the same torment, and know from the agony of their own experience how and when to give assistance.

Despite what many tell us, there is nothing wrong in having guilt feelings. We are in fact often guilty, and it is as well to admit this. We must recognize that we are very often weak, fully intending to do what is right, and failing to do it. But, however odd it may seem to say so, it is not altogether wrong to cry out against God, even to accuse Him of injustice. It is certainly not something to be recommended, but honesty before God takes precedence over all other Christian duties. Every counselor knows full well that only when someone is entirely frank, even when this is expressed in fury, contempt, and bitterness of heart, is it possible to give really effective help. Besides, how much worse our situation would be if there were no one to cry out against, no governing authority against whom to rebel!

Thanking and Hoping

We have already discussed the giving of thanks, but in this final section we must for a moment return to it, because it goes hand in hand with hope. In giving thanks we look back to the past, to all that is recorded in the Bible, to all the benefits that have accrued in the centuries since then, and to our own personal past. In thanksgiving we look also to the present, and certainly in this country to the manifold causes for rejoicing that surround us. In hope we continue this process into the future, and certify our confidence that God does not change, that His mercies are everlasting, and new every morning. We proclaim our conviction that our salvation, once achieved by Christ nearly two thousand years ago, can never now be annulled. Hope is of all human activities the most authentic proclamation to the world of the absolute reality of God and at the same time His infinite mercy.

There are, of course, many men and women in the world, far too many, who find that they are left with no other hope than death. As they lie helpless in prison, as they are brought day after day to the torture chamber, as they and their families die inch by inch from hunger, as they suffer the agonies of an incurable disease and are kept alive only by machines, they long for death as those lost in the pitiless desert long for water. Yet for very many of them, as for Job, the death they long for does not come. Some sadistic prison guards in totalitarian countries keep the prisoners alive for no other reason than that they may be tortured again.

This is indeed a grim note on which to conclude this book, but it would be less than honest to conceal it. These people exist in our world, and they are far too numerous. Even one would be too many, and they are a multitude. They are helpless, and it is left to us, the more fortunate, not only to express the hope they cannot utter, but also to be their hope. It falls to our lot to pray for them without ceasing, and to sustain them by our prayers, and at the same time to bring out into the full light of day the brutal and universal fact of human suffering, and to seek by the power of the Spirit to overcome evil by good.

> That word above all earthly powers,
>   No thanks to them, abideth;
> The Spirit and the gifts are ours
>   Through him who with us sideth:
> Let goods and kindred go,
> This mortal life also;
> The body they may kill:
> God's truth abideth still,
>   His kingdom is for ever.
>   Martin Luther, 1529
>   (trans. Frederick Hedge, 1852)

SELECT BIBLIOGRAPHY FOR
FURTHER READING

Based upon suggestions and comments made by the student contributors and the two authors.

GENERAL

Bainton, Roland. *A Short History of Christianity and Its Impact on Western Civilization*, 2 vols. New York: Harper & Row, 1966. An enjoyable treatment by an eminent scholar of Luther and Erasmus.

Barrett, David B., ed. *World Christian Encyclopedia: A Comparative Survey of Churches and Religions in the Modern World*, A.D. *1900–2000*. New York and London: Oxford University Press, 1982. An invaluable work of reference with maps, statistical tables, and pertinent secular information.

Bettenson, Henry, ed. *Documents of the Christian Church*. 2d. ed. New York and London: Oxford University Press, 1967. A useful compendium of a variety of materials, though tending to stress the English church.

Bloesch, Donald G. *Essentials of Evangelical Theology*, 2 vols. San Francisco: Harper & Row, 1978, 1979. This surveys, from a somewhat conservative stance, the topics of God, authority, salvation, human life, ministry, and hope.

Booty, John E. *The Church in History*. New York: Seabury Press, 1979. This is an elegant short study, forming part of a helpful series sponsored by the Episcopal Church for use in schools and discussion groups.

Cross, F. L., and E. A. Livingston, eds. *The Oxford Dictionary of the Christian Church*, 2d. rev. ed. New York and London: Oxford University Press, 1978. An indispensable work of reference, with updated bibliographies.

Feiner, Johannes, et al. *The Common Catechism*. New York: Seabury Press, 1975. An ecumenical primer on the basic Christian beliefs.

Gonzales, Justo. *A History of Christian Thought*, 3 vols. Nashville: Abingdon Press, 1971–1975. A comprehensive and balanced survey by a Third World theologian, writing from a Protestant position.

Johnson, Paul. *A History of Christianity*. New York: Atheneum, 1979. A very readable one-volume survey from the beginnings of Christianity to the present. Written in a sharp, somewhat popular style.

Lewis, C. S. *Mere Christianity*. New York: Macmillan Co., 1952. An admirable introduction to the main tenets of the Christian faith, written with great clarity and elegance.

McBrien, Richard P. *Catholicism*, 2 vols. Minneapolis: Winston Press, 1980. Surveys the meaning of being a Roman Catholic, in both traditional and modern terms. Includes primary documents, bibliographies, chapter summaries, and discussion questions. (Available also in a condensed form.)

Vidler, A. R. *Soundings: Essays Concerning Christian Understanding*. New York: Cambridge University Press, 1963. Contains eleven chapters, written by different authors, dealing with a large number of the subjects discussed in this book. Very easy to read.

1
FAITH AND BELIEF IN THE WORLD OF TODAY

Cupitt, Don. *The Worlds of Science and Religion*. London: Sheldon Press, 1976. A helpful short book that discusses in straightforward language whether science has destroyed religion, and whether a scientific standpoint can coexist with, or be a substitute for, a religious code.

Dixon, W. MacNeile. *The Human Situation*. Harmondsworth, Eng.: Penguin Books, 1937. These Gifford Lectures are at the same time profound and witty. Full of fascinating ideas, they are a joy to read.

Donovan, Peter. *Religious Language*. London: Sheldon Press, 1979. A short and interesting book about "religious *language-use*, just as much as religious language, to show that the emphasis is less on the words themselves than on what is being done with them."

Heim, Karl. *Christian Faith and Natural Science*. Translated by Neville Horton Smith. London: SCM Press, 1953. A scholarly and profound study of the difference between two worldviews: the scientific and the religious.

Hesse, Mary B. *Science and the Human Imagination: Aspects of the History and Logic of Physical Science*. London: SCM Press, 1954. A helpful introduction to the development of some aspects of modern scientific thought and their relation to religious thought.

Smith, Wilfred Cantwell. *Faith and Belief*. Princeton, N.J.: Princeton University Press, 1979. Examines the phenomenon of personal piety and of obedience to the Ultimate.

Steuer, Axel D., and James Wm. McClendon, Jr., eds. *Is God God?* Nashville: Abingdon Press, 1981. Ten essays in response to the question: What is, who is God? How can one know the true, adequate, proper *God-Concept*? Valuable, but not easy to understand.

Torrance, Thomas F. *Christian Theology and Scientific Culture*. Belfast: Christian Journals Ltd., 1980. A series of four lectures, concerned with "the deep mutual relation and respect of Christian and scientific thought for each other."

2
THE AUTHORITY OF SCRIPTURE

Achtemeier, Paul J. *The Inspiration of Scripture: Problems and Proposals*. Philadelphia: Westminster Press, 1980. A sympathetic study of the varying views on biblical inerrancy, which nevertheless in the end concludes that literal inerrancy of the Bible is a misleading concept.

Austin, M. R. "How Biblical Is the Inspiration of Scripture?" *The Expository Times* 93 (December, 1981): 75–79. A helpful article for those anxious to disentangle some of the difficulties of the subject.

Barth, Markus. *Conversation with the Bible.* New York: Holt, Rinehart and Winston, 1964. An excellent short study of the question of the interpretation of the Bible in the modern world and the problem of biblical authority in the light of modern critical and analytical studies. Strongly recommended.

Countryman, William. *Biblical Authority or Biblical Tyranny?* Philadelphia: Fortress Press, 1981. An explanation of biblical authority that criticizes both the fundamentalist and the purely critical reading and use of Scripture.

Gilson, Etienne. *Reason and Revelation in the Middle Ages.* New York: Charles Scribner's Sons, 1938. A valuable study of medieval religious thought, both Christian and Muslim.

Hauerwas, Stanley. "The Moral Authority of Scripture," *Interpretation* 34 (October 1980): 356–70. Shows how the community's morality is based in Scripture.

Henry, Carl F. H. *Revelation and the Bible.* Grand Rapids: Baker Book House, 1959. A serious and scholarly defense of the traditional conservative understanding of the revealed Word in the Bible.

Mesters, Carlos. "The Use of the Bible in Christian Communities of the Common People." In *The Challenge of Basic Christian Communities,* edited by Sergio Torres and John Eagleson. Maryknoll, N.Y.: Orbis Books, 1981. A Brazilian Roman Catholic priest examines the use and meaning of the Bible in rural church communities, and biblical interpretation in different cultural contexts.

Niebuhr, H. Richard. *The Meaning of Revelation.* New York: Macmillan Co., 1941. A classic treatment of the subject, concise and easy to read. Essential.

Smalley, Beryl. *The Study of the Bible in the Middle Ages.* Notre Dame, Ind.: University of Notre Dame Press, 1970. A valuable survey of the various schools of interpretation, literal and symbolic, now mostly lost.

3
ONE GOD AND
FATHER

Grant, Robert. *The Early Christian Doctrine of God.* Charlottesville, Va.: University of Virginia Press, 1966. Treats the developing Christian understanding of God in the context of the contemporary Hebrew and Hellenistic world.

King, Robert H. *The Meaning of God.* Philadelphia: Fortress Press, 1973. Discusses the concept of God in several religions, and examines the idea of the relationship between God and Christ. A good book to read.

Macquarrie, John. *Thinking about God.* New York: Harper & Row, 1975. Written in straightforward language, this covers a wide range of problems involved in attempting to think about the infinite God, and different approaches to these problems. Strongly recommended.

Niebuhr, H. Richard. *Radical Monotheism and Western Culture.* A classic study of the idolatry and polytheism characteristic of the self-proclaimed monotheism of the Western world.

Visser t' Hooft, Wilhelm. *The Fatherhood of God in an Age of Emancipation.* Geneva: World Council of Churches, 1982. A very thoughtful and sympathetic short study

228 THE FAITH OF CHRISTIANS

of the problem of paternalism in the present age of human affirmation. A helpful
introduction to the subject.

Watt, W. Montgomery. *The Reality of God.* London: SPCK, 1957. An excellent short
and simple introduction to a very complex subject.

Wolfson, Harry A. *The Philosophy of the Church Fathers*, 2d. rev. ed. Cambridge,
Mass.: Harvard University Press, 1964. Important essays by a renowned Jewish
thinker on the Christian understanding of God.

4
CREATOR AND
CREATION

Barton, George A. *Christ and Evolution.* Philadelphia: University of Pennsylvania
Press, 1934. A short and easy-to-read book, which presents straightforward explanations to many areas of concern considered in the present book.

Birch, L. Charles. *Nature and God.* London: SCM Press, 1965. Much emphasis is
placed on the theme of the first chapter, "The Universe: a Machine or a Birth." Easy
to read, this book offers a fresh look at the concept of creation.

Frost, Robert C. *The Mystery of Life.* Plainfield, N.J.: Logos International, 1981. Written by a biologist, this book gives a scientist's view of Christianity, presenting it in
the form of a series of questions: the Why? Who? When? Where? What? and How?
of life.

Gibbs, John G. *Creation and Redemption.* Leiden: E. J. Brill, 1971. This looks at Paul's
interpretation of creation and redemption, and how they are related to each other.
It is, however, not easy reading.

Hayes, Zachary. *What Are They Saying about Creation?* New York: Paulist Press, 1980.
Part of a useful series, this book gives an overview of the biblical and theological
treatments of creation, and the human place in the world in light of the challenges
from philosophy and the positive sciences.

Schaeffer, Francis A. *No Final Conflict.* Downers Grove, Ill.: Intervarsity Press, 1980.
A helpful booklet by a well-known conservative scholar, stressing that science, history, and the Bible can co-exist without conflict.

Westermann, Claus. *Creation.* Philadelphia: Fortress Press, 1974. An excellent short
book, which should be required reading for anyone who wishes to understand the
biblical perspective on creation.

5
JESUS OF NAZARETH—SON OF MAN
AND SON OF GOD

Anderson, Charles C. *The Historical Jesus: A Continuing Quest.* Grand Rapids: Wm.
B. Eerdmans, 1972. A scholarly and serious work, clearly written from a somewhat
conservative position. Contains much valuable information.

Boff, Leonardo. *Jesus Christ Liberator: A Critical Christology for Our Time.*
Maryknoll, N.Y.: Orbis Books, 1978. A Latin American theologian presents a portrait of Jesus, based upon a radical reading of the Bible.

Dodd, C. H. *The Founder of Christianity.* New York: Macmillan Co., 1970. An outstanding brief work dealing with the question: What do we really know about Jesus?
How do we know it?

Dyson, A. O. *Who Is Jesus Christ?* London: SCM Press, 1969. A difficult but rewarding book that examines the problems in the ideas about Jesus of such contemporary theologians as Rudolf Bultmann.

Green, Michael, ed. *The Truth of God Incarnate*. Grand Rapids: Wm. B. Eerdmans, 1977. Essays on the following topics: Jesus in the New Testament; Jesus and History; Jesus, God Incarnate.

Hall, Thor. *The Evolution of Christology*. Nashville: Abingdon Press, 1982. A brief, well-argued, and usually nontechnical study of the development of deeper understandings of the nature and work of Jesus. Two suggestive concluding chapters on how we should understand the work of God through Christ in the modern space age.

Mackey, James P. *Jesus: The Man and the Myth*. New York: Paulist Press, 1979. Although the book was not written primarily for scholars, but for the pastoral priest and the inquiring layperson, it is by no means easy reading. Yet it is worth struggling with, since it contains much excellent material.

Manson. T. W. *The Servant-Messiah*. Grand Rapids: Baker Book House, 1977. A quite excellent book. Short, easy to read, it throws much light on the person of Jesus.

Pagels, Elaine. *The Gnostic Gospels*. New York: Vintage Books, 1981. Elegantly written, this is an admirable introduction to the question of gnosticism and the writings of Gnostic Christians, whose views were ultimately rejected by the early church.

Ziesler, John. *The Jesus Question*. London: Lutterworth Press, 1980. A very helpful introduction to the problem of who Jesus really was—both scholarly and easy to read.

6
THE WORKS AND WORDS
OF JESUS

Anderson, Charles C. *The Historical Jesus: A Continuing Quest*. Grand Rapids: Wm. B. Eerdmans, 1972. A very helpful book, though more suitable for the moderately advanced student than for the beginner.

Beare, Frank W. *The Earliest Records of Jesus*. Nashville: Abingdon Press, 1962. Discusses in detail the mighty works done by Jesus, comparing the various Gospel accounts.

Davis, W. D. *Invitation to the New Testament: A Guide to Its Main Witnesses*. Garden City, N.Y.: Doubleday & Co., 1969. Beautifully written in everyday English, this is an invitation which no one wishing to understand the New Testament should refuse.

Hengel, Martin. *Crucifixion*. Philadelphia: Fortress Press, 1977. A mere ninety pages, this is a marvel of solid scholarship and clear presentation. It should not be neglected by anyone who wishes to understand the New Testament.

Hunter, A. M. *The Work and Words of Jesus*. London: SCM Press, 1950. The title of this chapter was stolen from this book, in admiration of the author's achievement. It was rightly described by another reviewer as "strong meat, excellently well served."

Kee, Howard Clark. *Jesus in History: An Approach to the Study of the Gospels*. New York: Harcourt Brace Jovanovich, 1970. A very clear and helpful introduction to understanding the Gospels and their background.

Lewis, C. S. *Miracles*. New York: Macmillan Co., 1976. A subtle and tightly constructed book concerning the existence of God and divine intervention in the lives of human beings, this is a model of clear and logical thought. Many readers are completely convinced by his argument, though others still have doubts in their minds at the end.

Swinburne, Richard. *The Concept of Miracle*. London: Macmillan & Co., 1970.

Defines miracle in various historical and modern senses, and discusses the problem of rationalization. A worthwhile book.

Sykes, S. W., and J. P. Clayton, ed. *Christ, Faith and History.* New York: Cambridge University Press, 1972. A collection of seventeen essays representing a wide variety of opinions concerning the nature and function of Jesus Christ.

Taylor, Vincent. *The Formation of the Gospel Tradition.* London: St. Martin's Press, 1968. Discusses the miracle stories, and argues that the basis for these can be found in tradition, influenced by popular stories and themes.

7

RESURRECTION

Badham, Paul. *Christian Beliefs About Life After Death.* New York: Harper & Row, 1976. An interesting and helpful survey of the biblical understanding of resurrection in the light of modern scientific knowledge, and in particular, modern studies of the human mind. Requires some background knowledge, but otherwise very readable.

Grillmeyer, Aloys. *Christ in the Christian Tradition: From the Apostolic Age to Chalcedon.* New York: Sheed & Ward, 1965. An encyclopedic treatment of developing concepts in early Christianity concerning the resurrected Christ.

Hellwig, Monica K. *What Are They Saying about Death and Christian Hope.* New York: Paulist Press, 1978. A very helpful little book on the subject of resurrection for people with only minimal background knowledge. Contains useful suggestions for further reading.

O'Collins, Gerald. *The Resurrection of Jesus Christ.* Valley Forge, Pa.: Judson Press, 1973. Gives a detailed analysis of the sources for the Christian belief in the resurrection and surveys modern interpretations, attempting at the same time to harmonize conflicting views.

Marxsen, Willi. *The Resurrection of Jesus of Nazareth.* Philadelphia: Fortress Press, 1970. A standard and authoritative study of the subject.

Torrance, Thomas F. *Space, Time and Resurrection.* Edinburgh: The Handsel Press, 1976. Designed for the general reader, this book examines the biblical understanding of both the resurrection and ascension of Christ, and argues that both are entirely consistent with (a) the nature and character of Jesus of Nazareth and (b) twentieth-century scientific thought.

Wilckens, Ulrich. *Resurrection.* Edinburgh: Saint Andrew Press, 1977. An excellent little book providing a helpful introduction to both the New Testament understanding of resurrection and also the Jewish concept of resurrection which lies behind the biblical accounts.

Williams, H. A. *True Resurrection.* New York: Holt, Rinehart and Winston, 1972. This short book is particularly helpful in that it discusses resurrection not only in the traditional sense of something happens after death, but as something which affects the whole of human life between birth and death.

8

THE HOLY SPIRIT

Cockin, F. A. *God in Action: A Study of the Holy Spirit.* Harmondsworth, Eng.: Penguin Books, 1961. A very helpful short book addressing the question of why, if the Christian church typifies the dynamic activity of the Holy Spirit, there should be so much division within it.

Minear, Paul. *Images of the Church in the New Testament*. Philadelphia: Westminster Press, 1960. Written by a distinguished scholar, this is an important study of the concept of the lordship of Christ over the church through the activity of the Holy Spirit.

Lampe, G. W. H. *God as Spirit*. New York and London: Oxford University Press, 1976. In these Bampton Lectures the author gives a general account of the relation of the Spirit of God and the spirit of man, as well as examining the church's relation to the Spirit.

Ramsey, Michael. *Holy Spirit*. London: SPCK, 1977. A brief, but very helpful study of this subject by the former Archbishop of Canterbury.

Taylor, John V. *The Go-Between God*. New York and London: Oxford University Press, 1979. A fascinating and suggestive study of the Holy Spirit as it is to be understood in modern-day terms. Essential reading for anyone interested in this subject.

Williams, Charles. *The Descent of the Dove*. New York: Meridian Books, 1956. A brief history of the church from the perspective of the activity of the Spirit. Beautifully written, this is a unique and important book.

9
THE HOLY AND UNDIVIDED TRINITY

Hodgson, Leonard. *The Doctrine of the Trinity*. London: James Nisbet & Co., 1943. Although written forty years ago, this remains a classic. It provides a helpful survey of the doctrine, examining both the biblical sources and the motives behind the later interpretations.

Lonergan, Bernard J. *The Way to Nicea: The Dialectical Development of Trinitarian Theology*. Philadelphia: Westminster Press, 1976. A historical study of a critical moment in the formulation of Christian dogma. The author is an important innovator in the field of theological method.

Sayers, Dorothy L. *The Mind of the Maker*. New York: Harcourt Brace Jovanovich, 1941. A fascinating study by a brilliant writer of the logical necessity of the Trinity concept, building her argument upon the analogy of human artistic creation.

10
SIN, SALVATION, AND REDEMPTION

Cherbonnier, E. LaB. *Hardness of Heart*. Garden City, N.Y.: Doubleday & Co., 1955. A helpful introduction to the subject, clarifying the traditional Christian understanding of sin, and bringing the Bible into modern focus.

Davies, D. R. *Down Peacock's Feathers*. London: Centenary Press, 1943. A delightfully written study of the Anglican General Confession, in which the author examines the nature of sin and repentance, leading to salvation. The readership should by no means be confined to Episcopalians!

Lewis, C. S. *The Great Divorce*. New York: Macmillan Co., 1946. In what is certainly one of his best books, C. S. Lewis gives an imaginary pictorial account of entering eternity through death, and of purgation and salvation in the afterlife.

Plaskow, Judith. *Sex, Sin and Grace: Women's Experience and the Theologies of Reinhold Niebuhr and Paul Tillich*. Lanham, Md.: University Press of America, 1980. Recent and relevant discussions of various interpretations of sin and salvation.

Shinn, Roger L. *Life, Death and Destiny*. Philadelphia: Westminster Press, 1957. Discusses sin and its consequences, as well as modern views on the relation of Christ to salvation. Very easy reading.

11
GOD AND HISTORY

Achtemeier, Paul, and Elizabeth Achtemeier. *The Old Testament Roots of Our Faith*. Nashville: Abingdon Press, 1962. Important for an understanding of the significance of the Mt. Sinai covenant for subsequent Israelite thought.

Baly, Denis. *God and History in the Old Testament*. New York: Harper & Row, 1976. This book, also written in collaboration with students at Kenyon College, provides a fuller picture of some of the ideas presented in this chapter.

Butterfield, Herbert. *Christianity and History*. New York: Charles Scribner's Sons, 1950. A brilliant series of lectures, showing how an understanding of history is essential for the Christian, since Christian faith and historical events are closely related.

Collingwood, R. G. *The Idea of History*. New York: Oxford University Press, 1956. A classic work, first published in 1946, but written about ten years earlier. Basic for any serious understanding of history.

Dodd, C. H. *History and the Gospel*. London: Hodder & Stoughton, 1964. Written with his usual felicity, this short book provides an excellent introduction to Christianity as a historical religion.

Edwards, David L. *Religion and Change*. New York: Harper & Row, 1969. A very important and provocative study of the changes wrought in religious thought by the development of science and the secularized society.

Richardson, Alan. *History, Sacred and Profane*. London: SCM Press, 1964. First delivered as the Bampton Lectures at the University of Oxford in 1963, this is a scholarly and serious study, but, like everything that Alan Richardson wrote, very clearly presented.

Rust, Eric C. *Towards a Theological Understanding of History*. New York and London: Oxford University Press, 1963. Written by a Baptist scholar to "show that the Christian revelation in salvation history does provide a coherent and comprehensive understanding of history," this is another very clearly written book.

12
CHRISTIANS AND THE
END-TIME

Averill, Lloyd J. "Is the End Near?" *The Christian Century* (19 January 1983): 45–48. A thoughtful essay questioning the current apocalyptic fervor.

Ellul, Jacques. *Apocalypse: The Book of Revelation*. Translated by George W. Schreiner. New York: Seabury Press, 1977. An in-depth study by a very distinguished French Protestant writer about the Book of Revelation, exploring the symbols and images, rather than attempting simply to decode the material.

Hick, John. *Death and Eternal Life*. New York: Harper & Row, 1976. A concise discussion of the wide range of ideas about heaven, hell, purgatory, etc., from early Christian times to the present.

Lindsey, Hal. *There's a New World Coming*. New York: Bantam Books, 1973. A detailed analysis of the Book of Revelation from the perspective of a born-again Christian.

Martin, James P. *The Last Judgment*. Grand Rapids: Wm. B. Eerdmans, 1963. Written from a Protestant Christian understanding of this subject, this is a helpful study, ending with a discussion of Ritschl's eschatology and rejection of a last judgment.

Martin, William. "Waiting for the End," *The Atlantic Monthly* 249 (June 1982): 31–37. A critical examination of the current emphasis on the end-time.

Pieper, Josef. *Death and Immortality.* New York: Herder & Herder, 1969. Worth reading especially for the treatment in chapter 3 of the question, What does the separation of body and soul mean?

13
CHRISTIAN WORSHIP

Barth, Karl. *Prayer and Preaching.* London: SCM Press, 1964. An excellent outline by the celebrated German theologian of the characteristics and function of both praying to God and proclaiming the Gospel.

Dix, Dom Gregory. *The Shape of the Liturgy.* London: Dacre Press, 1970 (1945). A reprint of a classic work on the subject of worship—both informative and inspiring.

Duffy, Regis. *Real Presence: Worship, Sacraments, and Commitment.* San Francisco: Harper & Row, 1982. The book relates sacraments to the human life cycle and to perspectives in recent psychological studies.

Hatchett, Marion J. *Sanctifying Life, Time and Space: An Introduction to Liturgical Study.* New York: Seabury Press, 1976. A study of the process of sanctification in various historical periods.

Moule, C. F. D. *Worship in the New Testament.* Richmond, Va.: John Knox Press, 1961. A detailed and comparative study of the New Testament understanding of the eucharist and of baptism. Authoritative and helpful.

Steere, Douglas V. *Prayer and Worship.* New York: Association Press, 1938. A very helpful introduction to the subject, clear and easy to read. The chapter on corporate worship is especially good.

Underhill, Evelyn. *Worship.* New York: Harper & Brothers, 1937. Another classic, and very worthwhile reading. The first part is particularly helpful in defining such terms as "sacrament" and "prayer."

14
THE MISSIONARY
IMPERATIVE

Cronin, A. J. *The Keys of the Kingdom.* Boston: Little, Brown & Co., 1941. A celebrated novel about a Scottish Roman Catholic priest who spends thirty-two years working as a missionary in a remote part of China. This book raises important questions about missionary methods and the Christian attitude to agnosticism and to adherents of other faiths.

Donovan, Vincent J. *Christianity Rediscovered: An Epistle from the Masai.* Maryknoll, N.Y.: Orbis Books, 1982. A short, extremely interesting book by a Roman Catholic missionary priest concerning the proper methods of winning men and women for Christ, and the often negative impact upon a tribal society of the traditional evangelism.

Hick, John, and Brian Hebblethwaite, eds. *Christianity and Other Religions.* Philadelphia: Fortress Press, 1981. A collection of very helpful essays by such distinguished scholars as Karl Rahner and Wilfred Cantwell Smith.

Kraemer, Hendrik. *The Christian Message in the Non-Christian World.* Grand Rapids:

Kreger Publications, 1963. First published in 1938, this is an admirably clear statement of the Barthian position that since Christianity is the one true faith, other religions must of necessity be false.

Ostling, Richard N. "The New Missionary: Proclaiming Christ's Message in Daring and Disputed Ways," *Time* 120 (27 December 1982): 50–56. This dispels many common and unfounded views about Christian missionaries and their methods, and shows what kind of changes are taking place amid the pressures of the modern world.

Neill, Stephen. *Christian Faith and Other Faiths: The Christian Dialogue with Other Religions* 2d. ed. New York and London: Oxford University Press, 1970. Originally written in 1961, this is a profound, sincere, and sympathetic study of a complex and difficult problem. Bishop Neill writes out of a lifetime of work in India and the ecumenical movement, and presents his ideas with admirable clarity.

Ridenour, Fritz. *So What's the Difference?* Glendale, Calif.: Regal Books, 1967. A brief survey of "Orthodox Christianity," i.e., the author's, and its "rivals," i.e., Roman Catholicism, Buddhism, Islam, Unitarianism, Christian Science, Judaism, Mormonism, and Hinduism. One of the contributors found it "excellent," but another termed it "superficial and tendentious."

Smith, Wilfred Cantwell. *The Faith of Other Men.* New York: Harper & Row, 1962. First given in the form of talks on Canadian radio, these brief introductions to other religions are very well worth reading.

Taylor, John V. *The Primal Vision: Christian Presence Amid African Religion.* London: SCM Press, 1963. Brief, but quite first class. The reviewer in *The Guardian* rightly said that "no anthropologist . . . and no politician . . . can afford to miss this profound, humorous, humane and prophetic book." He might well have added others to his suggested readership.

15
CHRISTIANS AND SOCIETY

Bennett, John C. *The Radical Imperative.* Philadelphia: Westminster Press, 1975. An articulate call for the churches in this country to assume their social responsibilities.

Berger, Peter L. *The Sacred Canopy: Elements of a Sociological Theory of Religion.* Garden City, N.Y.: Doubleday Anchor Books, 1967. Written by a distinguished sociologist, this presents a provocative, and often highly critical, picture of the function of religion in society and the part played by the churches in this country.

Brown, Robert McAfee. *Theology in a New Key: Responding to Liberation Themes.* Philadelphia: Westminster Press, 1978. A thought-provoking and at times disturbing treatment of liberation theology from the perspective of a First World theologian.

Haughey, John C. *The Faith That Does Justice: Examining the Christian Sources for Social Change.* New York: Paulist Press, 1977. Essays written from a Roman Catholic position on the biblical and historical attitudes to questions of social and economic justice.

Niebuhr, H. Richard. *Christ and Culture.* New York: Harper & Row, 1951. A very important treatment of the subject, written in a simple and lucid manner. Mandatory reading.

Niebuhr, Reinhold. *Moral Man and Immoral Society.* New York: Charles Scribner's Sons, 1932. Although written fifty years ago, this book remains a classic in the field, and is no less mandatory reading than his brother's book, listed above.

Silone, Ignazio. *Bread and Wine.* Translated by Harvey Fergusson II. New York: New

American Library, 1962. A picaresque depiction of prewar Fascist Italy, this novel is also a wider discussion of the relation of religion and politics.

Temple, William. *Christianity and the Social Order.* Harmondsworth, Eng.: Penguin Books, 1942. Another very valuable short book from an earlier generation. Clear, thought-provoking, and eminently worth reading.

16
THE CRISIS OF CHRISTIANITY
IN THE MODERN WORLD

Berger, Peter L. *A Rumor of Angels: Modern Society and the Rediscovery of the Supernatural.* Garden City, N.Y.: Doubleday Anchor Books, 1969. Written as a corrective to possible misunderstandings of his earlier book, *The Sacred Canopy,* Berger here argues for the authenticity of the persistent human belief in the supernatural.

Dewart, Leslie. *The Future of Belief: Theism in a World Come of Age.* New York: Herder & Herder, 1966. This is a somewhat dense treatise, though fortunately provided with a helpful index and footnotes. Its main thrust is an argument for the dehellenization of the Christian understanding of God.

Graham, Fred W., and James L. Goatley, "Issues in Science and Religion: The View from the Student Desk," *Religion in Life,* 49 (Summer 1980): 157–67. An interesting article which raises many important and stimulating questions.

Miller, Libuse Lukas. *The Christian and the World of Unbelief: A Comprehensive Critique of Modern Culture.* Nashville: Abingdon Press, 1957. A strong statement of Christian faith in the modern period by a profound student of Kierkegaard.

Robinson, John A. T. *Honest to God.* Philadelphia: Westminster Press, 1963. Somewhat hastily and indeed at times rather carelessly written, this short book by an Anglican bishop shocked a great many people when it first appeared. Despite its shortcomings, the ideas put forward are very worthy of serious consideration.

Schaeffer, Francis A. *A Christian Manifesto.* Westchester, Ill.: Crosswalk Books, 1981. A distinguished fundamentalist scholar traces the ills of modern society to modern humanism, and calls for a return to the traditional Christian foundations.

Thielicke, Helmut. *How Modern Should Theology Be?* Philadelphia: Fortress Press, 1969. This book presents some fascinating contemporary views of modern Christian dilemmas. Very interesting, and quick reading.

Vidler, A. D., ed. *Objections to Christian Belief.* New York: J. B. Lippincott, 1964. An interesting series of essays on the subject of the divergence between traditional Christian beliefs and modern worldviews.

Wiesel, Elie. *Night.* New York: Avon, 1969. Implied in this novel is the question of how modern Judaism or Christianity can proceed with "business as usual" after the appalling tragedy of the Holocaust.

17
DISCIPLESHIP

Bonhoeffer, Dietrich. *The Cost of Discipleship,* rev. ed. New York: Macmillan Co., 1967. A searching study of the role of the true disciple of Christ written by a celebrated German theologian who was executed for his role in the resistance to Hitler.

_____. *Letters and Papers from Prison.* Edited by Eberhard Bethge, translated by

Reginald H. Fuller. New York: Macmillan Co., 1953. Profoundly revealing evidence of the cost of discipleship in the time of Hitler.

Cooke, Bernard. *Ministry to Word and Sacraments.* Philadelphia: Fortress Press, 1976. A detailed account of the ordained ministry and other forms of communal service.

Ellsberg, Robert, ed. *By Little and Little: The Selected Writings of Dorothy Day.* New York: Alfred A. Knopf, 1983. Provides in her own words a portrait of this nonviolent social radical, who was a co-founder of the Catholic Worker movement.

Endo, Shusaku. *Silence.* Translated by William Johnston. New York: Taplinger Publishing Co., 1980. A historical novel about a seventeenth-century Portuguese priest in Japan who is forced to renounce Christ in order to save his flock from persecution. A masterpiece.

Lewis, C. S. *Surprised by Joy: The Shape of My Early Life.* New York: Harcourt Brace Jovanovich, 1973. The author's confessional narrative of the mysterious working of grace in his life, and how from being a convinced agnostic he became a no less convinced Christian.

Küng, Hans. *On Being a Christian.* New York: Doubleday & Co., 1976. A controversial, but profound and influential discussion of Christian belief and practice, designed for the puzzled inquirer. This is a long book, but very readable and full of excellent ideas.

Schillebeeckx, Edward. *Ministry: Leadership in the Community of Jesus Christ.* New York: Crossroad, 1981. A distinguished Dutch Roman Catholic priest examines the changing role and structures of ministry within the context of the whole Christian community.

Soelle, Dorothee. *Suffering.* Philadelphia: Fortress Press, 1975. Her understanding of suffering begins with the assumption that only those who themselves suffer will work toward the abolition of suffering.

Scott, John R. W. *Christian Counter-Culture: The Message of the Sermon on the Mount.* Downers Grove, Ill.: Intervarsity Press, 1978. In this clearly written book the author conducts the reader through a detailed study of the Sermon on the Mount, showing how completely different the life of a Christian must be from life lived according to the normally accepted standards of the secular world.

INDEX OF BIBLICAL REFERENCES

OLD TESTAMENT

237

APOCRYPHA

INDEX OF SUBJECTS

243

Wisdom, 103–4, 108
Word of God, 17–18, 171, 197
World Council of Churches, 184

World Missionary Conference, 184–85
Worship, 138, 169–79, 210